Madness, Medicine and Miracle in Twelfth-Century England

This book explores how madness was defined and diagnosed as a condition of the mind in the Middle Ages and what effects it was thought to have on the bodies, minds and souls of sufferers.

Madness is examined through narratives of miraculous punishment and healing that were recorded at the shrines of saints. This study focuses on the twelfth century, which has been identified as a 'Medieval Renaissance': a time of cultural and intellectual change that saw, among other things, the circulation of new medical treatises that brought with them a wealth of new ideas about illness and health. With the expanding authority of the Roman Church and the tightening of papal control over canonisation procedures in this period, historians have claimed that there was a rationalisation of the miraculous. In miracle records, illnesses were explained using newly-accessible humoral theories rather than attributed to divine and demonic forces, as they had been previously.

The first book-length study of madness in medieval religion and medicine to be published since 1992, this book challenges these claims and reveals something of the limitations of the so-called naturalisation of the miraculous. Throughout the twelfth century, demons continue to lurk in miracle records relating to one condition in particular: madness. Five case studies of miracle collections compiled between 1070 and 1220 reveal that hagiographical representations of madness were heavily influenced by the individual circumstances of their recording and yet were shaped as much by hagiographical patterns that had been developing throughout the twelfth century as they were by new medical and theological standards.

Claire Trenery completed her PhD at Royal Holloway, University of London, in 2017. She specialises in the history of madness and medicine, focusing on the twelfth century and the cultural and intellectual climate that accompanied the development of Scholastic learning in Western Europe. She has published articles on medieval madness, with particular attention to the impact of madness on the bodies, minds and souls of sufferers.

Madness, Medicine and Miracle in Twelfth-Century England

Claire Trenery

Routledge
Taylor & Francis Group
LONDON AND NEW YORK

First published 2019
by Routledge
2 Park Square, Milton Park, Abingdon, Oxon OX14 4RN

and by Routledge
52 Vanderbilt Avenue, New York, NY 10017

First issued in paperback 2020

Routledge is an imprint of the Taylor & Francis Group, an informa business

British Library Cataloguing-in-Publication Data
A catalogue record for this book is available from the British Library

Library of Congress Cataloging-in-Publication Data
Names: Trenery, Claire, author.
Title: Madness, medicine and miracle in twelfth-century England / Claire Trenery.
Description: Abingdon, Oxon ; New York, NY : Routledge, 2019. | Includes >bibliographical references and index.
Identifiers: LCCN 2018043020|
Subjects: | MESH: Mental Disorders—history | Mentally Ill Persons—history | saints | Religion and Psychology | History, Medieval | England
Classification: LCC RC450.E64 | NLM WM 11 FE5 | DDC 616.8900942—dc23
LC record available at https://lccn.loc.gov/2018043020

ISBN 13: 978-0-367-66197-7 (pbk)
ISBN 13: 978-0-8153-6745-1 (hbk)

Typeset in Times NR MT Pro
by Cenveo® Publisher Services

This book is dedicated to my family (Mum, Dad, Sara and Stanley) and to Peregrine Horden.

Contents

List of figures and tables

Figure

Tables

Acknowledgements

This monograph is drawn from research originally completed as part of my doctoral studies, which would not have been possible without funding from the Arts and Humanities Research Council and from Royal Holloway, University of London, for which I am very grateful. I would like to express my special gratitude to my PhD supervisor, Peregrine Horden, for his expertise, advice and patience, and for his continued guidance. I would also like to thank my PhD examiners, Bill MacLehose and Simon Yarrow, for their input in developing this project.

My thanks goes to all my friends and colleagues who have provided me with their encouragement and their expertise: Anne E. Bailey, Elma Brenner, Mariana Brockmann, Clive Burgess, Gordon Carrothers, Markus Daechsel, Joanne T. Edge, Klaus-Dietrich Fischer, Tamsin Gardner, Florence Eliza Glaze, Thomas Gloning, Monica Green, Jonathan Harris, Felicity Hill, Eleanor Janega, Hannes Kleineke, Rachel Koopmans, Harriet Mahood, Brian McLaughlin, Jennifer Neville, Marie-Christine Ockendon, Simon Thomas Parsons, Joanna Phillips, Katie Phillips, Hilary Powell, Miri Rubin, Ruth J. Salter, Sig Sønnesyn, Stephen Spencer, Véronique Thouroude, James Tuck, Maiike van der Lugt, Lena Wahlgren-Smith, Mark Whelan, Louise E. Wilson, Richard Wragg, and Barbara Zipser.

I am especially indebted to my parents, Gill and Colin Trenery, and my grandparents, Monica and George Slade, without whose love, guidance and financial support I would not have been able to complete this research. I am also very grateful to Sara Trenery for her unwavering support and to Stanley for his unconditional love.

List of abbreviations

AE	Adam of Eynsham, *Magna Vita Sancti Hugonis: The Life of Saint Hugh of Lincoln*, ed. and trans. by Decima L. Douie and David Hugh Farmer, 2 vols (Oxford: Clarendon Press, 1985)
BP	Benedict of Peterborough, 'Miracula Sancti Thomae Cantuariensis', in *Materials for the History of Thomas Becket, Archbishop of Canterbury*, ed. by James Craigie Robertson, 7 vols (London: Longman, 1875–85), II (1876), 21–281
Edmund Revised	Goscelin of Saint-Bertin[?], 'Miracles of St Edmund', in *Herman the Archdeacon and Goscelin of Saint-Bertin. Miracles of St Edmund*, ed. and trans. by Tom Licence (Oxford: Oxford University Press, 2014), pp. 127–303
GW	Gerald of Wales, *The Life of St. Hugh of Avalon, Bishop of Lincoln 1186–1200*, ed. and trans. by Richard M. Loomis, Garland Library of Medieval Literature A, 31 (New York, NY and London: Garland, 1985)
Herman	Herman the Archdeacon, 'Miracles of St Edmund', in *Herman the Archdeacon and Goscelin of Saint-Bertin. Miracles of St Edmund*, ed. and trans. by Tom Licence (Oxford: Oxford University Press, 2014), pp. 1–125
Metrical Life	*The Metrical Life of Saint Hugh of Lincoln*, ed. and trans. by Charles Garton (Lincoln: Honywood Press, 1986)
TM1	Thomas of Monmouth, *The Life and Miracles of St William of Norwich*, ed. and trans. by Augustus Jessopp and M.R. James (Cambridge: Cambridge University Press, 1896)
TM2	Thomas of Monmouth, *The Life and Passion of William of Norwich*, trans. by Miri Rubin (London: Penguin, 2014)
Vespasian B.IX	*The Book of the Foundation of Saint Bartholomew's Church in London*, London, British Library, MS

Cotton Vespasian B.IX. The miracles are not numbered in the manuscript, but each new miracle begins with an initial written in blue and decorated in red. I have numbered them for ease of reference.

WC William of Canterbury, 'Miracula Sancti Thomae Cantuariensis', in *Materials for the History of Thomas Becket, Archbishop of Canterbury*, ed. by James Craigie Robertson, 7 vols (London: Longman, 1875–85), I (1875), 137–546

All biblical references are from *Biblia Latina cum Glossa Ordinaria*, ed. by Adolph Rusch, 4 vols (Strassburg: the editor, 1480–81; repr. Brepols: Turnhout, 1992).

Open transliteration has been used for Arabic names and titles.

Introduction

> But what is easier, to give health of the mind or of the body? He who brought light to these corporeal eyes also restored a youth of Fordwich, Henry, to his mind. He had been insane for some days and had inflicted an unexpected wound of suffering upon his friends.[1] He was hauled to the saint with his hands tied behind his back. He was presented to the saint, although he struggled and cried out. He raved there all day but as the light of the sun receded, the light of reason little by little began to be restored. He spent the night in the church; the next day, his sanity returned.[2]

Henry of Fordwich was a madman who was believed to have been miraculously cured of his insanity when, in the early 1170s, he was brought to the tomb of Saint Thomas Becket in Canterbury Cathedral. His story was made known to the monks of Christ Church Cathedral Priory and recorded in one of two twelfth-century miracle collections that contain records of more than seven hundred miracles attributed to the saint. In the miracle collection, the record of Henry's cure follows that of Robert of Thanet, a blind man who miraculously recovered his sight.[3] His are the 'corporeal eyes' referred to at the beginning of Henry's miracle record where a comparison is made between physical and mental healing.

Within fifty years of its recording, Henry's miraculous healing had been immortalised in stained glass as part of a series of miracle windows that were produced to surround Becket's new shrine behind the high altar, where his remains were translated from their original tomb in the crypt. Eight hundred years on, this stained-glass representation of Henry can still be seen in two roundels in Canterbury Cathedral's Trinity Chapel, the easternmost part of the cathedral, where Becket's shrine stood until the Dissolution of the Monasteries in the mid-sixteenth century. To both the modern observer, unable to read the Latin inscription,[4] and the illiterate medieval pilgrim, Henry's madness and his return to sanity are nonetheless recognisable. As in the miracle record on which the stained glass is based, Henry's hands are bound behind his back. He is restrained by two men holding clubs. In the second roundel, Henry kneels beside Becket's tomb to give thanks for his cure. His cloak, previously dishevelled, hangs neatly over his shoulders. The

Figure 0.1 The cure of Henry of Fordwich, Window North IV, Trinity Chapel, Canterbury Cathedral. Photo taken by Gordon Carrothers and used with the kind permission of the Dean and Chapter of Canterbury Cathedral.

rope and sticks that were used to restrain him are displayed at the bottom of the panel, as no longer necessary.

Both the written record of Henry's cure and its stained-glass representation reveal something of twelfth-century understandings of madness. Different terms were employed to describe Henry's condition; the miracle record used the verb *insanire* (to be insane), whereas, in the inscription, Henry was 'amens' (out of his mind). The terms *insania* and *amentia* were used more or less interchangeably in English miracle records of this period. Both terms referred to agitated and sometimes violent mental[5] conditions, typical of the 'madness' encountered at saints' shrines. We rarely see those suffering from quieter mental conditions, like lethargy, receiving treatment at the hands of a saint. The Latin term *insania* was associated with foolishness and rage, and *amentia* was a state of being out of one's mind, which could refer to madness and also to excited or senseless behaviour.[6] The comparison with Robert of Thanet's corporeal ('corporeos') ailment distinguishes madness, as a condition of the mind, from blindness, as a condition of the body. It was Henry's mind (*mens*) that required the restoration of reason. Madness was made evident, in this case, through behavioural signs (struggling, crying out and raving) and was managed using physical restraint. Henry's madness, therefore, can be defined as a state in which the mind lacked reason, diagnosed by the observation of unusual behaviours, and an illness in the sense that it was contrary to health and necessitated a cure. Of course, this definition of madness cannot be broadly applied without comparison with representations of madness in other miracle texts. Nonetheless, it is a starting point.

This book explores how madness was distinguished and diagnosed in the Middle Ages as a condition of the mind and what effects it was thought to have on the bodies, minds and souls of sufferers, like Henry. Madness is examined through narratives of miraculous punishment and healing that were recorded at the shrines of saints. In the twelfth century, these miracle records largely contain second-hand accounts of pilgrims who travelled to various shrines in the hope that a saint would miraculously heal whatever ailment afflicted them. Except for a small minority of cases, usually when some indiscretion on the part of the supplicant meant that healing was denied, miracle collections only include accounts of those pilgrims who were successfully healed and not of the countless others who may have made appeals to saints. Several mad men, women and children were brought (sometimes forcibly) to saints' shrines by concerned and even desperate parents, friends or members of the wider community, and many were purportedly made sane by the saints. Monks also recorded miraculous punishments dispensed by their saints, though with far less frequency than they did miraculous cures in this period. Illness, including madness, was a common punishment for transgressions against the saint and the monastery that housed his relics.

The focus of this study is madness miracles of the twelfth century because this period has been identified as a 'Medieval Renaissance': a time of cultural change that saw, among other things, the expansion of England's great cathedrals, the development of canon law, the emergence of the concept of purgatory, the rise of the universities and the wide dissemination of Latin texts and translated Greek and Arabic works, which brought with them a wealth of new ideas.[7] With the expanding authority of the Roman Catholic Church and the tightening of papal control over canonisation procedures in this period, historians have claimed that there was a 'colonization of the miraculous by what we would now recognise as more rational procedures of inquiry into knowledge.'[8] The integration of Greek philosophy – via Arabic and then Latin translations – into Christian Scholasticism brought with it a 'systematic, naturalistic, and rationalistic analysis of the world from a non-Christian viewpoint'.[9] New understandings of the natural world led to a sharpening of its boundaries with the supernatural and the spiritual, which in turn led to renewed consideration of God's agency both within and beyond nature (i.e. through miracles).

Within this increasingly 'naturalistic, and rationalistic' setting, the influence of new medical ideas meant that conditions of the mind could be explained in relation to humoral imbalance (according to the theory, passed down from Hippocrates and Galen, that the body was regulated by balancing four humours, or fluids), rather than demonic possession (following the idea, manifest in the Bible, that the bodies and minds of humans could be taken over and controlled by malevolent agents of the devil). It has been suggested that, because of the impact of humoral medicine, madness was 'becoming naturalized and medicalized' in this period.[10] Nonetheless, as Catherine Rider has pointed out, the idea that demons could cause madness was not necessarily non-medical, and demonic possession was discussed by several medieval physicians as 'a medical condition, rather than (or as well as) a spiritual one'.[11]

Miracle collections were not medical texts and were very rarely compiled by physicians, so it is perhaps not surprising that, in miracle records like Henry's, we see no mention of humoral explanations for madness. Even so, as monastic men, miracle compilers were privileged with access to some of the most cutting-edge medical and scientific works of their day, and English monasteries housed one of the largest bodies of Latin medical literature in Western Europe.[12] Anne Bailey, in her analysis of hagiographical representations of madness, has argued that the influence of this new body of medical texts meant that 'stories of demons and *incubi* [demons that attacked and often sexually assaulted people in their sleep] may have been reshaped here and there for twelfth-century tastes'.[13] We are, however, left wondering whether 'tastes' differed from saint's cult to saint's cult or from miracle compiler to miracle compiler and what impact the reception of new ideas had on particular miracle collections. Did hagiographical representations of madness change over the course of the twelfth century in line with wider theological, intellectual and cultural developments? What influence did the particular circumstances of individual cults and the specific priorities and knowledge of the men who compiled miracles have on representations of madness in relation to broader chronological developments? How far was madness attributed to demons, and how (if at all) did the demons of the late eleventh century differ from those of the early thirteenth?

What is madness?

Historians of madness have long grappled with defining the scope of their field of study. All too often, medieval madness has been either simplistically equated with demonic possession or precariously compared to modern mental illness and even to specific modern psychological and neurological complaints.[14] Michel Foucault famously argued that the advent of psychiatry in the nineteenth century led to madness being categorised and investigated, and, for this reason, 'modern man no longer communicates with the madman' but instead 'delegates madness to the doctor'.[15] Foucault's madman was a social construct, defined by the reasoning society that had ostracised him.[16] Roy Porter, writing over forty years after Foucault, discussed madness in the eighteenth century as 'an extremely broad sociocultural category', not fundamentally a product of civilisation, as it was for Foucault, but manufactured only in the sense that 'society moulds basic human needs, wants, expressions into culture'.[17] More recently, historians have considered whether it is feasible – and indeed, useful – to associate conditions of the mind (which are reliant on interpretation, environmental factors and genetic inheritance) in two societies – modern and medieval – where the very nature of the mind itself is interpreted differently.[18]

In the present day, 'mental illnesses' are labelled, defined and treated in the spheres of psychiatry, neurology, homeopathy and religion, to name but a few. The terms we use to describe a lack or loss of reasoning capability are similarly varied: depression, anxiety, bipolar disorder, post-traumatic stress disorder, schizophrenia, obsessive-compulsive disorder. In the United Kingdom, psychiatrists largely diagnose mental health conditions based on the International Classification of Diseases (ICD-10), which is published by the World Health Organisation and allows practitioners to compare a patient's symptoms against standard symptoms that are listed for recognised conditions. For example, to be suffering from generalised anxiety disorder, a patient must experience some of the following symptoms in a 'generalized and persistent' way that is not restricted to a particular environment or situation: 'complaints of persistent nervousness, trembling, muscular tensions, sweating, lightheadedness, palpitations, dizziness, and epigastric discomfort'.[19] Evidently, there is room for interpretation here on the part on the diagnosing psychiatrist, but the diagnosis that a patient receives, nonetheless, has a direct impact on his or her psychiatric treatment and wider care (for example, when applying for disability benefits).

Those suffering from mental health conditions can also turn to alternative therapies, like acupuncture or aromatherapy, though few of these are recommended by the National Institute of Health and Care Excellence, and most are not funded by the National Health Service.[20] Furthermore, the diagnoses outlined in ICD-10 are not the only categorisations applied to those suffering from mental health conditions that are used to determine their mental state and appropriate care. For example, in order to be classified as legally insane and to enter a legal defence of insanity in relation to criminal charges, a person must be deemed to lack the ability to make a rational decision.[21] We thus diagnose mental health problems in relation to mental and physical states that we consider to be normal (legally normal, medically normal, socially normal, etc.).

'Madness is madness precisely *because* it makes (or is perceived to make) no sense, and hence poses problems of communication and of common meaning'.[22] Leigh Ann Craig's shrewd assessment of the challenges facing historians of madness is particularly relevant here. Should we, like Foucault, discuss madness as a purely social construct without organic reality? Or should we also consider that the language of madness is used to make sense of or communicate abnormality rather than to construct it? The concept of madness relies on a deviation from the norm and thus on subjective perceptions of normal behaviour. As far as possible, I approach madness from a medieval standpoint, using the terminology employed by medieval miracle collectors. Given that the source material is limited to second-hand representations of madness, this approach necessarily lends itself to a navigation of the cultural significance of madness from the perspective of contemporary understandings of rationality rather than a social engagement with medieval experiences of madness. I define 'madness miracles' as records of:

- states defined as *insania* or *amentia*.
- conditions typified by unusual behaviour.
- disorders of the mind in which reason was perceived to be lacking.

Many records contain only one or two of these components, and often, multiple categorisations of madness converge. Nonetheless, we should still investigate terminological distinctions. Was the madman different from the fool? Was the demoniac comparable to the lunatic?

Five case studies

My discussion takes the form of five thematic case studies, each based on an English cult that developed during the long twelfth century (c.1070–c.1220) and the miracles associated with it. A case-study format allows me to consider the various components of madness whilst acknowledging that hagiographers were not uniform in their approaches to recording miracles, which were influenced by the time and place in which they wrote. It is beyond the scope of this study to survey all miracles recorded in twelfth-century England. First and foremost, the miracle texts of the five cults I have chosen warrant discussion because they include a substantial number of madness miracles and references to madness.[23] The cults also represent a broad range of hagiographical perspectives, which lend themselves to comparison.

I address the five cults in chronological order so as to take into account broad chronological developments as well as the impact each cult had on those that followed it. Nonetheless, it will be shown that representations of madness were determined not so much by chronology as by the specific local context of each cult. I begin in Bury at the turn of the eleventh century, when attempts were being made to revive the Anglo-Saxon cult of Saint Edmund the Martyr. Under threat from Norman conquerors and the new and overbearing authority of the bishop of Norwich (the diocesan seat was moved from Thetford to Norwich in 1094), the monastic community at Bury sought to establish Saint Edmund as their patron and protector. Representations of madness in Edmund's miracles reflect this focus; madness was most often dispensed as a divine punishment that undermined and incapacitated the saint's (and the monastery's) adversaries. Within a decade of its completion, Edmund's miracle collection was completely rewritten, this time under the patronage of the bishop of Norwich, and the madness miracles indicate new episcopal priorities, which can be compared to the priorities of the previous collection.

Chapter 2 moves forward half a century to a very different cult facing a new threat. The *Life and Miracles of William of Norwich* was written in the wake of the Anarchy (1135-53) and is most well known for being the first written blood libel made against a Jewish community (the Jews of Norwich were accused of ritually murdering the prospective saint, William). Though William did not dispense insanity as a divine punishment, madness and irrationality were associated with the cruelty and savagery of the Jews, and the mad men and women who visited William's shrine were correspondingly particularly violent and savage.

The situation was very different for the next cult and the subject of Chapter 3: that of Saint Thomas Becket in Canterbury. Becket's cult flourished almost from the moment that the archbishop, murdered by four knights who claimed they were acting on the orders of King Henry II, spilt his blood in the cathedral on 29 December 1170. Two collections of Becket's miracles, compiled at Canterbury, comprise the largest surviving body of miracle records from twelfth-century England and contain especially varied accounts of madness. Some records were narrated by the miracle compilers themselves, and others were drawn from the letters of clerics and laymen who wrote to the monks, attesting to miracles that had been performed further afield. Nonetheless, madness was shown to be distinct, as a condition of the mind, from other conditions, like epilepsy, that had similar behavioural symptoms but affected the brain or limbs. Furthermore, despite the use of sophisticated medical terminology in Becket's miracle collections, the continued presence of demons is indicative of an enduring connection between demonic possession and madness.

Chapter 4 explores further the connections between madness and demonic possession and provides a counter-narrative to the so-called naturalisation of twelfth-century miracle texts. The foundation book of Saint Bartholomew's Church in London, compiled in the late twelfth century, contains records of miracles that occurred there during the lifetime of its founder, Rahere, as well as further miracles that were witnessed after his death, including four cases of miraculously-cured demonic possession. In the foundation book, the dysfunctionality of demonically-induced madness was vividly contrasted with Rahere's own feigned foolishness, which he adopted in the pursuit of spiritual well-being.

The final group of miracles was recorded in the thirteenth century, prior to and in celebration of the canonisation of Saint Hugh of Lincoln, and are the subject of Chapter 5. The record of Hugh's canonisation process itself does seem to reflect the naturalisation of madness that historians have observed in this period. In the canonisation report, mad people were referred to as *furiosi*, and demons were very rarely mentioned. Hugh's three *vitae*, however, contain varied and eclectic representations of madness and demonic possession, not dissimilar to those recorded in the twelfth-century miracle collections, though, in Hugh's case, many of the mad men and women were cured by the prospective saint during his lifetime and not posthumously, by means of his relics.

The miracles associated with all five cults were compiled within the monastic culture of their respective settings, which can be considered in terms of the monastic institutions that housed the shrines, the monastic libraries that the miracle compilers had access to, and the individual backgrounds of those hagiographers whose identities are known. All the cults were based in cathedral cities or large towns, and the miracles reveal engagement between the religious communities and the local people, as well as the influence of broader political and cultural changes. Four of the cults were fostered in Benedictine monasteries, where there was a marked commitment to learning and access to an education system that endorsed the secular arts (the learning of which was a form of mental discipline), as well as liturgical study, and made a significant contribution to the copying, transmission and preservation of texts.[24] The exception, Saint Bartholomew's Priory of Augustinian canons, was one of many such foundations made in England in the twelfth century, not necessarily to serve a local need, as they had in previous centuries, but rather to provide the canons with a more rigorous spiritual rule.[25] Given the fairly close proximity of the shrines, with four of the five located in central or eastern England (the exception being the cult of Hugh of Lincoln, which, nonetheless, had widespread appeal because of the bishop's influence in the royal court as well as in his own diocese), the miracle collections can be considered in relation to each other, to their local context and to their wider significance.

In previous studies of medieval insanity, historians have applied categories and distinctions across a large number of different medieval texts and made some generalisations about hagiographical representations of madness, which I address through close attention to the particular circumstances of individual miracle collections. Until now, there has been no concentrated, book-length study of representations of madness in medieval miracle records. As part of her overview study *La folie au Moyen-Âge*, Muriel Laharie undertakes an extensive, though far from exhaustive, study of miraculous cures of mad pilgrims in hagiographical texts. She lists a large number of saints who were recorded as having healed the mad; though, of the five saints examined in this book, only Saint Thomas Becket makes Laharie's list.[26] Laharie estimates that miraculous cures of the mad make up ten percent of miraculous cures recorded for the cults she reviews, or twenty to thirty percent if we include those who experienced madness-like symptoms as a result of other conditions and who thus did not primarily seek cures for their madness.[27] Using her list, Laharie makes several generalisations about mad pilgrims who were cured by medieval saints, some of which I have been unable to substantiate in the miracle texts I have looked at; for example, I have found no evidence that demoniacs were beaten by carers in an attempt to physically harm the demons inside them, though sufferers of both demonic and non-demonic madness were sometimes bound or otherwise restrained.[28]

Jean-Marie Fritz, in his review of hagiographical representations of madness in the twelfth and thirteenth centuries, concludes that the majority of mad individuals were portrayed as sinners and that madness itself was interpreted as a punishment for sin.[29] Again, I have found little evidence of this rationale in English miracles recorded after c.1100. I demonstrate that, whilst broad comparative studies of medieval madness, like Laharie's and Fritz's, highlight the importance of hagiographical material to the historical study of madness, detailed case studies of individual saints' cults allow for a nuanced engagement with representations of madness in medieval miracle records and challenge some of the established generalisations.

In recent years, medieval historians have focused on micro-studies of particular aspects of madness, whether it be a specific condition, as in Amy Hollywood's study of *melancholia*, or a specific sphere, as in Wendy Turner's evaluation of madness in English civil law. A case-study format is adopted in Sari Katajala-Peltomaa and Susanna Niiranen's edited volume *Mental (Dis)Order in Later Medieval Europe*, which delves into various aspects of medieval madness. The present work fits into this tradition and greatly extends the scope of the current historiography by comparing like sources from across the long twelfth century and thus building a picture of parallels and differences in their representations of madness. Madness miracles are not considered without contextualisation and attention to the importance of the wider dissemination and reception of ideas concerning madness in twelfth-century England.

Terminology

The language used by miracle compilers to describe madness was varied. In many cases, multiple terms were used within the same miracle account; many pilgrims were described as both 'insane' and 'possessed'. This variability is demonstrated in Table 0.1, which summarises the terms used to describe madness in the miracle records of the five cults studied in this book.

As Jackie Pigeaud cautioned in his study of ancient mental illness in the Greek and Roman worlds, historians must strive to avoid grouping ancient terminology into modern categories (religion, medicine, philosophy, etc.).[30] Since various theories concerning the natures of the body, mind and soul converged in twelfth-century England, I do not attempt to make categorical distinctions between them. It is nonetheless useful to briefly consider significant Latin terms and their common meanings in twelfth-century texts. None of these terms are defined in the miracle records, and it is not possible to provide definitions that adequately express the range of their use. The definitions in Table 0.2 present a foundation from which more detailed distinctions can be explored.

Medieval conceptions of madness were drawn partly from ancient models of the relationship between the body, mind and soul. The illustrious Persian physician known in the West as Avicenna (d.1037), who was influenced by Aristotle and whose treatise *De Anima* (*On the Soul*) was translated into Latin in the second half of the twelfth century, argued that man was separated from the beasts by his possession of a reasoning soul that

Table 0.1 Terms used to describe madness in the miracles of Edmund of Bury (two collections: one c.1070s–c.1090s; one c.1100), William of Norwich (c.1154–c.1155 and c.1173), Thomas Becket in Canterbury (two collections: 1170s), Bartholomew in London (c.1174–c.1189), and Hugh of Lincoln (three *vitae*: one c.1200s; one c.1213; one c.1220).

Latin term	*English definition*
a daemonio arreptus	seized by a demon
a daemonio vexatus	disturbed by a demon
alienatio capitis	alienation of the head
alienatio mentis	alienation of the mind
alienus	mad, rambling
amens	mad
amentia	madness
cerebri turbatione agitaretur	agitated by a disturbance of the brain
debachando/ debachantis	Bacchic (in reference to the pagan cult of the Roman god Bacchus, associated with drunkenness and wanton euphoria), raving
energumenus/a	demonically possessed
frenesis	frenzy
furere	to rave (in madness or anger)
furia	rage, fury, raving madness
furiosus	mad, furious, frantic
furor	rage, fury, raving madness
in mentis excessus	withdrawal in the mind (possible reference to the ecstasy of Benjamin, Psalms 67:28)
insania	insanity
insanire	to be insane
insanus	insane
hebes	foolish, stupid (not necessarily mad, but could refer to seemingly irrational behaviour)
mania	mania
mente captus	taken in the mind
plenam daemonio	filled with a demon
rabies	rabies (not necessarily associated with a bite from a rabid dog – more commonly a reference to raving madness)
stupor mentis	mental confusion, bewilderment

was able to comprehend God.[31] This idea resonated with Christian writers who were interested in the role that man's reason played in his relationship with God.[32] Medieval theologians were repeatedly drawn to the question of how the immaterial, reasoning soul was able to control the material body. At the forefront of medieval debates, and particularly influential in medical writing from the twelfth century, was the theory that the soul governed the body by means of a third substance, which E. Ruth Harvey has termed the 'inward wits'.[33] These inward wits, also known as reasoning spirits or *pneumata*, were material but consisted of a substance finer than any other element, which allowed the soul to express its intentions through the physicality of the body.[34] Stoic philosophy (from the Hellenistic school founded

Table 0.2 Definitions based on the survey of Latin terms used in British sources from the sixth to the sixteenth century carried out by R.E. Latham and others (1975–2013).

Latin term	*English definition*
anima	the incorporeal soul
animus	the mind or heart as the seat of thought and emotion
cerebrum	the physical brain
cor	the physical heart, or the heart as the seat of the mind
corpus	the physical body as distinct from the mind
mens	the mind, encompassing human reason and intellectual activity
spiritus	could indicate incorporeal human reason, or another incorporeal spirit, such as a demon

in Athens in the third century BC) placed the source of *pneumata* in the heart. Emotional changes (known as 'accidents of the soul') brought about increased pressure and heat in the chest cavity, which were then transferred, via these *pnuemata*, to the rest of the body, causing imbalance.[35]

The Stoic model of the reasoning spirits, or the *mind*, was widely applied in both a literal and a metaphorical sense in Old English texts of the ninth century and earlier. However, the transmission of cardiocentric theories waned after the tenth century with the much-increased circulation of Patristic texts, originally written by early Christian theologians in the first five hundred years after the death of Christ. This increase is most evident in English Benedictine monasteries, which received and copied texts from Frankish houses of their order.[36] Many Church Fathers, most notably Augustine of Hippo, were influenced by the writings of Plato, who differed from the Stoics and who argued that the incorporeal human soul itself was rational (as opposed to the rational, and corporeal, *pneumata*), thus blurring the boundaries between the mind and the soul.[37] As an impairment of rationality, madness could therefore be interpreted as a medical condition (in the sense that it impaired the corporeal reasoning faculties and could be treated by the application of human medicines) or a spiritual condition (in the sense that it impeded the rational soul's comprehension of God and required spiritual care) or as a mixture of the two.

Some of the works of the great medical writers of the classical age – Hippocrates (fifth century BC) and Galen (second century AD) – had been translated into Latin as early as the sixth century, but scholarly interest in their theories was renewed and added to by the translation of Arabic medical material from the late eleventh century in and around the medical schools in Salerno (modern-day Italy). The basis of the Hippocratic model of the body lay in the regulation of the four humours (blood, red/yellow bile, phlegm and black bile) within the body in the pursuit of health. The circulation of translated Hippocratic and Galenic texts in England from the eleventh century introduced another model of human reason that would challenge cardiocentrism: the association between the mind and the brain.[38]

In ancient medicine, four main conditions could lead to 'a mental disturbance', caused by humours in the brain becoming imbalanced.[39] These were *phrenitis* (frenzy), *lethargos* (lethargy), *mania* (mania) and *melancholia* (melancholy). The distinctions between these conditions were largely physical; for example, frenzy and lethargy were associated with excess heat and accompanied by fever, whereas mania and melancholy were not.[40]

Medieval madness could also be brought on by spiritual failings and, less often, by spiritual purity (as in the Byzantine 'holy fool', which will be discussed in Chapter 4). The spiritual and moral significance of madness is made particularly evident in the biblical narrative of Nebuchadnezzar, the Babylonian king whose loss of reason caused him to live as one of the beasts but who, upon restoration to his senses and to his kingdom, was brought closer to God (Daniel 4:31–3).[41] Nebuchadnezzar provided an archetype for literary and symbolic interpretations of madness.[42] Penelope Doob has identified three medieval tropes drawn from this archetype: 'the Mad Sinner', 'the Unholy Wild Man' and 'the Holy Wild Man'.[43] All three tropes discern the cause of the madness in question: whether it was a punishment for sin, a result of demonic interference or conferred by divine blessing. The third group, those blessed by divine madness, do not feature in miracle collections, most likely because they were not seeking cures for their conditions, and they would have distracted from the prominence of the saint in the narrative. The first group – the mad sinners – however, were the recipients of miracles; in some cases, the infliction of madness itself – rather than its cure – was interpreted as a miraculous occurrence. Saints were capable of inflicting madness as a punishment for sin or as a means of redemption.

Nonetheless, the majority of the mad people in this study were innocent victims, and many of them had fallen prey to demons. The Bible – both in the Old Testament and, more prolifically, in the New Testament – provides ample examples of demonic illness and demonic possession as well as a precedent for the exorcism of demons by holy men.[44] Biblical representations of demoniacs would almost certainly have influenced monastic miracle compilers. One of the many miraculous cures performed by Christ was that of a man from Gerasenes who was possessed by a demon (Mark 5:1–21). This man exhibited extreme strength, had to be chained and cried out day and night: symptoms that were frequently echoed in hagiographical accounts of both demonic and non-demonic madness. Once the man had been cured by Christ and the demons had been expelled, these strange behaviours stopped and his mind was made sane/healthy ('sanae mentis') (Mark 5:15). Three noteworthy precedents were set here: demons were capable of inflicting damage on the mind; such damage made itself apparent through the strange physical appearance and actions of the afflicted person; and such an affliction could be healed through divine intervention (in this case, through the person of Christ). There was, therefore, certainly a basis in medieval Christian theology for comparing madness and demonic possession in the context of miraculous healing as states that affected the mind and were characterised by similar symptoms.

In the twelfth century, there was no clear-cut concept of the 'supernatural', as distinct from the 'natural', and humoral and demonic explanations of madness were not posited at two ends of a spectrum as 'natural' and 'supernatural'.[45] If demons were able to manipulate the physical world around them (and this too was the subject of contention[46]), it could be reasoned that they were also able to manipulate a person's humours, resulting in humoral imbalance and sickness. So too could they take advantage of an individual already weakened by humoral imbalance. Many medieval physicians were aware of these theories and their relevance to the practical treatment of insane and possessed patients.[47] As Robert Bartlett has pointed out, medieval approaches to the natural world were certainly not uniform or even consistent, and were, in fact, akin to the discordant beliefs regarding the nature of the modern world that many people hold today.[48] Twelfth-century miracle compilers explored the connections between demonic possession and madness, often associating, and even equating, both sets of terminology. It was not always necessary for miracle compilers to precisely diagnose conditions, as physicians were required to do in order to prescribe appropriate cures, so long as it could be shown that a miracle had taken place.

Working with miracles: a review of the relevant historiography

Anyone trying to understand medieval miracle records stands on the shoulders of giants. I discuss just a few whose work is most relevant to the present study. The past forty years, following the publication of Peter Brown's groundbreaking study *The Cult of the Saints*, have seen historians open their minds to the use of hagiography as both a literary and a historical source.[49] Even so, we have only scratched the surface of what this vast volume of material can offer. The present work brings to the table a new way of approaching miracle records that allows me to trace how understandings of madness, as a particular condition, changed over time. It is important, however, that miracle collections are not simply mined for snippets relating to insanity and that madness miracles are explored in the context in which they were recorded and in relation to corresponding contemporary material.

Overview studies

Within the climate of increased historical interest in the miraculous cures performed at medieval shrines that developed in the 1970s and '80s, emerged two overview studies that attempted to use details from hagiographical records to construct social histories of the cult of saints from the perspectives of medieval pilgrims. The first of these studies was Ronald Finucane's *Miracles and Pilgrims*: a statistical survey of around three thousand miracle accounts recorded in England in the period 1066 to 1300.[50]

Finucane was careful not to draw too hasty conclusions from his statistical analysis, stressing the 'diversity' of medieval shrines and the fact that 'each saint's cult had its own history', but he did use his findings to make comparisons between cults; did more women visit a certain shrine over another, or did certain saints specialise in healing certain conditions?[51]

Whilst Finucane's approach provides a systematic review of a vast number of sources, something is lost in the analysis of the individual hagiographer. The shortcomings in his broad statistical methodology are particularly evident in his examination of medieval medicine, which he appraises in modern terms: for example, by comparing medieval cauterisation to modern-day acupuncture therapy.[52] In such instances, Finucane's conclusions would benefit from closer attention to medieval terminology and to what the language used in miracle texts can reveal about their composition and the conditions they represent. His analysis of madness is cursory and focuses predominantly on demonic possession.[53] He also argues that 'contemporaries usually made no distinction between epilepsy and insanity', which is something that I challenge in Chapter 3.[54] Finucane concentrates on the beliefs of the uneducated majority who, he suggests, submitted to the procedures used by medieval physicians in their 'desperate ignorance'.[55] What is missing from his consideration is the sometimes substantial medical knowledge of hagiographers themselves, which surely influenced their notions of healing and their portrayals of popular medicine.

Similarly, in his 1985 study of miracles recorded in France in the eleventh and twelfth centuries, Pierre-André Sigal pays limited attention to the context of his sources or to the hagiographical perspectives of those who compiled them.[56] What he does do, first and foremost, is highlight the usefulness of miracle collections as sources for social history, particularly through his in-depth consideration of various medical conditions. Unfortunately though, like Finucane's, his statistical analysis is rather limited in this regard by his use of modern categories of illness, including distinctions between mental and neurological conditions that traverse medieval boundaries.[57] In his section on mental illnesses ('les affections mentales'), he proposes that all bouts of aggression from mentally ill pilgrims were connected with demonic possession because of the inhuman barking, roaring, howling and blaspheming that accompanied them.[58] My examination of violent madness provides multiple examples that contradict this claim. In Chapter 2, I analyse violent madness in the *Life and Miracles of William of Norwich* in relation to conceptions of violence throughout the text as a whole, and I demonstrate that, in order to fully appreciate representations of madness in miracle collections, we cannot simply extract particular details from a record without paying attention to its cultural, intellectual and literary settings.

Benedicta Ward has focused her attention on the intellectual theory behind miracles and hagiographers' understandings of the miraculous. She separates miracle collections into two types, roughly based on their chronology and the role of the saint within the text. The 'traditional' (pre-twelfth-century) miracle collection was written in a monastic environment that lacked secular security. The saint acted as protector, promoting monastic interests and avenging wrongs through his or her miracles.[59] The second category, 'modern' miracles, Ward argues, became more prominent in the twelfth century, when there was no longer a need for spiritual protection, and monasteries turned their attention towards attracting pilgrims to shrines in search of cures for their ailments.[60] Admittedly, this summary is a simplification of Ward's model, and it is important to note that she allows for variations from shrine to shrine.[61]

Ward's intellectualist approach to the study of miracles does present some limitations. In contrast to Finucane and Sigal, she concentrates on the composition of miracle narratives rather than the recipients of cures themselves. Whilst she provides much-needed context for the cult of saints, and for Finucane and Sigal's studies, her argument could be extended by further consideration of the individual context for each saint, cult and hagiographer within the milieu of theories put forward by churchmen like Augustine, to whom she pays specific attention. Ward's original thesis has been developed by historians, who have reflected on the internal functioning of the cult of saints within this theological framework but also extended their gaze to the practical environment for the recording of, and belief in, the miraculous. Robert Bartlett, for example, has observed that the 'distinctive features' of individual cults are evidence of the diversity and malleability of hagiographical texts, which established local appeal whilst also conforming to the expectations of their genre.[62] By taking five cults from across the long twelfth century as case studies, I demonstrate that geographical, social and cultural contexts are just as important as chronological context when considering the focus of a cult and the way in which a miracle collection was constructed. Ward's chronological model has the potential, if not applied carefully, to obscure the nuances within and distinctions between twelfth-century miracle collections. In my case studies, I pay close attention both to the local demands of the monastic and wider community and to the broader demands of the changing genre of hagiography.

Periodisation: hagiography in the twelfth and thirteenth centuries

Simon Yarrow has championed a move away from Finucane's abstract consideration of sources without much by way of context and chronology and from Ward's intellectual approach to texts that are in fact reflective of community beliefs. He adopts a novel methodology that takes into account 'the social as well as the intellectual setting of the miraculous.'[63] Yarrow focuses on twelfth-century England, which, as he identifies, was undergoing a shift in its approach to the miraculous, partly because of the influence of events at Canterbury. Both the translation, in 1091, of six abbots to shrines in Saint Augustine's Abbey and the murder of Thomas Becket in the cathedral in

1170 prompted further translations elsewhere as well as the compilation of larger miracle collections.[64] Nonetheless, Yarrow argues that Ward's designation of the twelfth century as the start of the 'modern' age of miracles is problematic given that many twelfth-century miracle collections contain elements that she would classify as 'traditional'. It is more useful, he suggests, to place greater significance on the economic and social context of individual cults rather than on a chronological category.[65] The present study provides further validation of this approach and explores how the social and cultural context of a cult impacted the ways in which madness was represented in its miracle records.

Rachel Koopmans has proposed an alternative chronology to Ward's for twelfth-century recording of the miraculous in which she identifies phases of social and cultural development. She evaluates miracles recorded between the Norman Conquest and the end of the twelfth century, during which time, she argues, a 'miracle-collecting mania' developed in England.[66] Whilst no event caused a clear-cut break, she contends that this period can be divided into two phases of miracle collecting:

- c.1080–c.1140: Medium-sized collections, monastic miracles
- c.1140–c.1200: Long collections, more interest in the stories of the laity[67]

The second phase coincided with a growing concern across Western Europe to commit the customs and stories of the past and present to writing.[68] It is this second phase (c.1140–c.1200) with which this book is primarily concerned, though features of the earlier phase persisted in miracle collections throughout the twelfth century. Koopmans contends that the increasing inclusion of complicated medical terminology in miracle texts is illustrative of the changing position of the saint in twelfth-century England as well as the increasingly rigorous process of miracle recording and the introduction into English monasteries of medical ideas from, for example, the schools in Salerno.[69] Nonetheless, an examination of the terminology used to describe states of madness reveals that twelfth-century hagiographers drew on various authorities and that 'medical' or 'natural' concepts of suffering had not yet acquired the autonomy that they would in later centuries.

Both André Vauchez and Michael Goodich have traced perceptions of authority in thirteenth-century miracle texts, as papal control of the theory and practice of canonisation increased. According to Vauchez, miracles that could be recorded and verified by the papal curia were preferred to those in locally-compiled collections.[70] Goodich argues that stringent proofs demanded of miracles by the curia reflect growing concern with the tricks of the devil and with heresy as well as the rise of Scholasticism, which sought to resolve disparities between ancient and Christian philosophies through reasoned debate.[71] Nonetheless, in her 2011 doctoral thesis, Louise Wilson observes that canonisation processes applied similar methods for authenticating and recording miracles as those used by hagiographers and miracle compilers.[72] The rigorous recording of the miraculous that can be seen in the thirteenth century is perhaps not, therefore, the result of increased papal control and is instead illustrative of the adaptation of the cult of saints to the demands of contemporary legal and medical expectations. The twelfth century, in this regard, presents a more complicated picture than the thirteenth, since it was the period in which hagiographers were expanding their collections and experimenting.

Charles Burnett has argued that, whilst there was a change in approaches to learning in the West, the 'introduction of so many new texts in most fields of learning during the twelfth century made it simply impossible for one person to master them all', and this diversification led to the increased specialisation of knowledge and vocabulary in particular fields.[73] It is important to consider the impact of both increased standardisation and increased specialisation on the monks who compiled miracle texts. These monks would likely have been aware of shifting intellectual trends but would not have been experts in a particular field.[74] For this reason, it is necessary to take a threefold approach when evaluating the wider theological and intellectual context of miracle accounts compiled in the twelfth century. I explore representations of madness in relation to chronological shifts in medieval attitudes towards knowledge, to the dissemination of general and specialised texts on a local monastic level, and to the individual reception of these ideas by miracle compilers.

On a similar line to Burnett, Carl Watkins has suggested that changes in attitudes towards sin, penance and purgatory in the twelfth and thirteenth centuries may not have sprung from learned theological debates and may instead have been the result of growing interaction between the Church and the laity (for example, through preaching).[75] In theological texts, references to purgatory, as a distinct location in which souls awaited ultimate salvation through intercessory prayers made for them on earth, have not been found before the twelfth century.[76] However, even before the term 'purgatory' entered theological discourse, the idea of possible salvation for those who were not saints and monks brought with it an increased concern with individual piety and closer scrutiny of the relationship between ordinary Christians and God. The opportunity for redemption prompted the gradual replacement of the avenging God of the Apocalypse with the just God of the Last Judgement.[77] At the same time, heavenly compassion became more evident on earth through miraculous healings of the sick. As part of the expansion of hagiographical writing in twelfth-century England, miracle texts provide a unique glimpse of the changing relationship between the individual and the divine. Established associations between madness and sin were challenged by the saint's developing role as a purveyor of salvation: something that can be seen in the miraculous cures of mad pilgrims.[78]

Medieval records of these miraculous cures incorporated what modern readers would classify as both medical and religious elements.[79] I maintain that both elements were intrinsic to medieval interpretations of health, which was holistic in the sense that physical, mental and spiritual well-being were inherently reliant on one another. Therefore, when considering medieval illness, it is important not to impose modern distinctions and categories. We should also remember that medieval understandings of health and sickness were changing throughout the twelfth century as part of wider theological and intellectual developments and that reception of ideas depended on chronological, geographical and individual circumstances, which I take into account in each of my case studies.[80] To use the words of Matthew Mesley, we should '[insert] the miraculous back into the broader trends and developments of the medieval world'.[81]

The tradition to which miracle collections belong is very much one of public interaction with the sacred. Miracle records represent the miracle compiler's interpretation of collective behaviour and not his individual expression of piety. The involvement of the community can be seen, in the twelfth and thirteenth centuries, through increased attention to the testimony of witnesses, especially as papal canonisation procedures became more formalised. There was greater demand for a truthful and credible representation of communal events, and the hagiographer's engagement with his community – both monastic and secular – was vital to his collection. It is time to revive Finucane and Sigal's interest in the pilgrim whilst taking into account recent scholarship emphasising the importance of the context of individual saints' cults and the recording and dissemination of collective knowledge.

Notes

1. It is not clear from the Latin ('amicis suis inopinatum doloris vulnus inflixerat') whether Henry's friends were emotionally hurt by witnessing his suffering or whether he had physically attacked them, though I am inclined to go with the former.
2. BP, II.13, p. 66 ['Sed quid est facilius, dare salutem mentis an corporis? Qui oculos hujus corporeos illuminavit, juvenem de Fordwico Henricum menti restituit. Insaniverat diebus aliquot et amicis suis inopinatum doloris vulnus inflixerat. Colligatis a tergo manibus, ad sanctum trahitur; sancto, renitens licet atque reclamans, praesentatur. Ubi tota die insaniens, recedente luce solis, lucem rationis paulatim recuperare coepit. Pernoctavit in ecclesia; sanissimus in crastino remeavit'].
3. Ibid., II.12, p. 65.
4. 'He arrives out of his mind. He prays and departs sane' ['Amens accidit. Orat, sanusq[ue] recedit'].
5. The term 'mental' here refers to conditions affecting the 'mind', as it was understood in the Middle Ages, and should not be equated with the modern terms 'psychiatric' or 'psychological'.
6. Latham et al., V, 1397; Ibid., I, 76.
7. Haskins, pp. 6–7.
8. Yarrow, p. 1.
9. Bartlett, *The Natural and the Supernatural*, p. 31.
10. Boureau, p. 123.
11. Rider, pp. 48–49.
12. Green, p. 221.

13. Bailey, p. 252.
14. For example, see Clarke or Kemp.
15. Foucault, p. xxviii.
16. Ibid.
17. Porter, pp. 9–10.
18. In order to avoid retrospective categorisations, historians have focused on micro-studies of specific conditions as defined by individual medieval writers (for an example, see Jacquart's study of *phrénitis*).
19. ICD-10, F41.1.
20. 'Complementary and Alternative Therapy', *Mind*.
21. [1843] UKHL J16, 8 ER 718.
22. Craig, p. 732.
23. There is scope to extend this investigation to include additional cults. For example, the miracles of the Virgin Mary were experienced across England, and multiple shrines claimed her patronage, such as those at Evesham and Malmesbury. Despite some local attention, the largely decentralised nature of the Marian cult means that it is too broad to make a case study of here. The Virgin had a universal and a local appeal. For this reason, records of her miracles are wide-ranging, both geographically and chronologically, and were witnessed from Glastonbury Abbey to Jerusalem, and from the time of Augustine of Hippo (fl. early fifth century) onwards. Whilst local cults should be placed within the context of wider Marian devotion, 'local versions of Mary' were developed to meet the needs of individual communities [Rubin, pp. 52–53]. The cult(s) of the Virgin would therefore make an interesting study of their own, in which local distinctions could be compared to wider patterns. Nonetheless, for the purposes of this book, representations of madness in the Virgin's miracles are too few to draw meaningful comparisons. For example, in William of Malmesbury's *Miracles of the Blessed Virgin*, which was compiled in the 1130s and drew on other collections of the Virgin's miracles, there are only two brief references to madness: not enough to form a worthwhile case study [in miracle 27, a cleric of Pisa 'in amentia' takes on a large family inheritance, and in miracle 50, Saracens at Ramlah, 'in insania', try and fail to deface an image of the Virgin].
24. Clark, pp. 189–90.
25. Knowles, pp. 174–75.
26. Laharie, pp. 174–89.
27. Ibid., p. 192.
28. Ibid., p. 190.
29. Fritz, p. 222.
30. Pigeaud, p. 9.
31. Avicenna, V.1, fol. 22v; Harvey, p. 33; Ibid., p. 47.
32. Harvey, pp. 2–3.
33. Ibid., pp. 5–6.
34. Ibid., p. 5.
35. Ibid., p. 6; Lockett, p. 5.
36. Lockett, pp. 423–29.
37. Ibid., pp. 182–83.
38. Ibid., pp. 440–43.
39. Singer, p. 27.
40. Ibid.
41. Though Nebuchadnezzar's condition was not described as 'madness', upon raising his eyes to heaven, his senses were restored ('sensus meus redditus'). Thus, his previous state can be identified as one in which he lacked reason.
42. Doob, p. 58.

43. Ibid., p. 55.
44. To name but a few examples; in Job 2:7, Satan inflicts Job with boils; in Matthew 4:24, Christ is said to be able to heal both demoniacs and those suffering from other diseases; in Acts 8:7, Christ's disciples continue his exorcisms after his ascension to Heaven.
45. The Latin term 'supernaturalis' is rarely found in sources before the late twelfth century [Bartlett, *The Natural and the Supernatural*, pp. 2–7].
46. Bartlett, *The Natural and the Supernatural*, pp. 76–77.
47. Demaitre, pp. 136–37.
48. Bartlett, *The Natural and the Supernatural*, p. 2; Ibid., p. 33.
49. Brown, p. 1. Brown encouraged further historical analysis of hagiographical material, claiming that 'the full implications of what it meant to contemporaries to join Heaven and Earth at the grave of a dead human being has not been explored as fully as it deserves.'
50. Finucane, p. 9.
51. Ibid., pp. 11–13.
52. Ibid., p. 61.
53. Ibid., pp. 107–9.
54. Ibid., p. 107.
55. Ibid., p. 60.
56. Sigal, p. 13. The majority of the miracles used in Sigal's study come from the period 1050 to 1150 and from the region between the Seine and the Meuse. Nonetheless, little is said about the impact of chronological and geographical distinctions on the miracle collections themselves.
57. Ibid., pp. 236–43.
58. Ibid., pp. 236–37.
59. Ward, p. 36.
60. Ibid., p. 67.
61. Ibid.
62. Bartlett, *Why Can the Dead Do Such Great Things?*, p. 347; Ibid., p. 637.
63. Yarrow, pp. 9–10.
64. Ibid., pp. 7–8.
65. Ibid., p. 10.
66. Koopmans, p. 2.
67. Ibid., pp. 3–4.
68. Ibid., p. 3.
69. Ibid., pp. 193–98.
70. Vauchez, p. 35.
71. Goodich, p. 120.
72. Wilson, 'Miracle and Medicine', p. 177.
73. Burnett, p. 373.
74. As Wilson points out, though hagiographers may have been familiar with 'new learning', they were 'by no means at its speculative cutting edge', and, therefore, miracle texts present an amalgamation of 'practical knowledge, natural philosophy, medical theory and theology' ('Conceptions of the Miraculous', p. 101).
75. Watkins, pp. 32–33.
76. Le Goff, p. 135.
77. Ibid., p. 232.
78. Watkins, p. 31.
79. Thouroude has questioned whether the illnesses described in miracle texts should be thought of as 'medical conditions' at all or whether they should instead be read as representations of experiences (pp. 233–34).
80. My approach here aligns with that taken by the contributors in Matthew Mesley and Louise Wilson's edited volume, *Contextualizing Miracles in the Latin*

West, which explores the chronological context of saints' cults in relation to thematic explorations of contemporary beliefs and culture. Such an approach calls for an examination not of the veracity of miracles themselves but of the precedents surrounding their recording.

81. Mesley, p. 15.

Bibliography

Primary

Avicenna, 'De anima, qui sextus naturalium dicitur', in *Avicene perhypatetici philosophi, Opera in luce redacta* (Venice: Bonetus Locatellus for Octavianus Scotus, 1508), fols 1^r–21^v

Benedict of Peterborough, 'Miracula Sancti Thomae Cantuariensis', in *Materials for the History of Thomas Becket, Archbishop of Canterbury*, ed. by James Craigie Robertson, 7 vols (London: Longman, 1875–85), II (1876), 21–281

William of Malmesbury, *The Miracles of the Blessed Virgin Mary*, ed. and trans. by Michael Winterbottom and R.M. Thomson, Boydell Medieval Texts, 1 (Woodbridge: Boydell, 2015)

Secondary

Bailey, Anne E., 'Miracles and Madness: Dispelling Demons in Twelfth-Century Hagiography', in *Demons and Illness from Antiquity to the Early-Modern Period*, ed. by Siam Bhayro and Catherine Rider, Magical and Religious Literature of Late Antiquity, 5 (Leiden: Brill, 2017), pp. 235–255

Bartlett, Robert, *The Natural and the Supernatural in the Middle Ages* (Cambridge: Cambridge University Press, 2008)

———, *Why Can the Dead Do Such Great Things? Saints and Worshippers from the Martyrs to the Reformation* (Princeton, NJ and Oxford: Princeton University Press, 2013)

Boureau, Alain, *Satan the Heretic: The Birth of Demonology in the Medieval West*, trans. by Teresa Lavender Fagan (Chicago, IL: University of Chicago Press, 2006)

Brown, Peter, *The Cult of the Saints: Its Rise and Function in Latin Christianity*, rev. edn (Chicago, IL: University of Chicago Press, 2015)

Burnett, Charles, 'The Twelfth-Century Renaissance', in *The Cambridge History of Science*, ed. by David C. Lindberg and Ronald L. Numbers, 8 vols (Cambridge: Cambridge University Press, 2002–2018), II: *Medieval Science*, ed. by David C. Lindberg and Michael H. Shank (2013), pp. 365–384

Clark, James G., *The Benedictines in the Middle Ages* (Woodbridge: Boydell, 2011)

Clarke, Basil, *Mental Disorder in Earlier Britain* (Cardiff: University of Wales Press, 1975)

'Complementary and Alternative Therapy', *Mind: A Registered Charity in England (no.219830)* <http://www.mind.org.uk/information-support/drugs-and-treatments/complementary-and-alternative-therapy/what-are-they/?o=6829>

Craig, Leigh Ann, 'The History of Madness and Mental Illness in the Middle Ages: Directions and Questions', *History Compass*, 12 (2014), 729–744

Demaitre, Luke, *Medieval Medicine: The Art of Healing, from Head to Toe* (Santa Barbara, CA: Praeger, 2013)

Doob, Penelope B.R., *Nebuchadnezzar's Children: Conventions of Madness in Middle English Literature* (New Haven, CT and London: Yale University Press, 1974)

Finucane, Ronald C., *Miracles and Pilgrims: Popular Beliefs in Medieval England* (New York, NY: St. Martin's Press, 1977; repr. 1995)

Foucault, Michel, *History of Madness*, ed. by Jean Khalfa, trans by. Jonathan Murphy and Jean Khalfa (London and New York, NY: Routledge, 2006)

Fritz, Jean-Marie, *Le discours du fou au Moyan Âge, XIIe–XIIIe siècles: Étude comparée des discours littéraire, médical, juridique et théologique de la folie* (Paris: Presses Universitaires de France, 1992)

Goodich, Michael E., *Miracles and Wonders: The Development of the Concept of Miracle, 1150–1350* (Aldershot: Ashgate, 2007)

Green, Monica, 'Salerno on Thames: The Genesis of Anglo-Norman Medical Literature', in *Language and Culture in Medieval Britain: The French of England, c.1100–c.1500*, ed. by Jocelyn Wogan-Browne (Woodbridge: York Medieval Press, 2009), pp. 220–231

Harvey, E. Ruth, *The Inward Wits: Psychological Theory in the Middle Ages and the Renaissance*, Warburg Institute Surveys, 6 (London: Warburg Institute, 1975)

Haskins, Charles Homer, *The Renaissance of the Twelfth Century* (Cambridge, MA and London: Harvard University Press, 1927)

Hollywood, Amy, 'Acute Melancholia', *Harvard Theological Review*, 99 (2006), 381–406

International Statistical Classification of Diseases and Related Health Problems, 10 (2016), <http://apps.who.int/classifications/icd10/browse/2016/en#>

Jacquart, Danielle, 'Les avatars de la phrénitis chez Avicenne et Rhazès', in *Maladie et maladies: histoire et conceptualisation. Mélanges en l'honneur de Mirko Grmek*, ed. by Danielle Gourevitch (Geneva: Droz, 1992), pp. 181–192

Katajala-Peltomaa, Sari, and Susanna Niiranen, eds, *Mental (Dis)Order in Later Medieval Europe*, Later Medieval Europe, 12 (Leiden: Brill, 2014)

Kemp, Simon, *Medieval Psychology* (New York, NY: Greenwood Press, 1990)

Knowles, David, *The Monastic Order: A History of Its Development from the Times of St Dunstan to the Fourth Lateran Council, 943–1216* (Cambridge: Cambridge University Press, 1950)

Koopmans, Rachel, *Wonderful to Relate: Miracle Stories and Miracle Collecting in High Medieval England* (Philadelphia: University of Pennsylvania Press, 2011)

Laharie, Muriel, *La folie au Moyen-Âge, XIe–XIIIe siècles* (Paris: Le Léopard d'Or, 1991)

Latham, R.E., et al., eds, *Dictionary of Medieval Latin from British Sources*, 17 fascicules (London: Oxford University Press, 1975–2013)

Le Goff, Jacques, *The Birth of Purgatory*, trans. by Arthur Goldhammer (Chicago, IL: University of Chicago Press, 1984)

Lockett, Leslie, *Anglo-Saxon Psychologies in the Vernacular and Latin Traditions* (Toronto, ON: University of Toronto Press, 2011)

Mesley, Matthew M., 'Introduction', in *Contextualizing Miracles in the Christian West, 1100–1500: New Historical Approaches*, ed. by Matthew M. Mesley and Louise E. Wilson, Medium Ævum, 32 (Oxford: Society for the Study of Medieval Language and Literature, 2014), pp. 1–15

Pigeaud, Jackie, *La maladie de l'âme: Étude sur la relation de l'âme et du corps dans la tradition médico-philosophique antique* (Paris: Société d'Édition Les Belles Lettres, 1981)

Porter, Roy, *Madmen: A Social History of Madhouses, Mad-Doctors & Lunatics*, 2nd edn (Stroud: Tempus, 2004)

Rider, Catherine, 'Demons and Mental Disorder in Late Medieval Medicine', in *Mental (Dis)Order in Later Medieval Europe*, ed. by Sari Katajala-Peltomaa and Susanna Nirranen, Later Medieval Europe, 12 (Leiden: Brill, 2014), pp. 47–69

Rubin, Miri, *Emotion and Devotion: The Meaning of Mary in Medieval Religious Culture* (Budapest and New York, NY: Central European University, 2009)
Sigal, Pierre-André, *L'homme et le miracle dans la France médiévale (XIe–XIIe siècle)* (Paris: Cerf, 1985)
Singer, P.N., 'General Introduction', in *Galen: Psychological Writings*, ed. by P.N. Singer (Cambridge: Cambridge University Press, 2013), pp. 1–41
Thouroude, Véronique, 'Sickness, Disability, and Miracle Cures: Hagiography in England, c.700 – c.1200' (unpublished doctoral thesis, University of Oxford, 2015)
Turner, Wendy J., *Care and Custody of the Mentally Ill, Incompetent, and Disabled in Medieval England* (Turnhout: Brepols, 2013)
[1843] United Kingdom House of Lords Decisions [UKHL] J16, 8 ER 718, <http://www.bailii.org/uk/cases/UKHL/1843/J16.html>
Vauchez, André, *Sainthood in the Later Middle Ages*, trans. by Jean Birrell (Cambridge: Cambridge University Press, 1997)
Ward, Benedicta, *Miracles and the Medieval Mind: Theory, Record and Event 1000–1215*, rev. edn (Philadelphia: University of Pennsylvania Press, 1987)
Watkins, C.S., 'Sin, Penance and Purgatory in the Anglo-Norman Realm: The Evidence of Visions and Ghost Stories', *Past and Present*, 175 (2002), 3–33
Wilson, Louise E., 'Conceptions of the Miraculous: Natural Philosophy and Medical Knowledge in the Thirteenth-Century *Miracula* of St Edmund of Abingdon', in *Contextualizing Miracles in the Christian West, 1100–1500: New Historical Approaches*, ed. by Matthew M. Mesley and Louise E. Wilson, Medium Ævum, 32 (Oxford: Society for the Study of Medieval Language and Literature, 2014), pp. 99–125
———, 'Miracle and Medicine in Medieval Miracula ca. 1180 – ca. 1320' (unpublished doctoral thesis, University of Cambridge, 2011)
Yarrow, Simon, *Saints and their Communities: Miracle Stories in Twelfth-Century England* (Oxford: Oxford University Press, 2006)

1 Protection and punishment in the miracles of Saint Edmund the Martyr at Bury

> It happened at that time that a woman had fallen into the sheriff's disfavour through her involvement in a criminal case. Weak with womanish fear lest she be handed over to suffer the force of the law, she sought the holy martyr [Saint Edmund]'s protection, entered his sanctuary and stayed there, with the clerics' consent, next to the martyr's relics. When the judge [a sheriff named Leofstan of whom nothing is known aside from his name], whom we mentioned, discovered this, he presently decided upon a contest to show which of them was more powerful: the martyr, in freeing people, or the judge, in condemning them, so he instantly lined up his servants, bade them bring him the defendant and, (to compound his offence) in his madness ['rabide'], commanded them to violate the sanctuary, ignorant – the wretch – of the trouble such action would land him in. [...] There [at the boundary of the sanctuary], divine power made him lose his mind and be driven mad, thereby freeing the martyr's poor woman and distracting the attention of her captors, who were now more concerned with their punished lord than with seeing their impudent plans to completion.[1]

The fate of Sheriff Leofstan was recorded by a Bury monk sometime in the 1070s–80s, though the event itself is thought to have taken place during the reign of King Æthelred (r.978–1013 and 1014–16).[2] According to the miracle record, Leofstan never recovered his sanity, and, even after his death, his possessed corpse had to be sewn in a calf's skin and sunk in a lake to prevent its reemergence from the grave.[3] Such an undignified end was, as the miracle record makes clear, a divine punishment for breaking the sanctuary of Saint Edmund's shrine. Edmund's intercession served to defend those who sought his protection: in this case, an accused criminal and a 'weak' woman who could not defend herself against the sheriff's might. This chapter looks at madness as a divinely-inflicted punishment for sin and transgression. In miracle records like that of Leofstan, Saint Edmund was shown to protect the interests of the religious community at Bury by dispensing madness as a punishment and a deterrent.

Ostensibly, this miracle fits perfectly into Benedicta Ward's category of 'traditional' miracles, written in a monastic environment in which the saint provided protection for his monastery by miraculously avenging wrongs committed against them.[4] Saint Edmund promoted and protected his sanctuary by punishing transgressions. Nonetheless, it is important to place this miracle not only within a wider hagiographical typology but also within the context of late-eleventh-century Bury. Even within the broad category of 'traditional' miracles, we can see representations of madness evolving as they were influenced by contemporary philosophical, theological and medical learning. Saint Edmund's miracles provide a particularly rich case study for the concept of madness as a miraculous punishment. The collection in which Leofstan's miracle was recorded was entirely rewritten c.1100 under the likely patronage of Herbert de Losinga, bishop of Norwich (1091–1119).[5] The survival of both versions of the *De Miraculis Sancti Eadmundi* (that begun in the 1070s–80s and that of c.1100) allows for a comparison of the miracles from two perspectives through an examination of the intended audience of each collection:

- that of the Bury monks who were the likely intended audience for the earlier collection in which the above miracle was recorded
- that of the bishop who commissioned the new collection and who, along with the diocesan, had not appeared entirely favourably in the earlier collection

Of the five case studies that make up this investigation, the miracles associated with Saint Edmund at Bury were compiled the earliest. Bury is also the only location of the five at which new miracle collections were compiled for a pre-existing cult. This chapter reviews how political, cultural and intellectual developments in post-Conquest England influenced miracle collecting in Bury at the turn of the eleventh century and representations of madness in this context. The significance of madness as a punishment is explored in comparison to other divinely-inflicted illnesses, such as blindness or paralysis, which also feature in Edmund's miracle collections. Notably, Sheriff Leofstan's actions, even prior to his punishment, were labelled 'mad' ('rabide'), which alludes to the premise of *the punishment fitting the crime*, evident in the biblical aphorism of *an eye for an eye* (Deuteronomy 19:21 and Exodus 21:24).[6] From the perspective of the Bury monks, Leofstan had acted irrationally by breaking the sacrosanctity of Edmund's sanctuary, and he was fittingly punished with madness. Using this premise, I evaluate which transgressions were associated by Edmund's miracle compilers with madness, how the form of punishment paralleled the nature of the offence and in what ways Saint Edmund offered protection against such offences.

The post-Conquest miracles of Saint Edmund

The Anglo-Saxon cult and the Norman Conquest

Before we can turn to his miracles, we need to establish who Saint Edmund was and how he came to be associated with the monastic community at Bury. Saint Edmund of Bury, also known as Saint Edmund the Martyr and

Saint Edmund the King, was a ninth-century king of East Anglia who was martyred by Danish invaders in 869.[7] The near-contemporary *Anglo-Saxon Chronicle* recorded his defeat in battle but did not mention the martyrdom.[8] It is not clear when exactly Edmund's body was moved to Bury, though it was probably in the 890s, when a memorial coinage was issued for the saint.[9] The first hagiographical account of Edmund's life, *Passio sancti Eadmundi*, was composed by Abbo of Fleury (c.945–1004) in 985–87, possibly when he visited England and stayed at the nearby Ramsey Abbey.[10] The *Passio* proved to be extremely popular, influencing later accounts of Edmund's life and continuing to circulate well into the fifteenth century.[11] From the eleventh century onwards, Edmund's cult became crucial to Bury's self-identification as a powerful entity in East Anglia and as a formidable opposition to those seeking political power in its vicinity. In addition, the shrine was a large and fruitful place of pilgrimage and was arguably 'the most popular pilgrimage site in England' until the death of Thomas Becket in 1170 and his subsequent cult, which attracted pilgrims to Canterbury.[12]

Herman's De Miraculis Sancti Eadmundi

By 1070, eighty years had passed since Abbo had written his *Passio*, and Edmund's posthumous reputation needed updating. A new collection of miracles, entitled *De Miraculis Sancti Eadmundi*, was composed by a monk named Herman at the instigation of Baldwin, abbot of Bury (d.1097).[13] The collection was likely written in two parts: the first, sometime in the 1070s–80s and the second, in the 1090s.[14] Bury was fairly unusual in retaining its abbot through the Norman Conquest and for the entirety of the thirty-year period in which *De Miraculis* was compiled. Baldwin, a Frenchman with overseas connections in France and Italy, had served as physician to Edward the Confessor.[15] He would retain favour under the Norman kings, perhaps because of his medical skill; he continued to serve as a physician to both William the Conqueror and William Rufus.[16] Under Baldwin's continued guidance, Bury's cross-Channel interactions intensified, and the abbey strove to situate Saint Edmund's cult within this new pan-European environment.[17] In this context, the *vita* of the great English saint was rewritten by a German monk at the instigation of his French abbot.

It is likely that Herman, before coming to Bury, had trained at the abbey of Saint Vincent in Metz, where monks were encouraged to pay specific attention to the study of history.[18] His knowledge of historical writing, as well as his experience of the highly-meticulous keeping of relics at Saint Vincent's, which claimed to hold part of Saint Peter's chains among other relics, may have influenced his hagiography of Saint Edmund. He strove for detail and chronological accuracy by using chronicles and annals to give his work historical structure, and he chastised those who had previously neglected the saint.[19] According to Herman, Baldwin, in comparison with previous abbots, had made a considerable effort to revive the cult by spreading contact relics (parts of Edmund's clothing) across England and abroad and by commissioning Herman to compile a new miracle collection.[20] Admittedly, Edmund's cult may not have been in as dire a situation as Herman claimed, but it had, nonetheless, not yet reached the fame that it would under Baldwin.

In Herman's miracle collection, Edmund was not exclusively identified as a local saint but was shown to extend his patronage over all of East Anglia, and there is evidence to suggest that Herman strove to increase this sphere of influence. When reporting how Edmund's incorrupt body was transported to London following Danish attacks in East Anglia, Herman remarked that London 'gives birth to no saints and has none', subtly putting Edmund forward as a possible saint of London.[21] Even more ambitiously, having miraculously brought about the death of King Swein Forkbeard of Denmark (987–1014) and thus spared the Anglo-Saxon people from paying him tribute, Edmund 'had not only allayed the plight of the poor in his town but had even curtailed the ravenous invasion throughout the whole of England'.[22] Edmund stood as a protector for the entire kingdom.

The only surviving medieval copy of the full version of Herman's *De Miraculis* is in London, British Library, MS Cotton Tiberius B.ii, which can be dated to c.1100.[23] *De Miraculis* follows a copy of Abbo's *Passio*: the only two texts in the manuscript.[24] It is likely that both texts were copied together at Bury to provide a complete record of Saint Edmund's life and miracles there.[25] The manuscript is, however, incomplete and contains blank or partially blank folios (fols 69^{r}, 69^{v}, 77^{v}) for miracles that were presumably being revised when the manuscript was produced and were never added (perhaps because, by this time, the new version was being compiled).[26] Tom Licence has identified seven missing miracles attributed to Herman in Oxford, Bodleian Library, MS Bodley 240 (fourteenth century), though none of these miracles contain references to madness.[27] Tiberius B.ii ends mid-miracle, possibly because Herman died before being able to finish his collection.[28]

The revised miracle collection

Perhaps even whilst scribes were working on Tiberius B.ii, Herman's miracle collection was being rewritten. The revised collection of miracles survives in New York, Pierpont Morgan Library, MS M. 736. The manuscript was produced by a Bury scribe in the 1120s–30s, making this the latest possible date for the composition of the text it contains, though the most likely composition date is 1099–1100.[29] Though the compiler certainly had access to Herman's *De Miraculis*, the collection was completely rewritten, and new miracles were added.[30] One such miracle appears to show the demise of Herman himself, who was punished with sickness and death for his impropriety in displaying Saint Edmund's relics to the people, who had even been allowed (for a price) to kiss the martyr's blood-soaked clothes![31] The text also contains frequent critiques of Herman's rhetorical style, which 'craved the thrill of theatrical applause' and 'devote[d] undue attention to contriving witticisms'.[32] Neither is it complimentary of Bury itself – which was dubbed 'the tavern of the physicians', alluding to the medical enterprises of Abbot Baldwin and possibly of others in his brethren – which suggests that the compiler was not a Bury monk himself.[33]

Licence has suggested that the anonymous compiler of the revised miracle collection was Goscelin of Saint-Bertin, who had already composed several other hagiographies. One of these – his *Life of Saint Ive* – had been commissioned by Herbert de Losinga, the likely patron of the Bury collection.[34] Nonetheless, though the attribution of the Bury miracle collection to Goscelin is persuasive, it cannot be made with certainty since Goscelin's style could have been imitated by another hagiographer. It is beyond the scope of this chapter to confirm or refute Licence's claim, and Licence's analysis of the hagiographer's style and potential background can be used to explore his representations of madness without knowing his name. We shall call him 'the reviser'.

Whether Goscelin or another writing in a similar style, the reviser certainly presented a far more favourable picture of Bishop Herbert de Losinga than Herman had done, and the bishop's involvement in the commission of the revised collection seems likely.[35] E.M. Rose has speculated that de Losinga, lacking the patronage of a local saint at his new diocesan seat in Norwich, had attempted to move it to Bury, where Saint Edmund was already established as a local patron and protector.[36] The revised miracle collection may have formed part of the bishop's strategy to reshape Edmund's cult to his own advantage. The establishment of Edmund as a diocesan protector would have simultaneously augmented the bishop's temporal and spiritual authority and curbed the influence of the Bury monks who had been enjoying the benefits of divine favour. The bishop's plan to establish greater diocesan control at Bury was thwarted, as Herman had gleefully noted, when he was barred from officiating at Edmund's 1095 translation, a detail omitted from the revised collection.[37] It is clear from the compiler's own admission that he temporarily resided at Bury in the late eleventh/early twelfth century whilst completing his commission, but he does not seem to have been warmly welcomed by the monks, who may have opposed both the bishop's attempts to gain power and the revision of Herman's work so soon after his death.[38] The reviser lamented having to 'duplicate furrows only recently ploughed'.[39]

Madness miracles

Herman's miracle collection contains five accounts of madness (excluding single-sentence remarks and allusions to madness in general without mentioning a specific sufferer). The reviser rewrote four of the five (summarised in Table 1.1). The only madness miracle excluded from the revised collection was that of Ranulf, a Norman courtier.[40] Ranulf was confined to bed

Table 1.1 Summary of madness miracles in the two collections of the miracles of Saint Edmund of Bury compiled around the turn of the eleventh century (numbering according to Licence's 2014 edition).

Herman's collection	*The revised collection*
3: Sheriff Leofstan was sent mad by divine judgement after trying to remove a criminal woman from the sanctuary of Saint Edmund's shrine. He was possessed by a demon even after death, and his corpse had to be sunk in a lake.	I.3: A prefect named Leofstan (who had previously sneered at Edmund's miracles) was 'swollen with pride' when he ordered for a woman who was seeking sanctuary at Saint Edmund's shrine to stand trial. By way of the saint's vengeance, the prefect was seized by a demon and, after his death, either he or a demon in his likeness wandered the town until his corpse was sunk in a lake.
23: Edward the Confessor was visiting Bury and with him were several Danes, including a royal official called Osgod. Osgod approached Saint Edmund's tomb whilst drunk and went to lean irreverently on his axe. The axe was divinely thrown against a wall, and Osgod fell to the floor in a Bacchic frenzy. Under King Edward's instruction, the monks prayed for Osgod's reconciliation with the saint, and he recovered his senses except for the sense of touch in his hands, which was permanently lost as a reminder of his sin.	I.9: Osgod Clapa, a ferocious and proud Dane, tried to lean on his axe at Saint Edmund's shrine, but divine power tore it from his hands, and he was possessed by a demon. At the bidding of King Edward the Confessor, Osgod was exorcised with holy water by the abbot. The exorcism did not work, and Osgod was then carried to the saint's shrine, where he was restored but left with withered hands as a mark of his punishment.
34: Ranulf, a Norman courtier, was distracted by worldly affairs. His wandering thoughts led to an alienation of the head. He was confined to bed for eight days and could not eat, drink or sleep. On the eighth night, he fell asleep and encountered Edmund in a dream-vision. The saint pursued him on horseback. Ranulf begged forgiveness, and the saint marked him with the sign of the cross. He awoke, and putrid matter flowed out of his ears. He was then cured and became a monk.	
36: Robert de Curcun took part in the 1088 rebellion against William II. With the permission of his lord, he tried to seize the manor of Southwold, which belonged to Saint Edmund. A storm came upon Robert and his followers, and he went into a stupor. Robert dared not continue, but two of his servants, Turolf and Gyrenner de Mouneyn, did. One went mad and the other succumbed to frenzy.	I.15: With his reason overcome by greed, Robert de Curcun demanded the manor of Southwold from the sheriff, Roger Bigod. He set out with two knights, but a storm came upon them. Robert wisely abandoned the venture, but his two knights continued. One went mad and the other was seized by frenzy.

(*Continued*)

Table 1.1 Summary of madness miracles in the two collections of the miracles of Saint Edmund of Bury compiled around the turn of the eleventh century (numbering according to Licence's 2014 edition). (*Continued*)

Herman's collection	*The revised collection*
37: Wulmer returned from Rome and left an offering of marble at Saint Edmund's shrine as thanks for his safe passage. Once home, he went out of his mind and was ill for four days. It was thought that he was going to die, and he received the *viaticum*. He suffered for a further four days, unable to move. The next day was a celebration for Saint Edmund, and Wulmer was able to fall asleep. In his dream, he saw a dove that transformed into a man and cured him with a healing touch. Those keeping vigil thought that Wulmer must have been in a frenzy when he awoke and got up to go the church and give thanks. He gave more crystal marble to Saint Edmund and related his story to the monks.	I.16: The miracle begins with a long defence of dream-visions. Wulmer returned from Rome and went to give thanks to Saint Edmund. In the churchyard, he became cold and started trembling. His suffering increased, and, after four days, it was thought that he would die, so he was given the *viaticum*. He could not sleep or eat. After another four days, on the day of a feast for Saint Edmund, Wulmer fell asleep and dreamed of a white dove that transformed into a man and healed him. When he awoke and got up, his household thought that he had lapsed into insanity and was about to die. Instead, he went to the church to recount his story.

for eight days, unable to sleep or eat and suffering from alienation of the head ('capitis alienatione'). Ranulf's suffering was brought about because he had given in to distracting, worldly thoughts, which, Herman remarked, courtiers were prone to do. When he finally fell asleep, he was visited by a dream-vision of Saint Edmund, who touched him with his right hand and cured him. Upon awakening, 'putrid matter' flowed from Ranulf's ears, completing the cure, and later, he received the tonsure and became a monk at Bury. We can only speculate as to why the reviser chose to omit this miracle. Perhaps, since Ranulf's entrance into the monastic community at Bury served to highlight Edmund's patronage of the Bury monks, this message made Ranulf's story less attractive to Bishop Herbert de Losinga, who was seeking to strengthen diocesan ties with the saint and to curb the influence of the monastic community at Bury.

Aside from that of Sheriff Leofstan, sent mad for breaking Edmund's sanctuary, three madness miracles were recorded by both Herman and the reviser. The first recounted the divine punishment of a Dane called Osgod Clapa, whose irreverent behaviour at Saint Edmund's shrine caused his madness. Both accounts linked Clapa's mad behaviour with demonic possession.[41] Herman attributed the behaviour that led to Clapa's divine punishment to drunkenness (in a similar way to Leofstan, Osgod was 'unsound' ['incompetens'] *before* he was punished with madness), whereas the reviser condemned his pride ('tumidus').[42]

Another miracle record detailed the divine punishment of Robert de Curcun, his steward, Turolf, and a soldier, Gryenner de Mouneyn. Turolf and de Mouneyn were named by Herman but not by the reviser.[43] De Curcun had tried to take possession of the manor of Southwold, which belonged to Saint Edmund. In Herman's version, as the three men rode towards the manor, a storm broke and de Curcun was driven mad. The other men, not heeding the warning, continued onward and were also punished with madness. In the revised account, de Curcun himself wisely ('saniori') withdrew when the storm came upon the group and thus was not reprimanded. His unnamed companions, however, did not heed the warning and were punished; one went mad ('amens'), and the other was taken by frenzy ('frenesi').[44]

The final madness miracle is somewhat of an anomaly in that the sufferer described was not necessarily mad but was labelled by Herman as 'out of his mind' ('in mentis excessu').[45] According to Herman, a local man called Wulmer was overcome with faintness on his return from Rome and took to his bed for four days. His condition was deemed to be so dire that the parish priest was summoned and the *viaticum* was administered. For another four days he lingered, unable to move. After a total, then, of eight days, Wulmer eventually fell asleep and saw, in a dream-vision, a dove that metamorphosed into a beautiful man. The man touched Wulmer's right eyelid, opened it and told him he was cured. When he awoke, witnesses at first mistook his miraculous recovery for 'frenzy' ('frenesy' [*sic*]). The cured man gave an offering at Saint Edmund's shrine and reported his story to the brothers there. The revised version of the story is prefaced by a lengthy argument against those who did not believe in miraculous dream-visions.[46] The reviser did not describe Wulmer as 'out of his mind', but he did state that witnesses to the cure had thought that the invalid had 'lapsed into insanity' ('arreptus insaniret') when he suddenly leapt from his bed to give thanks at the church.

Madness as a punishment for transgressions against the saint

With the exception of Wulmer, all the cases of madness in the two collections were represented as divine retributions for transgressions made by the sufferers. Both miracle compilers, in some instances, drew parallels between transgression and punishment; madness punished 'mad' behaviour (i.e. actions that could be seen as 'irrational' because they contravened the saint's will). Madness was also debilitating enough to halt certain transgressions, such as that of Robert de Curcun and his followers. Madmen lost their respectability, making them socially as well as mentally incapable of continuing to attack Saint Edmund, whether it be by dishonouring his shrine or by seizing his manor. Seizing the saint's property was considered by Herman to be 'disreputable' ('inconueniens') in itself. As Robert's punishment, 'stupefaction was stamped on his face for everyone to see, for his state of mind left a physical impression'.[47] Madness, as a punishment for transgression, reinforced Edmund's protection of the monastic community by discrediting and disabling his opponents.

Leofstan

To set up Leofstan's miracle, Herman began by reminding his audience that he was writing during a 'time of grace' in which he and others could benefit from 'God's compassionate mercy'.[48] Periods of grace and mercy were referred to by Herman throughout his collection. Following biblical precedent (Psalms 102), he contended that God's mercy was bestowed on the world in appointed cycles.[49] Before the beginning of Edmund's miracles, the people lived in sin and thus did not 'enjoy their time of mercy'.[50] Here, Herman associated divine mercy with absence of sin. Sinfulness warranted the withdrawal of mercy, which left sinners more open to natural disaster or demonic attack, from which God's mercy could have spared them.[51] Referring to Scripture (Psalms 67:36 – 'God is wondrous in his saints'), Herman explained that, in Leofstan's case, God, the craftsman, had used Saint Edmund as a tool to bring about that which His kindness willed.[52] Thus, Herman established a historical and biblical context for the story, which he then dated specifically to 1 May.[53]

Both the setting of the miracle within the age of mercy and the date were omitted by the reviser.[54] Herman also used a biblical precedent (1 Thessalonians 4:6 – 'God will punish the perpetrators of all offences of this sort') to preface Robert de Curcun's miracle, and, again, the reviser omitted it.[55] Rather than focusing on the historical situation of each miracle in relation to God's mercy, the reviser structured his miracle accounts so as to clarify Edmund's miracles to the saint's critics.[56] In Leofstan's case, he offered a lengthy explanation for why Edmund performed this vengeful miracle, since, had he not, his sanctuary would have been degraded and he would have lost the respect that was necessary to protect his church.[57] It is noteworthy, nonetheless, that, in both miracle collections, Leofstan's suffering was justified by his behaviour, and the way in which he suffered was directly connected to his original transgression.

When performing his duties as a sheriff, Leofstan had a 'heart full of wickedness' and a 'fierce, wicked mind'.[58] When the accused woman fled to Saint Edmund's shrine, Leofstan 'in his madness, commanded [his servants] to violate the sanctuary' ('rabide iubet uiolari loca sancti').[59] Herman's use of the term 'rabide' here was no doubt purposeful given its associations with violent and frenzied behaviour.[60] Not only does the description foreshadow Leofstan's approaching madness, but it also vividly contrasts the sheriff's expected role to uphold peace and law. Further allusions to the illegitimacy of Leofstan's actions were made in Herman's description of his 'wicked servants', who did as he asked, 'driven by their devilish presumption'.[61]

As punishment, Leofstan lost his mind, which was perhaps the source of his wickedness, and went mad ('alienatione mentis eum infecit et amentia').[62] In this description, there is an apparent distinction between the terms *alienatio mentis* and *amentia*, unless Herman used like terms to emphasise Leofstan's fate. The terms were also used in conjunction in Saint Frideswide's miracles, compiled almost a century later, to describe a madwoman called Emelina, whose attempt at suicide was attributed to demonic suggestion.[63] The reoccurrence of various terms for madness throughout the twelfth century implies that there was a continued association between different terms and between madness and demonic possession. In the revised account of Edmund's miracles, Leofstan was 'possessed by a demon' ('possessus a demone') as punishment for his depravity ('prauitatis').[64] Herman, too, repeated the demonic imagery that he had previously applied to Leofstan's servants when he described the sheriff's own fate: 'he came to a bad end, possessed by a demon ['possessus a demone'] in life, and then similarly possessed as a corpse ['possidetur cadauer'] in death.'[65] Notably, it was 'divine power' ('uirtus deifica') that sent Leofstan mad, and it was this blow (*impetus*) that allowed a demon to possess him.[66] Though Leofstan's ultimate torment was demonic, its penal nature was highlighted by its divine source.

The power to exorcise demons lay with God alone, and Leofstan's continued affliction (even after his death) is indicative of the immoral state of his soul. Herman declared that Leofstan was 'despised in heaven and on earth' and was thus suspended between the two in the realm of demons, to which he fell prey.[67] Leofstan's luxurious earthly lifestyle (Herman accused him of abusing his position to 'increase his worldly possessions') was juxtaposed with his ignoble end: 'Not long held down by the grave's embrace, his body was sewn in a calf's skin and sunk in a lake'.[68] Leofstan met the same end in the revised account though, unlike Herman, the reviser hoped that the grisly punishment the sheriff had received would spare him at the Last Judgement.[69] In the revised account, Leofstan's fate delivered a moral message, and Saint Edmund provided both protection for his followers and the chance of redemption for his enemies. This message of redemption would become more prominent in hagiographical tracts as the twelfth century progressed. The reviser's representation of Leofstan as flawed but still ultimately redeemable is indicative of a move away from Herman's portrayal of the sheriff as irreconcilably doomed.

Additionally, ghost tales and stories of wandering corpses were especially prolific in the eleventh and twelfth centuries, and we can locate Leofstan's story within the trend towards recording such marvels for their fascination value as well as their moral message.[70] William of Newburgh, writing in the mid-twelfth century, incredulously recounted how a group of villagers had dug up a corpse and, to prevent it from terrorising the neighbourhood, had chopped it into pieces and burned it.[71] This course of action was not sanctioned by the local ecclesiastical authorities, and it is possible that the same was true for the disposal of Leofstan's body. Were this the case, it would certainly have been fitting that, having disregarded the ecclesiastical protection of Edmund's shrine, Leofstan's own body should be so ignominiously treated.

Osgod Clapa

Herman made the contrast between the vanity that accompanies transgression and the ignobility that comes with punishment even clearer in the miracle of Osgod Clapa. Clapa arrived at Edmund's shrine adorned 'head-to-toe in a graceful outfit of wild animal skins'; this oxymoron is a joke on Herman's part as well as an allusion to the barbarism of the Danes.[72] Clapa wore 'armlets' on both arms and carried a 'gilt-inlaid axe'.[73] Hinting at the moral of his story, Herman explained that 'later, this graceful get-up was turned to his infamous disgrace'.[74] Clapa's disgrace came when he attempted to lean irreverently on his axe whilst waiting at the shrine (note that the gilt-inlaid axe itself played a role in his downfall) and was reduced, 'out of his wits, [to rolling] around on the ground as though suffering Bacchic mania'.[75] The reference to Bacchus (the Roman god of wine) is particularly relevant given Herman's description of Clapa's previous behaviour as 'intoxicated' ('infrunitus') and his claims that the Dane was 'drunk out of his wits' ('incompetens stupefactus').[76]

The reviser removed the drunken element of the story and instead concentrated on Clapa's extravagant dress (as Herman had) and his 'wicked deeds'.[77] Following Herman's account, the reviser explained that divine power flung the Dane's axe from his hand as he attempted to lean on it, but, in the revised account, there was no mention of Bacchic mania. Instead, Clapa was 'possessed by a demon', which nonetheless caused similar physical symptoms to those described in Herman's account; he 'fell to the ground, groaning in distress [...] endlessly writhing and making various noises'.[78] The connections drawn between Osgod Clapa's madness and demonic possession were not unusual, and parallels between madness and demonic possession were frequently noted in both hagiographical and non-hagiographical texts of this period. Herman labelled Clapa a 'demoniac' ('energuminus') when explaining the method used to cure him (chanting psalms and reciting a litany).[79] The reviser stated that the abbot had attempted to 'expel the unclean spirit by saying rites of exorcism and pouring holy water over the invalid'.[80] This attempt had not worked (undermining the abbot's authority, which may have met with Bishop Herbert's approval), and Clapa was brought to Edmund's tomb, where the psalms and litanies were performed.[81]

Though Clapa was 'restored to health' ('recuperatus'), according to Herman, he never regained all his senses and forever lost the strength in his hands.[82] It was a fitting punishment to lose the sense of touch given the sensual ('sensualiter') nature of his sin (his worldly pride and irreverence towards the saint).[83] The reviser reported that Clapa's hands remained withered as a permanent reminder of his arrogance.[84] Both miracle compilers thus connected wickedness and improper behaviour with the punishment of madness as well as with a physical impairment of the hands. For Herman, madness was strongly associated with senselessness, and, for the reviser, demonic possession could be linked to wicked deeds. Osgod Clapa was permanently reminded of his sin and prevented from further sin by losing the sense that had led to his material transgression; he could no longer wield the axe that he had carried so irreverently at Edmund's shrine, nor could be proudly adorn himself with armlets.

Osgod was certainly not the only Dane to suffer at Edmund's hands. The saint acted on several occasions to protect the people of Bury and the surrounding area from Danish violence. The Danish leader, Swein, was struck down by the martyr with a lance in a miraculous vision and killed.[85] Swein's death meant that the people of Bury – and, in fact, all the poor of England – were spared from paying the tribute that he had imposed on them.[86] Another Dane was punished with blindness for lifting the cloth that covered Edmund's tomb to look underneath.[87] Again, the punishment was made to fit the transgression; blindness punished a man who had looked where he should not. Herman also connected the Dane's swollen eyes with his swollen arrogance.[88] Edmund's punishment of the Danes was perhaps a timely reminder, in the last decades of the eleventh century, for any Normans who might have thought to undermine the power of an Anglo-Saxon saint. The reviser, writing slightly later, related the blind Dane's punishment to the concept of sin more generally, explaining that Edmund 'achieved the salvation of souls by curing afflictions', whether these 'afflictions' came in the form of disease or illness or whether they were the result of sin and transgression, which could be rectified through bodily suffering.[89]

Robert de Curcun

Miraculous punishments dispensed by Edmund also served a practical purpose: the defence of his abbey and its rights. Madness was used as a punishment for those who had attempted to usurp the rights of the abbey or to undermine the prestige of Edmund's shrine. The individuals who were struck by madness, like Sheriff Leofstan and Osgod Clapa, were often important and powerful men, and their punishments not only acted as forms of vengeance and deterrents to others but also incapacitated them and made them unable to continue their disputes. Robert de Curcun had made his desire to take the manor of Southwold (used for the monks' provisions) known to his lord, Roger Bigod, who had granted his permission for de Curcun to graze his horses there.[90] The miracle took place during the 1088 rebellion against William Rufus, at which time 'soldiers [coveted ...] their lord's possessions'.[91] Bigod himself had been removed from his post as sheriff of Norfolk by William so had no authority to grant de Curcun's request.[92] In the rebellion against the king, Herman provided a parallel example of taking something that is not yours to take, emphasising the nature of the transgression in the case of Southwold.

Notably, in the revised account, which was written after Bigod's reappointment as sheriff in 1091, Bigod did not grant his permission for de Curcun to take the manor and stated that it belonged to Saint Edmund.[93] De Curcun, too, decided not to challenge the saint, and it is significant that two unnamed knights transgressed and were punished in the revised account, which was written when it might have been imprudent to criticise named individuals who had been restored to the king's favour. The reviser's disassociation of both Bigod and de Curcun from wrongdoing and madness emphasises the humiliation of madness as a divine punishment. Madness certainly seems to have been something that noblemen would not have wanted their names associated with.

De Curcun's miracle demonstrates how, in the face of secular unrest, Edmund was called upon to provide physical protection for the monastic community at Bury. Monastic patrons, like Edmund, could prove powerful allies in land disputes with the nobility.[94] Patrick Geary has identified the involvement of saints in secular disputes as particularly heightened during the period 800–1100, though his focus is on late-Carolingian and post-Carolingian Francia, with which, granted, both Herman and the reviser (if he was indeed Goscelin of Saint-Bertin) may previously have had some connection.[95] At a time when local authority was gradually being replaced with more centralised secular authority, relatively-rich monastic cult centres were both a target for plunder-seeking nobles and an alternate focus of power that could provide some form of stability and protection in the region.[96] Saint Foy, whose miracles were compiled c.1030–c.1050, protected her monastery at Conques (in southern Francia and on the pilgrimage route to Compostela) from the frequent assaults of a nobleman called Hector who 'preyed ruthlessly on the holy virgin's lands', and from another called Arnold who 'plundered everything the holy virgin possessed that was near his own property, taking farm animals and household goods as spoils.'[97] Simon Yarrow has argued that, likewise, Herman's miracle collection was very much framed 'to serve the needs of his present' and to provide a record of the abbey's legal privileges as upheld by Edmund.[98] This agenda was also evident in Herman's representation of Abbot Baldwin's disputes with Bishop Herbert de Losinga concerning the bishop's claims against the abbey, which were discussed above in relation to the translation of Edmund's relics, which Herbert was blocked from officiating. Though not every nobleman could be intimidated by the threat of spiritual reparation, a public display of the saint's vengeance – such as that inflicted on Robert de Curcun, which, as mentioned, was 'stamped on his face for everyone to see' – could provide a focus for public opposition.[99]

Madness was as effective as a visual deterrent as physical punishment, but it also left the victim legally undermined. Though evidence of the legal management of the insane in this period is sparse, twelfth-century legal texts did discuss provisions for the mentally incapacitated. Such individuals were to be placed under the legal care of a guardian and, in this way, lost their freedom to function independently in society.[100] De Curcun's accomplices, Turolf and Gryenner de Mouneyn, were not only punished by their madness; they were incapacitated by it. Herman reported that 'with their minds befuddled, they dared not make any further attempt of that kind on the manor'.[101] Madness would certainly have undermined de Curcun's claim to use the land at Southwold as well as his reputation as a soldier. Edmund had used madness to incapacitate a powerful challenger, both legally, to counter the permission given by Bigod, and socially, by damaging de Curcun's reputation. Leofstan's punishment had a similar effect to de Curcun's. Not only was Leofstan's madness/possession a visual deterrent to his soldiers, but it also distracted them and allowed their captive – the criminal woman – to escape.[102] Leofstan's breaking of Edmund's sanctuary was a clear secular violation of monastic authority. Such clashes were not uncommon in the tenth century when kings began to tighten their control over sanctuary rights.[103]

Edmund's saintly duty towards the monastic community at Bury included the protection of their property. Bartlett argues that 'relations between followers and saints were modelled on the bond between lord and dependent'.[104] The *patrocinium* (duty as a patron) that tied a saint to his community was exercised by the superior lord (the saint) over the inferior subject (the monastery).[105] The protection that Edmund afforded Wulmer on his journey to Rome was described as 'patrocinatori', or that afforded 'by the patron'.[106] As patrons, saintly lords could take the part of a monastic community in legal disputes with secular powers.[107] Certainly, during the 1088 rebellion, the monks of Bury seem to have been unable to rely on judicial protection for their manor and, instead, achieved their own justice through bringing social pressure to bear on de Curcun and his followers. Land disputes of this type were portrayed as not only unjust but also senseless. When a different Norman courtier seized another of Edmund's manors, Herman described him as 'taking leave of his senses' ('datus in reprobum sensum').[108] The reviser made the purpose of the punishment inflicted by Edmund on de Curcun's followers very clear, though he excluded de Curcun himself, claiming that the courtier had 'opted for a wiser course' (note the contrast between wisdom and madness) and abandoned the venture: 'Thus Edmund cast down the arrogant wrongdoers and the greedy usurpers from the heights of their audacious presumptions, avenged their wrongs, and asserted his lordship'.[109]

The narrative of punishment and patronage was carefully constructed in both collections. For Herman, a Platonist model of natural balance merged with his biblical framework of periods of grace and mercy. During such periods, God delivered divine punishments to protect the community of His saint, Edmund. Herman's concept of avenging wrongs fits with a Platonist understanding of the world-soul, in which all natural things were in harmony with each other.[110] The minds of de Curcun and his followers were made to echo the natural chaos of the storm that preceded their madness.[111] Herman emphasised this connection and gave it a Christian twist by repeating the transgressors' fear that the storm had been generated by God and

Saint Edmund.[112] The revised collection left out the Platonic rhetoric and focused instead on the connection between sin, punishment and salvation. Perhaps the reviser had noticed the complication that a Platonic-Christian model of the world-soul, which operated through natural balance, left less room for the direct intervention of God in human affairs in a way seemingly contrary to nature (i.e. through miracles).[113] The disparity in Herman's and the reviser's approaches to madness as a punishment can be viewed in terms of the revival of Platonism at the turn of the eleventh century and its mixed reception from Christian writers.[114]

The first half of the twelfth century saw works of Platonic and Neo-Platonic origin, which had been known before, take a more central role in theological debate.[115] Perhaps the most influential of these Platonic texts was the *Timaeus*, an account of the cosmos set in the format of a debate in which Socrates and Timaeus were contributors. Only the first part – that detailing the formation and nature of the cosmos – was known in the Middle Ages.[116] Justin Stover has identified at least seventy individual twelfth-century writers who discussed the *Timaeus*, and he concludes that knowledge of Platonic ideas was becoming 'familiar, even commonplace' in the Latin West.[117] By the second half of the twelfth century, Bury almost certainly had a copy of the *Timaeus*.[118] It is therefore possible that Herman was able to engage with Platonist ideas in Bury or that he had encountered them elsewhere, either in Latin translation or via Latin commentaries.

Knowledge of the *Timaeus* in the West was heavily influenced by the philosopher Calcidius's Latin translation and commentary, which reached the peak of its influence c.975–c.1125.[119] Calcidius (fl. fourth century) allowed for some influence of the body over the mind, for example, in the irrational minds ('inrationabilem mentis') of children.[120] Lack of reason and intellectual feebleness ('imbecillitatem') in the young, which gave way to bodily impulses, could also extend to the mad, who too lacked reason.[121] For Herman, these connections between body, mind and soul aligned with his concept of natural balance. The damaged souls of transgressors were reflected in their damaged minds and the grotesque physicality of the symptoms of madness. The journey that de Curcun and his followers had undertaken to seize the manner was, in itself, 'stupid' ('stolidum'), and they were 'foolish' ('hebetes') for taking part in such a venture.[122] The term 'hebetes' was frequently employed in the works of Cicero (fl. first century BC), himself a Platonist.[123]

Punishment was carefully balanced against transgression to emphasise the connection between the two. In the case of madness, transgressions were deemed to be nonsensical. Punishment prevented the continuation of the transgression, provided a public example for would-be transgressors and served a practical purpose in legally and socially undermining the transgressor. Herman's heavy classical rhetoric would become less popular during the twelfth century when descriptions of individual miracles were generally shorter and hagiographers were more open to the possibility of salvation for the laity. The reviser, writing only a few decades after Herman, criticised his 'rhetorical ornaments' and set out to restore 'Christian simplicity and homely faith' to Edmund's miracle record.[124] The revised collection portrayed punishment both as a means to spiritual salvation and as a vehicle for punishing the actions of sinners, concentrating, in the case of Osgod Clapa for example, on the wicked deeds of the transgressor.

Madness as a punishment for sin

Herman and the reviser emphasised Edmund's role as Bury's patron through the miraculous punishments he inflicted on those who had wronged the abbey. There was also a concern, in both collections, to highlight the sins of such transgressors. Osgod Clapa was punished for his arrogance or pride ('fastu').[125] Swein, the Danish leader who had tried to exact a tribute from the people of East Anglia, was compared to the blasphemous Julian the Apostate and Edmund to Saint Mercurius, who slew him.[126] In both of these cases, it was not only the actions against Edmund that warranted punishment but also the sins from which these actions stemmed. This emphasis on the personal sins of the protagonists perhaps served to highlight that their punishments were justly deserved. Not only were their challenges to the abbey or to Edmund's authority wrong, but their characters were ultimately flawed by sin. It was this sin that caused them to contest the abbey's jurisdictional rights and that warranted divine punishment.

The sins of the Danes, including Osgod Clapa

The relationship between sin and divine punishment is particularly clear in Herman's account of a Dane who was punished with blindness:

> the swelling arising from his arrogance ['arrogantiae'] was turned into a corrective, as God and the saint won the sinner over and drove the Dane to repent tearfully, abjectly seeking mercy in the hope of securing forgiveness he did not deserve; and because God does not spurn a contrite and humble heart (and because the hardest hearts often prove the most pliant in response to favour), the Dane's prayer was answered and his sight restored.[127]

It was the Dane's pride that made him show irreverence towards the saint. This sin required forgiveness, and his irreverent actions needed God's pardon.

Osgod Clapa, in flaunting his pride at Edmund's shrine, was shown to have indulged in earthly pleasures above spiritual pursuits, endangering his soul. Herman's detailed description of Clapa's extravagant jewellery and appearance has already been discussed. It was echoed by the reviser, who depicted the Dane 'all dressed up in clothes woven with gold, sporting golden bracelets and a gold-inlaid axe, slung Danish-style from his shoulder'.[128] Herman's Clapa was 'puffed up with pride' ('cum fastu superbie'), and the reviser's had a 'rigid body and swollen mind' ('corpore rigidus et mente tumidus'). With this description, the reviser drew a parallel between Clapa's outward appearance and his inner immorality.[129] This parallel was made permanently visible in Clapa's withered arm, which, according to the reviser, never recovered.[130] Pride, expressed through human arrogance, was – to borrow a phrase from Kiril Petkov – the 'benchmark of illegitimacy' because it denied God's supremacy.[131] By acting thus against God, the actions of the proud man were seen as immoral and illicit.[132] The association of Osgod's actions with pride, therefore, confirmed Edmund's legitimacy by presenting irreverence towards him as irreverence towards God.

For Herman, Clapa's miraculous punishment served a dual purpose:

> [Clapa] has clearly lost his mind ['mentis alienationem'], either that God may be glorified – as the words of the gospel bear witness in the case of the man born blind – or because God, together with His saint, desired to punish him, seeing that the wretch plotted evil.[133]

The biblical reference is to John 9:3, which discusses why a certain man was born blind. The man's blindness was said to be the result of neither his parents' sins nor his own sins but was brought about by God so that His workings could be shown in the world. Herman's inclusion of this reference in Clapa's miracle, and his repetition in the final line that Clapa 'makes the necessary reparation for his sensual sin, so that God may be glorified in all things', emphasises that, whilst sins could be punished miraculously, the ultimate purpose of all miracles was to promote the glory of God. Miracles could appear as contrary to nature but were, in fact, indicative of God's power within nature, in line with Platonic theories of the world-soul.[134] This Platonic-Christian conception of the miraculous was drawn from the writings of Augustine (fl. early fifth century) and was widely known in the period 1000–1215.[135] Herman used Clapa's punishment and his partial healing to highlight the consequences of irreverence but also to encourage further reverence by glorifying God.

Ranulf

The miracle of Ranulf (excluded from the revised collection) is particularly illustrative of Herman's approach to miraculous punishment and healing. It is possible that the miracle's construction around a Platonist-Christian framework of natural balance was the reason for the reviser's omission of it. The account is centred on Ranulf's military lifestyle, implying that there was a connection between his life as a soldier and his madness.

> Riding along in a wild way, he thought too much upon things that were wrong and too little on the things of God, because, in the manner of courtiers, he pursued those other things, which pertain to this world.[136]

Ranulf's preoccupation with worldly things, whilst not abnormal for a courtier, had compromised him spiritually. Herman argued that the strength of those who inflicted evil on the servants of God should be laid to waste (Daniel 3:44). This argument perhaps reflects his monastic judgement of courtiers, who, as we have seen in Edmund's other miracles, could pose a threat to monastic power. The biblical narrative from which this argument is drawn describes the miraculous deliverance of three Jewish men who had been sentenced to be burned alive for refusing to worship the gold icon of King Nebuchadnezzar, himself a well-known example of the power of God exemplified through madness. Whilst the Jewish men were spared and were able to walk in the flames unharmed, the flames devoured the king's men who had thrown them into the furnace. Like the king's men, Ranulf had rejected the true God by absorbing himself in worldly affairs.

Ranulf's spiritual transgression was directly connected to his punishment. Herman wittily explained how, wrapped up in worldly affairs, 'the foolish soldier strayed', as a result of which 'straying, he was taken by alienation of the head.'[137] Having been plagued by sleeplessness, after eight days, he was finally able to sleep and was then cured via a dream-vision. The dream-vision was distinctly military. Ranulf was fleeing on horseback from the saint, who was also mounted and wielding a spear. Edmund struck him in the back with his spear, causing him to fall off his horse and then 'loomed over him like a warrior about to kill him'.[138] It was only upon hearing Ranulf's pleas for forgiveness that Edmund's persona abruptly changed, and he healed the fallen courtier. The putrid matter ('putrida sanie') that was expelled from Ranulf's ears when he awoke from his dream cleansed him physically and symbolised the spiritual cleansing of his worldly thoughts.[139]

Mirroring Edmund in the dream-vision, Ranulf then converted from a military to a religious life and received the tonsure.[140] Here, Ranulf transcended the trifunctional system of three orders, made up of *those who pray, those who fight and those who toil* by moving from one order to another.[141] Similarly, Edmund himself transcended military and monastic boundaries in his demonstration of both military and saintly virtue. The limits of the three orders were being questioned in the second half of the eleventh century, with Benedictine reformer, Peter Damian calling for worldly warriors to become warriors of Christ, a concept also envisaged in the call for the First Crusade (1095).[142] Herman hinted that Ranulf had perhaps strayed from his true occupation long ago, as he had previously been 'schooled in religion'.[143] Once again, Ranulf's wandering lifestyle was associated with his wandering mind. Where he strayed spiritually, he also strayed mentally.

Wulmer

Wulmer, who, according to Herman, went 'out of his mind' and was left bedridden for eight days, cannot be said to have neglected to care for himself spiritually, as Ranulf had. Returning from Rome, Wulmer went to Saint

Edmund's shrine to give thanks for his safe journey and offered a piece of marble inlaid with crystals.[144] As one of the saint's villeins ('villano eius'), Wulmer was protected by the sanctuary that Edmund offered his community.[145] The reviser stated that, before leaving for Rome, Wulmer had 'knelt down to entrust himself to the protection [or sanctuary] of his lord, St Edmund'.[146] Just as a secular lord would provide some form of protection for his villeins, so too did Edmund provide physical and spiritual protection for his community. The reviser's Wulmer, upon his safe return from Rome, 'duly went to thank his patron and give what he had vowed, plus a spontaneous gift'.[147] He was in the churchyard, about to go home, when he fell ill.[148] There was no suggestion that Wulmer had been at fault or that his illness was an act of divine punishment. According to the reviser, Wulmer's neighbours were incredulous that

> a man strong enough to escape so many dangers, scrapes with death, and the countless frauds of the wicked on his vast, circuitous journey by land and sea, should suddenly be shipwrecked, as it were, upon reaching a safe harbour in a tranquil port.[149]

Despairing for his life, and to protect his soul, Wulmer received the *viaticum*.[150]

Similarly, in Herman's version of the story, no precise cause was provided for Wulmer's illness, and perhaps it was ascribed to chance. Earlier in his collection, Herman had explained that, 'if reason [*ratio*] is lacking, God's mercy reinstitutes it at the right time'.[151] Wulmer's cure certainly came at an opportune moment, or the 'right time'. Eight days after Wulmer fell ill, there was a celebration to commemorate the discovery of Saint Edmund's incorrupt remains. A miraculous cure would certainly have brought greater prestige to the festivities, and Herman underlined this connection by musing that perhaps the saint 'wished to do the sick man a good turn or enhance his [Edmund's] special day with joy'.[152]

Herman emphasised the wonder of the cure by pointing out that Wulmer's condition could not have been rectified by contemporary medicine. Revisiting the theme of periods of mercy, which underlies his collection, he explained that

> Any Hippocrates can cook up some medicine with his potions, either to cure the sick after a very long wait or to alleviate their suffering a little bit. This saint of ours, however, whose pure heart seeks nothing but God's mercy, will rapidly deliver a cure wherever the worthy sick are in need of one.[153]

The reference to Hippocrates is reminiscent of a moment earlier in the collection when Herman discussed a cure provided by Abbot Baldwin for Bishop Herfast of Thetford's swollen eye, which had been injured in a riding accident. For Herman, human fate was determined by God, and God's favour was a precondition for medicine's effectiveness. He knew some technical medical vocabulary, describing, for example, Baldwin's use of 'cauteries and eye ointments'.[154] However, he attributed Baldwin's cure of Bishop Herfast's putrid eye not to medicine but to the miraculous intervention of Saint Edmund: 'Not even Hippocrates or Galen, if they were alive, could handle this case, unless God's mercy came to their aid.'[155] Wulmer, having received the *viaticum*, had certainly been close to death.[156] Nonetheless, as one of Edmund's 'worthy' villeins, Wulmer was under the saint's protection. Healing was, as Herman explained elsewhere in the collection, afforded to the saint's 'people' ('suorum': his devoted followers, including the monastic community at Bury) for their protection, just as the punishment of wrongdoers protected their interests: 'To his people [Edmund] was the most faithful patron, but to any that opposed him and his people he was an indefatigable adversary.'[157]

Contemporary medical texts, held at Bury, acknowledged that earthly practitioners were sometimes limited to alleviating a patient's suffering without being able to cure him or her. Michael Gullick has identified English hands and a Bury pressmark in Sloane 1621, an eleventh-century medical manuscript.[158] The manuscript was originally produced on the Continent (possibly France) and probably came to Bury with Baldwin or during his time there.[159] Debby Banham has distinguished in the contents of Sloane 1621 examples of '"new medicine" that appeared in England from somewhere around the middle of the eleventh century.'[160] She uses the term 'new medicine' to indicate medical theory regarding the origin of disease, technical medical vocabulary (in Latin but with a Greek basis) and references to medical authorities, like Hippocrates and Galen, which, as we have seen, Herman made on more than one occasion in his collection.[161] Both Herman and the reviser used terms for madness that can be found in the Hippocratic corpus: *frenesis*[162] and *mania*.[163] The turn of the eleventh century saw an increased circulation of 'new' medical literature, influenced by Greek humoralist texts, which had been translated via Arabic into Latin and which had an impact both on hagiographical writing and on wider conceptions of madness. In Sloane 1621, the majority of folios contain an *antidotarium* (recipe collection), which was added to by several hands and seems to have been intended for practical use at Bury.[164] The final recipe in the Bury *antidotarium* gives advice on how to ease the suffering of a dying patient with a recipe called 'the power of God'.[165] This recipe is indicative of a practical awareness of the limitations of medical healing and a spiritual concern for the well-being of the patient, something that is evident in Herman's declaration that even Hippocrates and Galen needed the assistance of God's mercy.[166] It is likely that Herman's references to Hippocrates and his comparison of medical and divine healing were based on his understanding of 'new' medicine and were meant to be understood by his readers at Bury in this light.[167]

Herman explained that Wulmur's sudden recovery was so unexpected, given the limits of earthly medicine, that his neighbours believed him to be suffering from 'frenzy' ('frenesy' [*sic*]), which had caused his sudden movement when before he had been as still as a tree trunk ('truncus'). They feared that they might have to hold him down.[168] Similarly, in the revised account, when Wulmer got out of bed and dressed, 'no doubt his amazed household told each other that he had finally lapsed into insanity ['arreptus insaniret'] and would rapidly expire'.[169] Here, there is an implied connection between madness and increased or unexpected movement; previously, Wulmer had been bedbound, and then suddenly, he was able to stand. The increased strength of the mad, which sometimes had to be contained by force, was frequently mentioned in both hagiographical and medical texts of this period. Patients suffering from frenzy could require strong binding because of their physical strength, which explains the people's fear, expressed in Herman's account, that Wulmer would need to be restrained.[170] Additionally, the revised account implies that madness could precede death even if it was not itself the cause of death (the reviser did not record that Wulmer went 'out of his mind', only that those around him may have *thought* he had gone mad and was about to die). A comparable episode can be seen in a miracle recorded at Reading in the twelfth-century collection of the miracles of the Hand of Saint James.[171] The count of Boulogne was struck by an arrow (sent as a divine punishment) in the kneecap. He was taken to his lodgings, where he became increasingly ill, was seized by a demon and died.[172] The count's physical weakness, as well as the corruption of his soul, had left him more open to demonic attack, as had also been the case for Sheriff Leofstan in Edmund's miracle collections. Wulmer, in the eyes of his neighbours, was in a state of physical weakness and was therefore more open to the delusions of madness.

Alternatively, if we consider Herman's use of the term 'in mentis excessu' to describe Wulmer's mental state, it can be argued that Wulmer's out-of-mind experience was divinely inspired but may not have been recognised as such by his neighbours. The phrase 'in mentis excessu' appears in Psalms 67:28 to describe the youth Benjamin in a state of ecstasy.[173] Jerome (fl. late fourth/early fifth century) and Augustine interpreted this passage as a prophetic reference to the conversion of Paul, who descended from the tribe of Benjamin and was divinely healed from sudden blindness via a vision before becoming a vessel for the Holy Spirit (Acts 9).[174] Psalms 67 also refers to the wonders of heaven, where 'if you sleep among the midst of lots, you shall be as the wings of a dove covered with silver, and the hinder parts of her back with the paleness of gold' (verse 14) and proclaims that 'God is wonderful in his saints' (verse 36).[175] This biblical imagery was employed by Herman when Wulmer received a dream-vision of Saint Edmund in the form of a dove, which transformed into a man and healed the sick man by touching his right eyelid (perhaps echoing the divine healing of Paul's blindness).[176] By drawing associations between Wulmer's vision of Saint Edmund and the biblical precedent of divine healing via dream-vision, Herman emphasised the divine nature of Wulmer's spiritual encounter and glorified Edmund as a vessel through which God's wonders could be observed.

Herman also used Wulmur's miracle to critique non-Christian literature by providing an alternative rhetoric of saintly metamorphosis to supersede Ovid's *Metamorphoses*.[177] When Edmund, in Wulmer's dream-vision, transformed from a dove into a beautiful man, Herman exclaimed

> O wondrous new metamorphosis! Nothing like this appears in Ovid's works! For this is a spiritual transformation, beneficial to man, while his are fleshly and give rise to illicit laughter.[178]

Herman's styling of Saint Edmund as the 'metamorphosed man' ('uir metamorphosicus') meant that his audience could experience the drama – and even the humour – of a classical (and, more importantly, pagan) tale but within a framework that would provide spiritual benefits.[179] Whilst Wulmer enjoyed the benefit of the saint's protection and healing, the audience were shown the power of God's mercy.

The reviser discarded Herman's references to classical literature and, perhaps because of this omission, felt that he needed to provide an alternative justification for his inclusion of Wulmur's miracle in his collection. Though he did not use the phrase 'in mentis excessu', the reviser was compelled to justify at length that Wulmer's vision was not a delusion. Herman's allusions to Psalms 67 were far less direct than the reviser's lengthy justification, and it is possible that the veracity of the miracle had been questioned before it came to be revised. In the face of an opposition that failed to see that dreams could be miraculous, the reviser explained that there were two types of dream, 'illusion and revelation', and that 'men of experience and caution' were able to discriminate between the two.[180] In contrast to divine dream-visions, 'ineffective dreams come from the spirit of illusion, and [...] mocking phantasms ['fantasiarum'] plague deluded minds'.[181] The term *fantasia* was likely used here to denote the imaginative faculty of the mind.[182] During sleep, both the senses that supplied the imaginative faculty and the reason that aided interpretation were inactive, leaving the sleeper open to misinterpretations and delusions.[183]

There is a noteworthy parallel between the insanity that Wulmer's neighbours perceived in his miraculous cure and the imaginative impairment that critics believed to be his dream-vision. The reviser explained that when 'the body relaxes in sleep, however, the spirit enjoys a period of freedom' in which it is able to perceive something of the divine that it ordinarily would not.[184] Following Herman's account, the reviser indicated that Wulmer experienced this freedom when, in his dream-vision, he saw a white dove fly into his house. The dove then changed into a handsome man, who later identified himself as Saint Edmund, spoke compassionately with Wulmer, touched his right eyelid with two fingers and cured him.[185] Whether added for rhetorical flourish or reflective of actual cynicism, the reviser's defence of this miracle illustrates how accusations of delusion and insanity could be used to undermine, as they had also done for the saint's own enemies

(Leofstan, Osgod Clapa, Robert de Curcun). Nonetheless, as the reviser pointed out, Wulmer's health (upheld by the testimony of many) stood as proof of the miracle, and it was the cynics themselves who ought to 'come to their senses and be saved'.[186]

Madness was represented as a punishment for sin in both collections, and the transgressive nature of sinful behaviour was reflected in the wandering of the mind. The process of suffering from madness and then receiving a miraculous cure could work as a form of redemption, echoing the madness of Nebuchadnezzar, whose seven years of madness humbled him before God (Daniel 4:16–25). Ranulf, through his madness and cure, was set back on the right track and adopted a monastic lifestyle. The infliction and cure of madness, as with other ailments like blindness, was a visible manifestation of God's (and Edmund's) power to punish wrongdoers and to protect His community. The reviser's construction of Wulmer's miracle was particularly striking in this sense, for he observed delusion not in Wulmer himself but in those who questioned the power of miracles.

Conclusion

Both collections of the miracles of Saint Edmund of Bury reveal different, though not entirely incompatible, approaches to punishment and protection. In Herman's collection, God's favour was displayed in periods of mercy in which He worked miracles through His saints. Edmund's miracles took place during one such period. In order to receive a cure, a sick person had to be worthy of God's favour. The most worthwhile lifestyle was a spiritual one, though Herman did not deny the importance of other responsibilities; medicine, for example, functioned within nature as part of God's divine order.

In order to retain natural balance, transgressions required punishment. To emphasise this concept of balance, there was a strong correlation between the nature of the transgression and its accompanying punishment. When madness was dispensed as a divine punishment, the mind of the transgressor had already deviated by defying the saint, committing sin, or both. Madness, as a punishment, matched the transgression of unreasonable behaviour, just as the Dane who looked where he should not was punished with blindness. Madness also served the practical purpose of socially, and often legally, undermining the transgressor, thus halting the transgression and protecting the monastic community of the saint. Both punishment and cure, then, were, above all else, demonstrations of God's power, which protected the worthy from the transgressions of sinners and from the diseases of nature.

When the reviser came to rewrite the miracle collection, he shifted its focus. Unlike Herman, he was not writing from within the community at Bury but instead composed his work under the patronage of the bishop. For this reason, he was less concerned than Herman with the immediate needs of the Bury monks and the punishment of those who had undermined them. Madness was not connected with the senseless actions of transgressors as much as it was with the wicked deeds of sinners. God, through Edmund, delivered punishments and performed cures as a form of protection; punishment on earth protected the soul from further suffering after death, and miraculous cures protected the recipients from suffering earthly afflictions. Madness, both as a divine punishment and as an illness to be miraculously cured, was a cause of suffering. The reviser, writing in Herman's shadow, was aware of his own critics. Those who lacked the sense to comprehend God's miracles suffered in their ignorance and their alienation from God.

This case study of two miracle collections written in quick succession has drawn attention to the crucial role of the individual hagiographer in the construction of madness in his collection. Herman and the reviser were influenced by their respective intellectual backgrounds and by their perceptions of Edmund's role as a saint and patron. Nonetheless, patterns and similarities have emerged in their representations of madness:

- The signs and symptoms of madness affected sufferers physically and mentally.
- Madness could be connected with demonic interference.
- Those perceived as mad or possessed could require restraint.
- Madness brought the morality of a sufferer into question, and there was concern for the state of his or her soul.

The emphasis placed by each hagiographer on the role of madness in individual miracles was reliant on his conceptions of punishment and cure, which were influenced by the precedent of earlier writers (ranging, for the reviser, from the Bible to Herman himself) and by the contemporary agenda of the miracle record.

As we move into the twelfth century, we will observe three new cults, developing in very different contexts. In nearby Norwich, in the mid-twelfth century, the cult of pseudo-martyr William of Norwich emerged from the turmoil of the Anarchy and amidst growing anti-Semitism. In Canterbury, in the 1170s, the cult of Saint Thomas Becket was rapidly gaining momentum, and the prestigious Benedictine priory at Christ Church produced the two largest collections of miracles that England had seen. In the wake of Becket's cult, in London, which, as Herman had noticed, had no saint of its own, the new Augustinian priory of Saint Bartholomew attempted to draw on the reputation of the great apostolic saint in constructing its own foundation legend. I examine the roles of earthly and spiritual suffering in relation to madness in the miracles of these three saints, paying close attention both to the characteristics of individual collections and to the emerging patterns within madness miracles. In the next chapter, we will see the connection between mad behaviour and immorality, evident in Edmund's miracles, applied to a new cause in the *Life and Miracles of William of Norwich*.

Notes

1. Herman, 3, pp. 10–13. The numbering of both Herman and the reviser's miracles is according to Licence's edition.
2. Ibid., p. 11, n. 59.
3. Ibid., pp. 12–13.
4. Ward's argument is discussed in more detail in my Introduction. 'Traditional' miracle collections reflected the requirements of early monastic communities for saintly protectors who avenged wrongdoings with miraculous punishments (Ward, p. 36). According to Ward (p. 67), there was a shift in the twelfth century towards 'modern' miracle collections in which the just and compassionate saint performed miraculous healings.
5. Licence, 'Introduction', in *Miracles of St Edmund*, pp. xiii–cxxxi (p. cxii and p. cxiv). The diocesan seat was moved from Thetford to Norwich in 1094.
6. Herman, 3, pp. 12–13. The significance of the term 'rabide' is returned to below.
7. Bale, p. 1.
8. Gransden, 'Edmund', para. 1 of 8.
9. Licence, 'Introduction', in *Miracles of St Edmund*, p. xix.
10. Gransden, 'Edmund', para. 3 of 8.
11. Bale, p. 3.
12. Ibid., p. 4.
13. Gransden, 'Composition and Authorship', p. 10.
14. Licence, 'Introduction', in *Miracles of St Edmund*, pp. liv–lix; Herman, 23, pp. 62–63. There is some ambiguity as to when Herman wrote the first part of his collection. Herman himself stated that he laid down his pen at the end of chapter 24 and concluded with a 'brief epitome' of the kings named in the Anglo-Saxon Chronicle from Saint Edmund to William I, which suggests that he was writing soon after the Norman Conquest. However, the fact that William the Conqueror was specifically referred to as 'William I' might mean that Herman was in fact writing during the reign of William II Rufus (1087–1100).
15. Licence, 'Introduction', in *Bury St Edmunds*, p. 2.
16. Banham, p. 226.
17. Bates, p. 21.
18. Licence, 'The Cult of St Edmund', p. 104.
19. Ibid.; Herman, 1, pp. 4–5; For Herman's use of the Anglo-Saxon Chronicle, see Licence, 'Introduction', in *Miracles of St Edmund*, pp. lxix–lxxi; an example is Herman, 2, pp. 4–5.
20. Licence, 'The Cult of St Edmund', p. 107; Licence, 'New Light', p. 94. Baldwin and Herman may have previously known each other through connections between Saint Vincent's and Saint-Denis, where Baldwin had been a monk.
21. Herman, 15, pp. 34–35.
22. Ibid., 8, pp. 24–25.
23. Thomas Arnold collated Tiberius B.ii and Paris, Bibliothèque nationale de France, MS latin 2621 (an abbreviated version of Herman's miracles that was probably intended for wider circulation) in his edition of Saint Edmund's miracles, published in 1890 in *The Memorials of St Edmund's Abbey*. Arnold's edition contains a number of errors, some of which were noted by Antonia Gransden in her 1995 list of *corrigenda*, and several more of which are highlighted in Licence's new edition and translation, which is used for this study.
24. See Gransden, 'Composition and Authorship', pp. 2–6 for a detailed analysis of the manuscript.
25. Licence, 'Introduction', in *Miracles of St Edmund*, p. xci.
26. Ibid.

27. Herman, 'The Missing Miracles', p. 337.
28. Licence, 'History and Hagiography', p. 526.
29. Licence, 'Introduction', in *Miracles of St Edmund*, p. cix and p. cxii.
30. Ibid., p. cx.
31. Edmund Revised, II.5, pp. 286–99.
32. Ibid., I.0, pp. 128–29.
33. Ibid., II.1, pp. 242–43.
34. Licence, 'Introduction', in *Miracles of St Edmund*, pp. cxiv–cxxvii.
35. Ibid., cx–cxiii. Since Herman's death is recorded in the collection and he died in 1097/98, this is the earliest date for its composition. Abbot Baldwin died in 1097, and, after his death, the office of abbot was left vacant for two years, during which time the abbey was administered by the diocesan bishop, Herbert de Losinga. The dispute over the abbacy that started in 1100 is not mentioned in the text, leading Licence to conclude that it was compiled before 1100. The compiler claims that he is writing on the orders of a prelate ('prelatiue auctoritatis iussione'), and the only prelate in office with influence over Bury between 1097 and 1100 was Herbert de Losinga.
36. Rose, p. 95.
37. Edmund Revised, II.2, pp. 244–47; Herman, 40, pp. 114–17.
38. Licence, 'Introduction', in *Miracles of St Edmund*, pp. cxiv–cxv. The reviser writes of being in 'exile' at Bury from which he can 'depart' after completing his commission.
39. Edmund Revised, II.4, pp. 270–71.
40. Herman, 34, pp. 94–99.
41. Ibid., 23, pp. 58–59; Edmund Revised, I.9, pp. 208–11.
42. Herman, 23, pp. 56–57; Edmund Revised, I.9, pp. 208–9.
43. Herman, 36, pp. 100–103; Edmund Revised, I.15, pp. 226–29.
44. Edmund Revised, I.15, pp. 228–29.
45. Herman, 37, pp. 104–5. Licence translates as a 'mental attack'.
46. Edmund Revised, I.16, pp. 228–33.
47. Herman, 36, pp. 102–3 ['Cuius signum stuporis in eius uisu denotare postea potuit omnis, cuius est mens aliquomodo physicalis'].
48. Ibid., 3, pp. 10–11.
49. Licence, 'Introduction', in *Miracles of St Edmund*, p. lxii; Herman, 2, pp. 8–9.
50. Herman, 2, pp. 8–9.
51. Licence, 'Introduction', in *Miracles of St Edmund*, p. lxiii.
52. Herman, 3, pp. 10–11.
53. Ibid.
54. Edmund Revised, I.3, pp. 142–43.
55. Herman, 36, pp. 100–101; Edmund Revised, I.15, pp. 226–27.
56. Licence, 'Introduction', in *Miracles of St Edmund*, pp. cxxvi–cxxvii. For an example, see Edmund Revised, I.16, pp. 228–33.
57. Edmund Revised, I.3, pp. 142–45.
58. Herman, 3, pp. 10–11 ['cor plenum nequitie', 'animo truci ac deteriori'].
59. Ibid., pp. 12–13.
60. Latham et al., XIII, 2644. In the miracles of Saint Frideswide, *rabies* was defined as 'furoris amentia' (p. 584).
61. Herman, 3, pp. 12–13 ['apparitores deteriores', 'ausu demonico permoti'].
62. Ibid.
63. *Miracles of St Frideswide*, p. 574.
64. Edmund Revised, I.3, pp. 142–45.
65. Herman, 3, pp. 12–13.
66. Ibid.
67. Ibid., n. 63.

68. Ibid., pp. 10–13.
69. Edmund Revised, I.3, p. 144.
70. Schmitt, pp. 60–62.
71. Ibid., p. 83.
72. Herman, 23, pp. 56–57.
73. Ibid.
74. Ibid.
75. Ibid. ['amens prosilit ad terram, uolutans humo uelut maniam passus debachando']. Licence translates as 'as though struck uncontrollably mad in a Bacchic frenzy'.
76. Ibid.
77. Edmund Revised, I.9, pp. 206–9 ['nefandis'].
78. Ibid. ['miseras emittens uoces in terram eliditur {...} uariis motibus ac uocibus incessanter agitari'].
79. Herman, 23, pp. 58–59.
80. Edmund Revised, I.9, pp. 208–9 ['dictis exorcismis, aque consecrate aspergine perlustrans egrotum, impurum demonem pellere nitebatur'].
81. Ibid., pp. 210–11.
82. Herman, 23, pp. 58–59; Isidore of Seville, XI.i.18, p. 232. In Isidore of Seville's *Etymologies*, the fifth sense was touch.
83. Herman, 23, pp. 58–59.
84. Edmund Revised, I.9, pp. 210–11.
85. Herman, 9, pp. 24–25.
86. Ibid., 8, pp. 24–25.
87. Ibid., 17, pp. 36–37.
88. Ibid.
89. Edmund Revised, I.5, pp. 170–71.
90. Licence in Herman, 36, pp. 100–101, n. 375; Licence, 'Introduction', in *Miracles of St Edmund*, p. cxi, n. 408. De Curcun is identified as Bigod's tenant in Domesday Book.
91. Herman, 36, pp. 100–101.
92. Wareham, para. 2 of 3.
93. Edmund Revised, I.15, pp. 226–27.
94. Geary, pp. 78–81.
95. Ibid., pp. 15–22.
96. Ibid.
97. Bernard of Angers, IV.16, p. 204 and C.2, p. 223.
98. Yarrow, p. 32.
99. Geary, p. 20; Herman, 36, pp. 102–3.
100. Turner, pp. 32–35.
101. Herman, 36, pp. 102–3 ['cum mentis stupore, non ulterius in predicto manerio ausi sunt simile quid attemptare'].
102. Ibid., 3, pp. 12–13.
103. Hyams, p. 95; Licence in Herman, 3, p. 12, n. 60.
104. Bartlett, p. 464.
105. Ibid.
106. Herman, 37, p. 104.
107. Bartlett, pp. 464–65.
108. Herman, 26, pp. 64–65.
109. Edmund Revised, I.15, pp. 228–29 ['Sic EADMVNDVS impios arrogantes, et auidos peruasores a presumptionis audacia deiecit, iniuriam uindicauit; ius proprium uendicauit].
110. Licence in Herman, 36, pp. 100–101, n. 373.
111. Ibid.; Calcidius, 'Timaeus Platonis', 43a, p. 38.

112. Herman, 36, pp. 102–3.
113. Licence, 'The Cult of St Edmund', pp. 125–26.
114. Ibid., p. 126.
115. Gregory, 'The Platonic Inheritance', p. 54.
116. Ibid., p. 77 and p. 54.
117. Stover, p. 13.
118. Thomson, p. 640.
119. van Winden, p. 1; Dutton, p. 184.
120. Sorabji, p. 157; Calcidius, 'Commentarius', p. 224.
121. Calcidius, 'Commentarius', p. 224. The extension of these characteristics to include the mad is my own inference.
122. Herman, 36, pp. 102–3.
123. For Cicero's influence on Herman, see Licence, 'Introduction', in *Miracles of St Edmund*, pp. lxxiv–lxxv.
124. Edmund Revised, I.0, pp. 128–29.
125. Herman, 23, pp. 56–57.
126. Ibid., 7, pp. 20–21, n. 93. The reference is likely taken from Ælfric's *Life of Saint Basil.*
127. Ibid., 17, pp. 36–37.
128. Edmund Revised, I.9, pp. 206–7.
129. Herman, 23, pp. 56–57; Edmund Revised, I.9, pp. 208–9. Licence translates 'corpore rigidus et mente tumidus' as 'puffed up in mind and body'.
130. Edmund Revised, I.9, pp. 210–11.
131. Petkov, p. 45.
132. Ibid.
133. Herman, 23, pp. 58–59.
134. Augustine, III.7–8, I, 138–40.
135. Ward, pp. 31–32.
136. Herman, 34, pp. 96–97 ['Equitans ergo effrenis queque de uia meditando nimis, parum que Dei sunt meditatur, quia palatinorum more mundi alia sectatur'].
137. Ibid. I have chosen a literal translation in order to analyse the terms associated with madness but Licence's translation captures Herman's amusing tone: 'As the devious soldier wandered astray in this way, his mind wandered deviously, he succumbed to wandering in the head, as he headed on his way' ['Dum sic deuius deuiat miles deuians, capitur capitis alienatione taliter itinerans']. Herman's use of *alienatio capitis* as opposed to the more-common *alienatio mentis* enables the alliterative rhythm of 'capitur capitis'. It also reflects an association between the mind and the head.
138. Ibid.
139. Ibid.
140. Ibid.
141. For an exploration of this theme and its occurrence in literature between the eleventh and thirteenth centuries, see Duby.
142. Ibid., p. 226.
143. Herman, 34, pp. 98–99.
144. Ibid., 37, pp. 104–5.
145. Ibid.
146. Edmund Revised, I.16, pp. 232–33 ['domini sui sancti uidelicet EADMVNDI supplex subiit asilum'].
147. Ibid.
148. Ibid.
149. Ibid.
150. Ibid.

151. Herman, 22, pp. 50–51.
152. Ibid., 37, pp. 106–7.
153. Ibid.
154. Ibid., 27, pp. 76–77 ['cauteriationibus ac colliriis']; For an analysis of Herman's medical vocabulary, see Licence, 'Introduction', in *Miracles of St Edmund*, p. lxxxvi.
155. Herman, 27, pp. 72–73.
156. Ibid., 37, pp. 104–5 ['morti proximo'].
157. Ibid., 25, pp. 64–65.
158. Gullick, p. 190; Banham, p. 228.
159. Banham, p. 229.
160. Ibid., p. 228.
161. Ibid., pp. 228–29.
162. Herman, 37, pp. 108–9; Edmund Revised, I.15, pp. 228–29.
163. Herman, 23, pp. 56–57.
164. Banham, p. 230.
165. Ibid., pp. 237–38.
166. Ibid.
167. Herman, 27, pp. 72–73.
168. Ibid., 37, pp. 104–9.
169. Edmund Revised, I.16, pp. 234–35.
170. Gariopontus, I.8, fol. 5^{r} ['in lecto ligentur et membra eis fortius constringantur quoniam fortes sunt'].
171. GCL, MS 1, fol. 175^{r}.
172. Ibid.
173. 'Ibi Beniamin adulescentulus in mentis excessu'.
174. Németh, p. 358.
175. Verse 36 is also referred to in Leofstan's miracle (discussed above).
176. Herman, 37, pp. 106–7.
177. Licence, 'Introduction', in *Miracles of St Edmund*, p. lxvi.
178. Herman, 37, pp. 106–7.
179. Ibid.
180. Edmund Revised, I.16, pp. 230–31 ['illusio uidelicet et reuelatio determinantur', 'prudentes et circumspecti uiri'].
181. Ibid. ['a fantastico spiritu somni ministrentur, atque fantasiarum ludibriis delusa mens agitetur'].
182. MacLehose, p. 82.
183. Ibid., p. 83.
184. Edmund Revised, I.16, pp. 230–31 ['uero somno corpus resoluitur, quodammodo spiritus libertatis otio perfruitur'].
185. Ibid., pp. 232–35.
186. Ibid., pp. 234–35; Ibid., pp. 228–29 ['resipiscant et saluentur'].

Bibliography

Manuscripts

Gloucester Cathedral Library (GCL), MS 1, fols 171^{v}–175^{v}

Primary

Augustine, *De Trinitate Libri XV*, ed. by W.J. Mountain, Corpus Christianorum, Series Latina, 50, 2 vols (Turnholt: Brepols, 1968)

Bernard of Angers, 'Liber miraculorum sancte Fidis', in *The Book of Sainte Foy*, trans by. Pamela Sheingorn (Philadelphia: University of Pennsylvania Press, 1995), pp. 39–261

Calcidius, 'Commentarius', in *Timaeus a Calcidio translatus commentarioque instructus*, ed. by J.H. Waszink, Corpus Platonicum Medii Aevi, Plato Latinus, 4 (Leiden and London: Brill, 1962), pp. 53–346

———, 'Timaeus Platonis', in *Timaeus a Calcidio translatus commentarioque instructus*, ed. by J.H. Waszink, Corpus Platonicum Medii Aevi, Plato Latinus, 4 (Leiden and London: Brill, 1962), pp. 1–52

Gariopontus, *Passionarius Galeni* (Lyon: n.p., 1526)

Goscelin of Saint-Bertin[?], 'Miracles of St Edmund', in *Herman the Archdeacon and Goscelin of Saint-Bertin. Miracles of St Edmund*, ed. and trans. by Tom Licence (Oxford: Oxford University Press, 2014), pp. 127–303

Herman the Archdeacon, 'De Miraculis Sancti Eadmundi', in *Memorials of St Edmund's Abbey*, ed. by Thomas Arnold, 3 vols (Cambridge: Cambridge University Press, 1890–1896), I (1890), 26–92

———, 'Miracles of St Edmund', in *Herman the Archdeacon and Goscelin of Saint-Bertin. Miracles of St Edmund*, ed. and trans. by Tom Licence (Oxford: Oxford University Press, 2014), pp. 1–125

———, 'The Missing Miracles', in *Herman the Archdeacon and Goscelin of Saint-Bertin. Miracles of St Edmund*, ed. and trans. by Tom Licence (Oxford: Oxford University Press, 2014), pp. 337–349

Isidore of Seville, 'The Etymologies', in *The* Etymologies *of Isidore of Seville*, trans. by Stephen A. Barney, W.J. Lewis, J.A. Beach and Oliver Berghof (Cambridge: Cambridge University Press, 2006), pp. 33–406

Miracles of St Frideswide, ed. by Josepho van Hacke, Benjamino Bossue, Victore de Buck and Antonio Tinnebroek (Brussels: Alphonsi Greuse, 1853), Acta Sanctorum, 8 October, pp. 568–589

Secondary

Bale, Anthony, 'Introduction: St Edmund's Medieval Lives', in *St Edmund, King and Martyr: Changing Images of a Medieval Saint*, ed. by Anthony Bale (Woodbridge: York Medieval Press, 2009), pp. 1–25

Banham, Debby, 'Medicine at Bury in the Time of Abbot Baldwin', in *Bury St Edmunds and the Norman Conquest*, ed. by Tom Licence (Woodbridge: Boydell, 2014), pp. 226–246

Bartlett, Robert, *England Under the Norman and Angevin Kings, 1075–1225* (Oxford: Oxford University Press, 2000)

Bates, David, 'The Abbey and the Norman Conquest: An Unusual Case?', in *Bury St Edmunds and the Norman Conquest*, ed. by Tom Licence (Woodbridge: Boydell, 2014), pp. 5–21

Duby, Georges, *The Three Orders: Feudal Society Imagined*, trans. by Arthur Goldhammer (Chicago, IL and London: University of Chicago Press, 1980)

Dutton, Paul Edward, 'Medieval Approaches to Calcidius', in *Plato's* Timaeus *as Cultural Icon*, ed. by Gretchen J. Reydams-Schils (Notre Dame, IN: University of Notre Dame, 2003), pp. 183–205

Geary, Patrick J., *Furta Sacra: Thefts of Relics in the Central Middle Ages*, rev. edn (Princeton, NJ: Princeton University Press, 1990)

Gransden, Antonia, 'The Composition and Authorship of the *De miraculis Sancti Eadmundi* Attributed to "Hermann the Archdeacon"', *The Journal of Medieval Latin*, 5 (1995), 1–52

———, 'Edmund [St Edmund] (d. 869), king of the East Angles', in *Oxford Dictionary of National Biography* <https://doi.org/10.1093/ref:odnb/8500>

Gregory, Tullio, 'The Platonic Inheritance', in *A History of Twelfth-Century Western Philosophy*, ed. by Peter Dronke (Cambridge: Cambridge University Press, 1988), pp. 54–80

Gullick, Michael, 'An Eleventh-Century Bury Medical Manuscript', in *Bury St Edmunds and the Norman Conquest*, ed. by Tom Licence (Woodbridge: Boydell, 2014), pp. 190–225

Latham, R.E., et al., eds, *Dictionary of Medieval Latin from British Sources*, 17 fascicules (London: Oxford University Press, 1975–2013)

Licence, Tom, 'The Cult of St Edmund', in *Bury St Edmunds and the Norman Conquest*, ed. by Tom Licence (Woodbridge: Boydell, 2014), pp. 104–130

———, ed., *Herman the Archdeacon and Goscelin of Saint-Bertin. Miracles of St Edmund* (Oxford: Oxford University Press, 2014)

———, 'History and Hagiography in the Late Eleventh Century: The Life and Work of Herman the Archdeacon, Monk of Bury St Edmunds', *English Historical Review*, 124 (2009), 516–544

———, 'Introduction', in *Bury St Edmunds and the Norman Conquest*, ed. by Tom Licence (Woodbridge: Boydell, 2014), pp. 1–4

———, 'New Light on the Life and Work of Herman the Archdeacon', in *Bury St Edmunds and the Norman Conquest*, ed. by Tom Licence (Woodbridge: Boydell, 2014), pp. 94–103

Hyams, Paul R., *Rancor and Reconciliation in Medieval England* (Ithaca, NY and London: Cornell University Press, 2003)

MacLehose, William F., 'Fear, Fantasy and Sleep in Medieval Medicine', in *Emotions and Health*, ed. by Elena Carrera, Studies in Medieval and Reformation Traditions, 168 (Leiden: Brill, 2013), pp. 67–94

Németh, Csaba, '*Paulus Raptus* to *Raptus Pauli*: Paul's Rapture (2 Cor 12:2–4) in the Pre-Scholastic and Scholastic Theologies', in *A Companion to St. Paul in the Middle Ages*, ed. by Steven Cartwright, Brill's Companions to the Christian Tradition, 39 (Leiden: Brill, 2013), pp. 349–392

Petkov, Kiril, 'The Cultural Career of a "Minor" Vice: Arrogance in the Medieval Treatise on Sin', in *Sin in Medieval and Early Modern Culture: The Tradition of the Seven Deadly Sins*, ed. by Richard G. Newhauser and Susan J. Ridyard (Woodbridge: York Medieval Press, 2012), pp. 43–64

Rose, E.M., *The Murder of William of Norwich: The Origins of the Blood Libel in Medieval Europe* (Oxford and New York, NY: Oxford University Press, 2015)

Schmitt, Jean-Claude, *Ghosts in the Middle Ages: The Living Dead in Medieval Society*, trans. by Teresa Lavender Fagan (Chicago, IL and London: University of Chicago Press, 1998)

Sorabji, Richard, 'The Mind-Body Relation in the Wake of Plato's *Timaeus*', in *Plato's* Timaeus *as Cultural Icon*, ed. by Gretchen J. Reydams-Schils (Notre Dame, IN: University of Notre Dame, 2003), pp. 152–162

Stover, Justin Anthony, 'Reading Plato in the Twelfth Century: A Study On the Varieties of Plato's Reception in the Latin West Before 1215' (unpublished doctoral thesis, Harvard University, 2011)

Thomson, R.M., 'The Library of Bury St. Edmunds Abbey in the Eleventh and Twelfth Centuries', *Speculum*, 47 (1972), 617–645

Turner, Wendy J., *Care and Custody of the Mentally Ill, Incompetent, and Disabled in Medieval England* (Turnhout: Brepols, 2013)

van Winden, J.C.M., ed., *Calcidius on Matter, His Doctrine and Sources: A Chapter in the History of Platonism*, Philosophia Antiqua, 9 (Leiden: Brill, 1959)

Ward, Benedicta, *Miracles and the Medieval Mind: Theory, Record and Event 1000–1215*, rev. edn (Philadelphia: University of Pennsylvania Press, 1987)

Wareham, A.F., 'Bigod, Roger (I) (d. 1107)', in *Oxford Dictionary of National Biography* <https://doi.org/10.1093/ref:odnb/2378>

Yarrow, Simon, *Saints and their Communities: Miracle Stories in Twelfth-Century England* (Oxford: Oxford University Press, 2006)

2 Managing the mad: violence, cruelty and restraint in the miracles of William of Norwich

> But as he was being dragged thither more violently ['uiolentius'] he burst his bonds, not by his strength but by that of the evil spirit ['maligni spiritus'], and, attacking his mother, he threw her to the ground and fastened his teeth in her throat. And he would certainly have killed her, had not the people run up and rescued her. Then, hissing through his teeth and glaring at the bystanders with savage ['toruis'] eyes, he pitiably tore at all whom he could reach. A crowd assembled; he was savagely ['crudeliter'] seized and bound, and, with his hands and feet tied together, was put down willy-nilly beside the holy tomb.[1]

Such was the dramatic arrival of an unnamed madman, who, we are told, was the son of a man called Richard de Needham, at the tomb of William of Norwich in around 1153. It was recorded by a Benedictine monk of Norwich Cathedral Priory, Thomas of Monmouth, in his *Life and Miracles of William of Norwich*. Richard de Needham's son was not the only mad pilgrim to arrive at William's shrine with his hands and/or feet bound. A madman named Ebrard Fisher had his hands tied behind his back and his feet chained in iron shackles, and a mad servant of the Norwich moneyers had to be bound in strong chains.[2] The *Life and Miracles* contains records of some of the most violent embodiments of madness across my five case studies, and, perhaps unsurprisingly, the violent mad men and women who were brought to William of Norwich's tomb were often violently restrained. The cult of William of Norwich is most well known today, as it was in the Middle Ages, for its violent beginnings in the horrific ritual murder libel made against the Jewish community in Norwich, who were accused of torturing and crucifying the boy 'martyr', and for the subsequent persecution that it inspired. Perhaps the particularly savage representations of madness in the *Life and Miracles* can, in part, be attributed to the violent context in which it was written. After all, the premise of the text itself, as well as the cult attached to it, hinged on a single act of violence – the alleged martyrdom of William of Norwich – since, besides his violent death, William had little claim to sanctity.

In William's miracles, compiled over fifty years after Edmund of Bury's, we see a markedly different representation of insanity; Thomas of

Monmouth did not portray madness as a divine punishment, dispatched by a defensive saint, but as an illness, often provoked by demons, that required the saint's miraculous healing. Nonetheless, whilst the majority of the cases of madness recorded in Edmund's late-eleventh/early-twelfth-century miracle collections were caused by divine punishment, Bury's madmen were not treated with the same levels of physical restraint as the mad men and women who came to Norwich and who, as we shall see, had been inflicted with madness without any transgression on their part. Many scholars, including Muriel Laharie in her study of mad pilgrims in miracle texts, have argued that the demonically possessed were more likely than other cure-seekers to be the recipients of beatings, which were aimed at the demons inside them.[3] Despite the violent treatment of several possessed pilgrims being recorded in the *Life and Miracles*, there is no evidence of this rationale being behind the binding and occasional beating of demoniacs. Instead, this chapter explores how representations of madness in the *Life and Miracles* were indicative of a new challenge faced by monastic shrine custodians: the management of insane and potentially violent pilgrims who were brought, often forcibly, into the presence of saints in the hope of a miraculous cure. The second half of the twelfth century saw a noticeable increase in the number of pilgrims recorded as visiting the shrines of saints who were now acclaimed for miraculously curing illnesses and afflictions rather than for punishing sins.[4] Whilst monastic miracle compilers, like Herman, who had recorded the miracles of Saint Edmund of Bury in the late 1000s, had distanced themselves from the laity, later compilers, like Thomas of Monmouth, keenly engaged with lay stories, which they committed to writing, not necessarily to be retold to laymen but to glorify and preserve the saint's healing miracles as an important manifestation of his sanctity.

Historical context

In moving from Bury in the early 1100s to Norwich in the 1150s, we have made a fairly large chronological leap. The Church in East Anglia was no longer under threat from Norman conquerors and, instead, faced a new, internal peril. When the pseudo-martyr William of Norwich met his untimely end in 1144, England was in the midst of a civil war between the Empress Matilda and Stephen of Blois. Only in 1153 – coincidentally, the same year that Richard de Needham's son received his miraculous cure at William's tomb – did Stephen secure his throne by promising the succession to Matilda's son, the future King Henry II. Lack of a stable royal authority (especially during Stephen's incarceration in 1141) led to local outbreaks of violence and a greater dependence on local authorities. In the 1140s, East Anglia witnessed some minor skirmishes between the king and prominent noblemen in the region, though, in Norwich itself, the prerogative of the sheriff, John de Chesney, seems to have been upheld.[5] The Church in East Anglia also appears to have experienced some instability, with Bishop

Everard of Norwich and Bishop Seffrid of Chichester reportedly being deposed by the king in 1145.[6]

What impact did this political and social instability have on Thomas of Monmouth, the cathedral monk who took it upon himself to record William's *Life and Miracles*, and his writing? Thomas Callahan has argued that, though the extent of monastic damage caused by the civil war may have been exaggerated, not least by the chroniclers themselves, many monastic writers were appalled that any holy place would be damaged or violated.[7] Evidence of Thomas of Monmouth's attitude towards the violation of Christian sacrosanctity can be seen in the *Life and Miracles* in his representation of the Norwich Jews, who he held responsible for William's violent death. William of Norwich had been found dead in Thorpe Wood (just outside of Norwich) on 24 March 1144 (Good Friday). He was twelve years old and had been working in Norwich as an apprentice skinner.[8] Thomas of Monmouth was not in Norwich at the time of the boy's death but had joined the Benedictine community there by 1150 at the latest.[9] According to Thomas's account, William had been tricked, through the offer of a job, into entering the home of a prominent Norwich Jew, where he was tortured and then crucified by members of the Jewish community, who then dumped his body in the woods.

In his prologue to the *Life and Miracles of William of Norwich*, Thomas of Monmouth stated that he intended to save William's memory from oblivion, and his efforts certainly went a long way to sustaining the popularity of the cult, which, by his own admittance, was waning after the initial discovery of William's body.[10] Nonetheless, unlike the Bury miracle compilers, who had also claimed to be writing to sustain the memory of their saint (Edmund), Thomas of Monmouth had far more to do than reshape and revive a pre-existing and well-established cult. Even at its peak in the 1150s, William's cult seems to have faced opposition from contemporaries. Thomas of Monmouth himself reported how the sheriff of Norfolk, John de Chesney, when he heard of the allegations against the Jews, had offered them protection in Norwich Castle, which was perhaps unsurprising given that he was the king's man, and the Jews were ostensibly under the king's protection.[11] More problematic was the opposition of Prior Elias, Thomas's superior within the Benedictine monastery of Norwich Cathedral, who objected to Thomas's ostentatious dressing of William's tomb, once the boy's body had been translated to the chapter house in 1150, with a cloth and a large candle, both of which the prior had removed (the candle was later restored when Elias was ordered to do so by William himself in a vision).[12] Revealingly, Thomas of Monmouth dedicated the second book of the *Life and Miracles* to combatting accusations that William had not died a martyr and was therefore unworthy of veneration, which shows that, even as its biggest supporter, he was aware of considerable hostility towards the cult. It is unlikely that the *Life and Miracles* itself was widely circulated (though the story it told spread across Europe). Only one copy of the text survives, in a manuscript that was likely produced for the Cistercian order, given certain stylistic observances, around 1200 (Norwich's own copies of the text were destroyed in a fire in 1272).[13] The manuscript now known as Cambridge University Library MS Add. 3037 was probably originally housed at Sibton Abbey in Suffolk, the only Cistercian house in East Anglia.[14] William of Norwich was predominantly a local saint, and the majority of pilgrims who came to his shrine were from Norwich itself or from the surrounding area.

Despite the modest scope of its contemporary circulation, the *Life and Miracles* has received considerable attention from scholars almost certainly because of its prominent place in the study of Jewish ritual murder accusations. The account of William's death is the earliest surviving written blood libel made against a Jewish community in the Middle Ages and is indicative of growing tensions between Christians and Jews. Miri Rubin suggests that the blood libel was very much fuelled by the fertile environment of Norwich during and immediately after the Anarchy, as well as by the 'creation of [Thomas of Monmouth] who saw the city and its possibilities afresh, as newcomers often do, and used his Jewish fellow newcomers as scapegoats.'[15] Christian antagonism towards England's Jewish population would violently intensify in the second half of the twelfth century, resulting in the murder of several Jews in London during the coronation of Richard I in 1189 and the massacre of an entire Jewish community in York in 1190. Gavin Langmuir speculates that Thomas of Monmouth's accusation of ritual child murder had such a lasting impact on the popular image of anti-Semitism that it went on to influence Luther and even Hitler.[16]

Given the significance of the *Life and Miracles* to the history of anti-Semitic thought, it is important to approach the text with due consideration of its continuing impact. In this book, all references to William of Norwich as a 'saint' and 'martyr' are made with the understanding that this is how he was referred to by Thomas of Monmouth and should in no way be taken as an acceptance of the blood libel claim. Nonetheless, whilst its lasting influence cannot be ignored, the *Life and Miracles* also needs to be looked at in the context in which it was written, locally and in its own terms. The miracles, which will be the subject of this chapter, are in Books Three to Seven of the text and are often overlooked by historians. These miracles should be considered in relation to Books One and Two (the account of William's life and death, and the accusation of ritual murder), but they also need to be understood in the context of twelfth-century miracle collecting, which their inclusion in this comparative study will go some way to addressing.

It is likely that Thomas composed Books One to Six of the *Life and Miracles* in 1154–55, shortly after arriving in Norwich.[17] Book Seven, the final book of miracles, seems to have been written at a later date, probably around 1173 (at the height of Thomas Becket's cult in nearby Canterbury, which is discussed in the next chapter), since William Turbe, bishop of Norwich, to whom the text is dedicated, died in 1174.[18] In his prologue to Book Seven, Thomas of Monmouth acknowledged that a considerable amount of time had elapsed since he had finished Book Six in 1155.[19] Only one madness miracle is recorded in Book Seven, and it is worth exploring whether the fifteen or so years between his recording of this case of madness and those in Books One to Six changed how Thomas of Monmouth represented the condition.

This chapter analyses how violent behaviour and violent intent were interpreted and portrayed in the text as a whole and in relation to reason and madness. Did the violent actions of mad pilgrims warrant, by twelfth-century standards, the treatment they received, and how were different types of violence (unpredictable, reactionary, justifiable) displayed in the text? Examining violence within this context presents an etymological challenge in that the meaning of the term 'violence' is relative both to the place and to the time in which it is applied. In twelfth-century England, perceptions of what constituted violence were different from those held today. It is therefore very important to pay attention to Thomas of Monmouth's own vocabulary and his interpretation of violence. Notably, the term *uiolentius* (with more violence/force) was applied most often to the actions of bystanders who bound mad pilgrims. At times, bystanders also acted *crudeliter* (cruelly/savagely), perhaps indicating the overzealous application of an otherwise necessary physical restraint. The mad themselves were described as *torvus* (wild) or as acting *crudeliter*, like those who restrained them. Similarly, when he commented on the acts of torture that the Jews were said to have performed on the young martyr, Thomas of Monmouth branded the perpetrators *crudeles* (cruel/savage) and additionally emphasised their 'maliciousness' ('malitie').[20] In the *Life and Miracles*, the saint's enemies (in this case, the Jews of Norwich and their defenders) were not punished with madness, but their conduct still resonated with the behaviour of the mad. The different expressions and experiences of violence recorded in the *Life and Miracles* suggest that Thomas of Monmouth's conception of violence extended not just to physical actions but also to the intentions of the perpetrator and the interpretation of their actions in relation to social norms and customs.

The 'savage' behaviour of the Jews

Many medieval *vitae* include aspects of violence, and the *Life and Miracles of William of Norwich* is no exception. The boy martyr's death was vividly described by his hagiographer, Thomas of Monmouth, with specific emphasis on the cruelty or savagery of the Jews. The great importance that Thomas placed on the violent nature of William's death probably stems from the fact that it was his death alone that gave him his saintly status. His short life had not been particularly exceptional and would not have warranted veneration had it not ended at the time and in the manner it was said to. With the successful cult of Saint Edmund at nearby Bury as inspiration, Thomas of Monmouth sought to establish William as a Christian martyr, whose violent death represented a renewed struggle against non-Christian adversaries. It is possible that the monks of Norwich envisaged William as a potential rival for Edmund, given the bishop of Norwich's repeated failure to assert his authority over Bury (discussed in Chapter 1) and Edmund's prominent international reputation and prestige.[21] Thomas constructed William's sanctity by juxtaposing the boy's Christian virtue and the Jews' malicious violence. William was a pious and Christian child. From the age of seven, he was devoted to abstinence, fasting when his elder brothers would not and celebrating the vigils of all the apostles and other saints. William was also depicted as exceptionally innocent, and it was this innocence that made him particularly susceptible to the trickery ('fraudis') of the Jews.[22] William's vulnerability, as an innocent child, was the antithesis of the Jews' cunning malice.[23] He was conceived as the embodiment of good qualities, marked by piety and innocence, which sharply contrasted the deceitful qualities of the Jews and increased the outrageousness of their violation, since, as a child, William had been unable to defend himself.

William's *Life and Miracles* was composed within the wider context of increasing concern for the frailty of children, epitomised in the image of the Christ Child.[24] The two focal points of Christ's life (his childhood and his Passion) were paralleled in William's *Life* through the descriptions of his childhood innocence and his crucifixion.[25] According to Thomas, the Jews waited to seize William whilst he was eating dinner, in imitation of the Last Supper. As a means of torture, the Jews placed a teasel in William's mouth and tied a knotted rope around his head, positioning the five knots (corresponding to the five wounds of Christ) on pressure points to cause maximum pain when the rope was pulled tight. William's head was shaved and stabbed with thorns, and the Jews tied him to a makeshift cross, made from wooden beams in their house, to mock the Passion of the Lord.[26] In a great clamour and vying to see who could kill him first, the Jews then attacked William, and the mortal blow was inflicted by a wound to his left side. To halt the severe blood flow from the wounds, the Jews poured boiling water over the corpse, which was subsequently placed in Thorpe Wood.[27] Throughout this section of the *Life and Miracles*, Thomas repeatedly emphasised the cruelty or savagery ('crudelitas') of the Jews' actions and the torment they caused.[28] The resemblance to Christ's death is very clear and was evidently intended to be so. Thomas referred to William as an 'innocent lamb' (Jeremiah 11:19), facing the wickedness of the Jews, thus rendering their actions a violation of his goodness.[29] This violation echoed what was understood to have been the Jews' ultimate act of violence, for which they were punished with living as a subservient underclass in a Christian society: the death of Christ.

James McCulloh has pointed out that the importance of the ritual murder accusation lies not simply in Thomas's invention but in the acceptance by the Christian population that the Jews were capable of such violence.[30] Israel Yuval has observed that Thomas of Monmouth, in composing his tale of ritual murder, was able to 'harness to local needs' a pre-existing perception of the Jewish population as dangerous.[31] The twelfth century marked a period of growing distrust of minority groups in England, especially religious minorities like the Jews, following the religious fervour of the First Crusade and the failures of the Second Crusade, which left the few survivors in debt, many disillusioned and others seeking a scapegoat.[32] Though there were clearly those who disagreed with Thomas's interpretation of events (he admits as much himself), there were also those who shared in his suspicions, including perhaps William's uncle, Godwin Sturt, who is said to have accused the Jews of his nephew's murder. The Jews themselves, when seeking the protection of the sheriff, anticipated the negative reaction of the Christian population towards them. By extension, Thomas's application of the term *crudeliter* to the actions of the Jews as well as to the ravings of the mad indicates that insanity continued to be associated with violent or sinful behaviour. This association leads us to question whether the cruelty of the Jews differed from the savagery of the mad and what the physical, mental and spiritual implications of madness were for its sufferers.

Behaving badly/behaving madly: were mad people violent?

In total, Thomas of Monmouth described eleven people in his collection who suffered from madness or madness-like symptoms (summarised below in Table 2.1), though not all of these occurrences resulted in a miraculous cure.[33] Like the son of Richard de Needham, the majority of these mad people exhibited extreme behaviour, and many were restrained by their families and friends or by worried bystanders. Behaviours associated with madness were clawing, wailing, tearing and attacking. Sufferers acted without control of their bodies or, as was more often the case in this miracle collection, whilst their bodies were under the control of demons. People who exhibited similar symptoms, though for reasons other than madness (such as grief or pain), were likened by Thomas of Monmouth to the insane and provide an interesting comparison to those who were truly mad. How did Thomas make it apparent that someone was not suffering from madness but was simply *acting madly*? Did the demoniacs who sought William's miraculous assistance present differently from sufferers whose madness was not associated with demons? Were there any mad people who did not exhibit the typical behavioural signs, and, if so, how was their madness represented?

The first mention of madness in the *Life and Miracles* is in Book I and refers to William's mother, Elviva's, extreme grief upon hearing of the death of her son. In an episode of deep emotional significance, Elviva's lamentations were used by Thomas of Monmouth to inspire sympathy in his audience and anger towards the Jews who had allegedly committed this crime. When told of her son's murder by various people, Elviva tore out her hair, wrung her hands and ran through the streets, weeping and wailing. Thomas described her as acting like a mad person ('tanquam amens').[34] Here, mad behaviour was equated with being out of control and was seen

Table 2.1 Summary of madness miracles in Thomas of Monmouth's collection of the miracles of William of Norwich.

Ref.	*Summary*	*Behaviour of mad person*	*Restraint of mad person*	*Description of healed person*
I.15	William's mother, Elviva, heard of her son's death and violently lamented it. Thomas described her as behaving 'like a mad person' ('tanquam amens').	She tore at her hair, clasped her hands, wept and wailed.	None.	None.
III.22	Ida, the wife of Eustace, a moneyer from Norwich, suffered from severe gout, the pain of which made her act like a mad person ('amens'). She offered a candle to William and, upon touching his sepulchre, appeared unimpaired.	Hideous shrieking.	None.	She 'appeared unimpaired' ('apparuit incolumis') and was able to leave the shrine without assistance.
IV.3	A possessed servant of the moneyers of Norwich was freed through prayers to the martyr.	Behaved badly.	Bound in strong chains.	The servant was 'freed' ('liberatus').
IV.13	The mad daughter of Eustace, a moneyer, was brought to the tomb and made healthy within an hour.	None.	None.	The girl was 'healthy/sane' ('sanam').
V.12	A peasant belonging to Simon de Hempstead was tormented by a demon for many days and then was made healthy and unimpaired by William.	None.	Bound hand and foot to the tomb.	He was 'healthy/sane' ('sanum') and 'unimpaired' ('incolumem').
V.13	A very violent man (the son of Richard de Needham and Silverun), who was possessed by a devil and had tried to kill his mother, was cured at the tomb.	Could not eat or sleep for six days, cried out in a horrible voice, refused to go to the tomb, broke his bonds, bit his mother's throat, gnashed his teeth, glared savagely.	Seven men were hardly able to chain him. He was bound for six days and dragged to the tomb.	Calm, quiet, asked to be unbound, able to eat and drink. Returned home with his parents and friends, sane ('sanus') and unimpaired ('incolumnis').

(*Continued*)

Table 2.1 Summary of madness miracles in Thomas of Monmouth's collection of the miracles of William of Norwich. (*Continued*)

Ref.	*Summary*	*Behaviour of mad person*	*Restraint of mad person*	*Description of healed person*
VI.4	Ebrard/Everard Fisher was vexed by an unclean spirit. He attacked people and blasphemed. He was cured after being tied beside William's tomb.	Broke his chains, tore at bystanders with his teeth and nails. Blaspheming and talking nonsense. Unable to sleep.	Hands tied behind his back, feet bound, brought to the tomb by a number of men.	Quiet, able to sleep and eat, healthy, joyful.
VI.5	Robert, a man suffering from bouts of madness, was brought to the tomb by his mother and was cured.	Shaking, seizing, fiery eyes, crying, stripping, unable to control himself, extreme strength.	Coaxed with soft words and brought to the tomb.	Returned home with joy ('cum gaudio').
VI.6	A woman called Sieldeware was possessed by a demon. She was bound and brought to the tomb by her friends. At the tomb, she seemed cured because the demon was afraid to attack her in front of the martyr. However, when she left, she went mad again. She was brought back to the tomb for a second time and was then permanently cured.	Resisted going into the church. Crying and wailing. Kicking the ground and trying to break her bonds with her teeth.	Four strong men struggled to drag her inside the church. Bound with her own veil and girdle.	Quiet. Able to sleep and eat. Her body grew in health and her soul in faith.
VI.8	Gilliva, a blind woman, suffered from severe pain during her miraculous cure and was compared to a mad person.	Collapsed, tore at her cheeks, rolled around and screamed.	None.	She received her sight and was able to rest following the great pain she had suffered.
VII.3	Robert, son of William de Crachesford, was disturbed in the brain ('cerebri turbati') and troubled by insanity ('laborantem insania'). He spent the night at William's tomb quietly with his friends and was cured.	None.	He was brought to the tomb by many people but was quiet when there.	He was 'healthy/sane' ('sanum').

as a physical manifestation of emotional trauma. Nonetheless, Elviva was not identified as mad; she was likened to a mad person. Her behaviour was not irrational because it was an accepted response to grief. Such actions as hair-pulling and lamenting were common visualisations of female grief and would no doubt have been recognisable as such to Thomas's intended audience.[35] William, as the Christ-like martyr, was mourned by his mother, just as Mary had grieved for the crucified Christ.[36] Maternal grief was typified by theatrical displays of emotion that made visible the mother's internal pain.[37] Such displays had a biblical precedent (Rachel weeping for her children, Jeremiah 31:15) and were repeated in other child murder stories, such as that of Little Saint Hugh, whose death in the mid-thirteenth century was attributed to Jews and whose mother purportedly frantically searched the Jewry, crying out for her child.[38] Elviva's mad behaviour was not a surprising reaction to grief and so did not contravene social expectations. Her behaviour was tolerated without resorting to restraint and was even used to inspire sympathy in others.

There are other examples in the *Life and Miracles* of people acting as though they were mad. Ida, the wife of Eustace, a moneyer from Norwich, reacted so forcefully to the severe pain of gout that people thought she had gone mad ('amens putaretur'). Her 'hideous shrieks' made her sound insane.[39] This graphic description of Ida's behaviour emphasised the severity of her physical pain, and, much as Elviva's heightened emotional state led to madness-like symptoms, Ida's extreme pain was associated with abnormal behaviour, such as screaming and rolling around. Gilliva, a blind woman, was also compared to a mad person whilst suffering the agony of her cure. Her eyes were struck with a fiery vapour, and she collapsed to the floor, tearing at her cheeks and rolling around as if in a fury (*furia*).[40] Like Ida, Gilliva let out terrible cries that were terrifying and filled the church.[41]

Extreme suffering was not, however, always negative. Lewin, an invalid from Wells, was so severely sick that he was on the brink of death. In his delirious state, he was guided by an angel in an ecstatic vision and witnessed both the horrors and the wonders of the afterlife.[42] Though Lewin was not described as being mad, his mind was said to have become separate from his body for the duration of the vision and was then reunited with it, in a scene paralleling the Last Judgement, at which point he was cured of his physical illness.[43] This separation of mind from body was enabled both by the extreme suffering of his illness and by the spiritual guidance of the angel. It was Lewin's tremendous resilience of spirit that enabled the cure of his physical body.[44] Lewin's strong spirit strengthened his body, whereas, for the moneyer's wife, Ida, her weak body weakened her mind.

Strength of spirit was again demonstrated in another miracle: that of a desirable virgin from Dunwich. Following the well-known virgin martyr trope, this young woman had chosen a celibate lifestyle and yet was pursued by many suitors, the most ardent of whom proved to be a demonic *incubus*.[45] The *incubus* tried to win her affection with various gifts and by so doing influenced her mind (*mens*). Nonetheless, her mind (*animus*) remained strong through its connection to Christ, and she refused the *incubus's* advances.[46] It is noteworthy that the term *mens* was used to describe the mind that was susceptible to demons, whereas the term *animus* was used to describe the mind that was strengthened by Christ. The term *mens* seems to have referred to the virgin's human ability to make judgements (whether or not to accept the temptations of the demon), and *animus* was the reasoning faculty by which she was connected to Christ; *mens* was the mind to which the human body was subject, and *animus* was the mind that was subject to Christ. Virgin martyrs often featured in the hagiographical writings of late antiquity (Agatha, Agnes, Lucy), and such stories continued to resonate in the Middle Ages, particularly in the twelfth and thirteenth centuries.[47] Notably, Thomas of Monmouth described several visions, experienced by Norwich monks and members of the laity, in which William of Norwich appeared alongside virgins, including the virgin martyr Saint Katherine.[48] Thomas used these visions to associate William with more-established saints and to remind his audience of William's own martyrdom (conspicuously, the sole reason for his veneration despite Thomas's account of his pious life). The demon's attempt to violate the virgin from Dunwich may have been a further subtle reminder of the violation of William's innocent body by his alleged killers, which, in turn, paralleled the Jews' supposed murder of Christ.

A comparable story appears in Book I of the *Life and Miracles*, and it is plausible that Thomas of Monmouth was conscious of the analogies that could be drawn between the events of William's life and martyrdom and the workings of his posthumous miracles. According to Thomas, in order to trick Elviva into entrusting her son, William, to their care, a messenger of the Jews lied that the boy would be taken to work as a servant in a large manor house and paid in silver for his service. Unlike the Dunwich virgin, whose mind remained steadfast in the face of the riches offered by the *incubus*, Elviva – the Judas to William's Christ – gave in to the temptation of the silver, and her 'mind ['animus'] was fiercely beaten'.[49] A second Judas can be seen in the Jews' messenger, who convinced Elviva to give up her son by his 'false snares of words' and his 'deceitful promises'.[50] Thomas of Monmouth was unsure whether the messenger was a Christian or a Jew but repeatedly referred to him as 'the traitor' ('traditor') and once, explicitly as 'Judas'.[51] Both 'Judases' – the mother and the messenger – embodied the sins of greed and deceit, which contrasted William's childhood innocence, as well as the Dunwich virgin's Christian chastity, and mirrored the perceived immorality of wealthy Jewish communities. In the miracle account, having failed to tempt the virgin, the evil spirit then began to torment her with violence ('uiolentia'), and 'it soon became known to all that it was a demon that was infesting her.'[52] Despite the infestation of the demon, the young virgin continued to resist his violence and was eventually liberated thanks to William's intercession.[53] Unlike other young people who were driven insane by the seduction of demons (we come across two such cases in Chapter 4, one involving a virgin who was portrayed very similarly to this one), the Dunwich virgin did not become mad. It was the *incubus* that acted violently and the virgin who remained resistant and pure in body, mind and soul.

To what extent, then, did the possessed take on the violence of the demonic tormentors that had violated their bodies and minds rather than display extreme force of their own making? Several pilgrims who were brought to be cured at William's shrine were described as being possessed. One common characteristic of demonic possession was that the sufferer was not able to or did not need to eat, drink or sleep, perhaps indicating that demons had assumed all bodily functions and that they themselves did not require food, water or sleep.[54] Likewise, demons were connected with the abnormal physical movements and behaviours of the possessed. A servant of the Norwich moneyers was seized by a demon ('demonio arreptus') and then behaved so badly ('male se habuit') that he had to be locked in irons.[55] Upon cure, the servant was 'freed' ('liberatus'), which suggests that his previous bad behaviour had been against his will.[56] Though the demon itself did not 'behave badly', its violation of the servant's body and mind caused his bad behaviour and resulted in him being restrained. Restraint itself was not necessarily violent, and, in this case, it was a logical and expected reaction to the servant's behaviour. In fact, all those present in their right minds had offered prayers of support for the young man.[57] Similarly, in another miracle, a peasant (*rusticus*) of Simon de Hempstead was tormented by a demon ('a demonio uexatum'). His hands and feet were bound despite there being no mention of violence or of his behaviour at all.[58] Evidently, an association between demonic possession and physical restraint prevailed, so much so that individual cases of restraint did not require specific explanation. For miraculously curing the peasant, Thomas of Monmouth credited William with being able to 'not only control the diseases of men, but also the wiles of devils.'[59] It was a clear mark of William's sanctity, and a further comparison between him and Christ, that he was able to expel the demons, which others had struggled to restrain.[60]

The necessity for restraint was all too apparent in many of Thomas's accounts of demonic possession. The son of Richard de Needham, who we met at the start of this chapter, was seized by a demon that gave him the strength of seven men and made him act so fiercely ('acriter') that he needed to be bound.[61] His violence continued, however, and, upon reaching the tomb of the martyr, he broke his bonds. Thomas specifically stated that the man's extreme strength came not from within him but from the demon that possessed him.[62] The strength that made his violence possible was inhuman and was contrary to normal human behaviour. The demon was 'evil' (*malignus*): the same term that had been used to describe the Jewish plot to kill William, thus drawing a parallel between the Jews and the devil.[63] The possessed man's inhuman violence escalated when he attacked his mother, Silverun, and tried to kill her by tearing her throat out with his teeth.[64] He then went on to attack anyone he could reach.[65] The man's actions were described using wild imagery to emphasise his disconnection from humanity and his subservience to the demon; he hissed through his teeth and looked at bystanders with savage eyes.[66] Similar language was used to describe Ebrard Fisher, who was violently mad and had to be brought to the tomb bound in iron shackles. When his shackles accidently broke, he savagely ('crudeliter') tore at those around him with his nails and teeth.[67] Like Richard de Needham's son, Ebrard was also possessed; he was tormented by a spirit ('uexatus spiritu').[68] Whilst at William's tomb, Ebrard repeated various blasphemies, and it was only by God's grace that he was eventually cured.[69]

Whilst demonic possession was the most common cause of violent madness in Thomas's collection, it is important to acknowledge that one violent madman, who came to the tomb with his mother, was not explicitly depicted as the victim of demonic attack, though demonic involvement cannot be ruled out since his symptoms mirror those of the other demoniacs, and some language that hints at possession was used to describe his condition. Robert was from the parish of Saint Michael Conisford in Norwich and had been suffering for some time with bouts of madness interspersed with periods of lucidity. Upon arriving at the church, he became tormented ('uexari'), and, when placed by the tomb, he began to display similar wild behaviour to those who were possessed: 'his eyes sent out fiery sparks, he made horrible sounds'.[70] Robert forgot his humanity ('hominem oblitus') and removed his clothes, contravening normal social behaviour without shame.[71] The madman also exercised 'great strength', which he was unable to control.[72] Robert was cured by William's intercession, and the madness of the Bacchic spirit ('debachantis spiritus insania') was driven from him.[73] Anne E. Bailey has argued that this miracle record is indicative of a shift that occurred in the twelfth century, whereby behaviours that were traditionally associated with demonic possession were increasing medicalised, and 'demonic possession' itself was transformed from a 'supernatural event into a medical one'.[74] Whereas, in Saint Edmund of Bury's late eleventh-century miracles, the demon that had possessed Sheriff Leofstan had been interpreted literally, resulting in the sheriff's possessed corpse being sunk in a lake, Robert's 'spirit' was an illness (*morbus*) that could be cured. Nonetheless, as Leofstan's case exemplifies, the etymological association between demonic possession and madness was not new in the second half of the twelfth century; as we saw in Chapter 1, Herman described Leofstan as suffering from 'madness' ('amentia') as well as being possessed by a demon ('possessus a demone').[75] Furthermore, Thomas's reference to Bacchus – also used by Herman to describe the madness of Osgod Clapa – demonstrates a continued linguistic association between insanity and the frenzy of Bacchus's pagan cult, and between demonic behaviour and non-Christian beliefs, something that would have been particularly pertinent given the accusations that Thomas had made against the Jews.[76]

In two accounts of madness, Thomas did not use any language pertaining to demonic possession. In the first, the mad daughter of Eustace, almost certainly the same moneyer who was married to Ida (who had suffered with severe pain from gout), was brought to the tomb and cured within an hour. She was not said to have been bound, and the only description given of her was that she was 'insanam'.[77] The lack of detail in this miracle record can perhaps be attributed to Thomas's poor memory; elsewhere in the collection, he admitted to lapses of memory when unable to recall a miracle recipient's name, and he may, likewise, have been unable to remember any further details of this girl's condition.[78] He was clearly referring back to a miracle that had occurred in the past because he prefaced the story with 'We also saw in those days'.[79]

The second case of non-demonic madness is in Book Seven of the *Life and Miracles*, which was written over fifteen years after the other six books. This large chronological gap might explain the evolution of Thomas's terminology, though, as shown in the next chapter, Thomas Becket's miracle collections, which were also compiled in the 1170s, contain several records of demonic possession. In this final case of madness, a clerk named Robert was described as being troubled by insanity ('laborantem insania') and disturbed in the brain ('cerebri turbati').[80] Notably, Robert was not the only madman whose insanity was connected with a problem in the brain. Ebrard Fisher's brain (*cerebrum*) benefitted from the restful sleep that he was able to obtain at William's tomb when spared from the torments of the demon that had vexed him.[81] There is no allusion to demons in Robert's miracle record, and Robert was specifically non-violent, exhibiting none of the signs that, in Thomas's other miracle records, were connected with demonic possession. Instead, he 'calmly' ('placide') spent the night at William's tomb and was cured in the early hours of the morning.[82]

Binding and restraining: were mad people treated with violence?

As Table 2.1 shows, all the mad men and women who acted violently at William of Norwich's tomb (and some who did not) were restrained or otherwise coerced into the martyr's presence. Their symptoms were seen to be savage or wild because they violated expected social norms. It is perhaps for this reason that relatives and bystanders saw the need to restrain them: to place some form of restraint on an otherwise unrestrained and powerfully violent body. As shown in the record of Richard de Needham's son's cure, the violence that mad people exhibited was often reflected back at them in the actions of observers. The mad son acted with increasing violence ('uiolentius') and even attacked his own mother, which resulted in him being savagely ('crudeliter') seized by bystanders and restrained.[83] The same term ('crudeliter') was used to describe the madman Ebrard Fisher when he attacked bystanders at the tomb.[84] Despite Thomas's tendency to portray mad people as innocent victims of illness, which was often demonically induced, the violence with which they were shown to be treated at William's tomb may reflect a continuingly negative moral perception of insanity, the type of which was seen in Edmund of Bury's miracle collections.

A possessed female pilgrim, Sieldeware, exhibited an unusual strength, similar to that of the male pilgrims examined above and equivalent to that of four sane men, who took hold of her with more violence ('eam uiolentius arripiunt'), then bound her with her own veil and girdle.[85] Sieldeware was the victim of a spirit ('spiritus') possession and was also described as being 'insane' ('insanam').[86] Yet she was treated with violence by her contemporaries. The violation by the demon provoked violent behaviour in Sieldeware (forceful refusal to enter the church), which then necessitated a violent response from the crowd. Whilst the crowd was able to restrain her temporarily, Sieldeware's violence had a demonic cause and demanded a spiritual cure. Thomas explained that the evil spirit feared the martyr and was afraid to cry out in his presence. In this way, William restored a sense of calm, so much so that it was believed that Sieldeware was cured, and she was removed from the tomb. Without the interference of the evil spirit, she 'restrained her foolish cries', but this self-restraint was lost when she was moved away from the saint.[87] As soon as the spirit had regained its confidence, it began to torment her again, and she beat the floor and tore at her bonds with her teeth. The abrupt changes in Sieldeware's behaviour highlight that it was the evil spirit that caused her violent symptoms and not Sieldeware herself. Sieldeware was eventually cured after being returned to the tomb and remaining there for three days, which, presumably, the spirit could not endure.

Other miracle records follow a similar pattern; the loss of the mind (to madness or to demonic possession) was often a sudden and violent occurrence in itself. In their reactions, sane observers met violence with equal violence, binding and restraining a mad man or woman. Only William's divine intervention could restore calm. The story of the Norwich moneyers' mad servant begins with the moneyers engaged in their work: an expected behaviour. Then, 'unexpectedly' ('subito'), the servant was seized by a demon ('demonio arreptus'). The use of the term 'arreptus' implies that the servant was taken by force.[88] During his demonic possession, the servant behaved badly ('male se habuit'), and this behaviour necessitated his restraint in strong chains ('fortibus uinculis').[89] The forceful response from the community was precipitated by the servant's bad behaviour, which itself was caused by the demon. In another miracle record, the possessed peasant of Simon de Hempstead was tormented ('uexatum') by a demon, then bound ('ligatum') and brought to the shrine, where he was made healthy and unharmed ('sanum et incolumem').[90] Particularly striking is the case of Richard de Needham's son, who was seized ('correptus') by a demon, and then, as we know, acted so fiercely ('acriter') that he almost killed his mother.[91] He was cruelly seized ('crudeliter arripitur') by bystanders at the shrine, who bound him.[92] Then,

> as soon as he touched the sacred spot, wonderful to say, neither by voice nor look did he show the least token of madness. After an hour had passed he gently and meekly asked to be loosed and was unbound by one of the servants of the Church. Thereafter, he behaved himself as quietly and tamely as if he had suffered no touch of madness.[93]

Contact with the saint's shrine had an instantaneous effect on the madman's behaviour, which was emphasised by the adverbs 'gently' ('blande'), 'meekly' ('humiliter'), 'quietly' ('placide') and 'tamely' ('mansuete'). Such terms directly contrast the adverb 'acriter', which was used to describe his actions when mad. Once cured, Richard de Needham's son was unbound ('solutus'), which demonstrates that his previous binding, though violent in its forcefulness, was necessary only to counter his own violent behaviour.

Similarly, Thomas of Monmouth provided no explicit justification for the removal of Sieldeware's veil and girdle or for the binding of a madwoman, perhaps because he felt that these actions did not need explanation and that the motives of the binders were obvious given the situation. It was Sieldeware's own forceful refusal to enter the church that elicited a response that involved unusual levels of force. The violent actions of bystanders were intended to help Sieldeware by enabling her to be brought to the protection of the saint's tomb. There was a long-standing precedent for forcibly restraining the insane; the biblical Gerasene demoniac was bound with chains and fetters, which he then broke (Mark 5:3–4). There was also a contemporary precedent for the bystanders' actions, which can be seen in twelfth-century social provisions for the management of the insane. Records of legal guardians being appointed for mad wards do not emerge until after 1250, and it is thought that such individuals were cared for by their families and communities (if at all) before this.[94] Brandon Parlopiano has found some evidence in legal texts of the twelfth century to suggest that the insane (at least, those with landed wealth) were dealt with in the same way as orphaned minors; their estates were to be managed but not appropriated by guardians.[95] Theoretically, guardians would be formally appointed, but family members would also take the responsibility of care upon themselves.[96] The *Leges Henrici Primi*, produced by an anonymous author, most likely in the early twelfth century, to record the legal practices of his day, states that 'their relatives should compassionately care for insane persons and dangerous people of this kind.'[97] Two inferences can be drawn from this statement. First, it supports the work of historians who have argued that madness was largely cared for within the home and that compassion was an important part of this care.[98] Conversely, it identifies the mad as dangerous people and insists upon the necessity of others taking responsibility for them, for the sake of their own welfare and that of others.

These legal beliefs and practices are very much reflected in the treatment of the mad at Norwich. Many of the mad pilgrims were described as being taken to the tomb, which suggests that they were assisted by other members of the community. The mad daughter of Eustace was led ('adduci') to the tomb, and Ebrard Fisher was similarly led ('adducitur') to the shrine by many men.[99] Richard de Needham's son was led ('adduceretur') to the tomb by his parents, and Robert came with his mother ('cum matre uenerat').[100] The presence of companions on journeys of pilgrimage was not unusual. Anne Bailey found that relatives, friends, villagers and strangers made up almost one quarter of the pilgrims recorded in sixteen twelfth-century English miracle collections, and it is likely that many more companions were not mentioned by the compilers.[101] In cases of madness, companions were almost always present, which suggests that they played a key role in the care and management of mad pilgrims. It was clearly an accepted practice for members of the mad person's family or community to assist in the process of their cure. Furthermore, the fact, as we have seen, that most of these pilgrims were bound demonstrates a recognition that they could be dangerous and needed to be contained by those caring for them. Sieldeware, for example, was bound and brought to the tomb by her friends/relatives.[102] In such cases, the mad were recognised as members of the community who needed special provision, and this status was reflected in their treatment at Norwich.

Community provision for the mad was also prescribed in canon law. According to Gratian's *Decretum*, a collection of canon law compiled in the mid-twelfth century, the mad were not to be excluded from the sacraments so long as they had expressed their desire to receive them prior to losing their sanity.[103] This recommendation could no doubt have been fairly loosely interpreted since, unless the sufferer had been born mad, it may often have been difficult to tell whether or not previous desire had been expressed. The mad were not rejected by the Christian community, and madness was not always conceived as a permanent state. Mad people had once been lucid and had the potential to become lucid again. Indeed, beneficed clergy were not expected to relinquish their positions if they succumbed to insanity. Instead, they were appointed a *coadiutor*, who would oversee their ecclesiastical duties until they recovered or passed away.[104] Conversely, as we saw in Chapter 1, in the late-eleventh-century miracles of Saint Edmund of Bury, Leofstan, a possessed sheriff, was shunned by both secular and ecclesiastical authorities and 'despised in heaven and on earth'.[105] Leoftan was unable to maintain his position as sheriff, was denied a dignified Christian burial and would not receive salvation at the Last Judgement.[106] Such restrictions were not placed on the mad in Thomas of Monmouth's *Life and Miracles*, in which mad pilgrims were physically restrained but were admitted to the church and were restored to full participation in the Christian community by the martyr.

Despite, on a few occasions, exacting vengeance on wrongdoers via miraculous punishment (for example, a monk called Richard died in agony after refusing to allow some ornate candles in his possession to be lit at the saint's tomb), William of Norwich was also shown to restore sinners to the Christian community.[107] In one miracle account, a sorceress came to William's tomb with a group of pilgrims from Cambridge. However, as she tried to approach the tomb, the saint miraculously prevented her from doing so because of her profane lifestyle. Becoming frustrated, the sorceress resorted to violence, pulling her headscarf off, tearing at her hair and face, beating her breast and trampling on the ground.[108] Such behaviour is reminiscent of Ebrard Fisher, the madman who tore at bystanders with his teeth and nails, or Robert, who removed his clothes at the tomb.[109] The sorceress was not described as being mad; her unnatural behaviour was the result of a tormented mind living in mortal sin ('sacrilega mente').[110] She was denied access to the saint because of her sin, whereas mad people, who were, despite their antisocial behaviour, allowed to approach the tomb, were not directly associated with sinfulness.

The mad approached the shrine as did other pious pilgrims and were not denied the saint's intercession. The crowd of onlookers that saw Sieldeware's mad ravings, including Thomas himself, pitied her, and Thomas personally asked the saint for assistance for her.[111] Madness was also recognised as a curable illness, and, through William's intercession and God's grace, the mad were returned to a state of sanity and wholeness. Sieldeware was healed with a heavenly remedy ('celeste remedium'), and the peasant belonging to Simon de Hempstead was made healthy and unimpaired ('sanum et incolumem').[112] Thus, despite their violence, mad people remained part of secular and religious society and were catered for within it. Sometimes, the nature of their conditions demanded communal management, and their miraculous cures are very much a reflection of their inclusion in a communal process that inspired public compassion.

Conclusion

In the *Life and Miracles of William of Norwich*, madness was detected by behaviour that violated normal social expectations in an extreme way, though, as we have seen, it was itself characterised by its own set of culturally-accepted representations. The behaviour of mad pilgrims arriving at shrines provided a spectacle, which drew the attention of onlookers and, presumably, of those who read and listened to miracle accounts. Recognised mad behaviours included 'savage' snarling, glaring and biting, as well as extreme physical strength. Such behaviours could, and sometimes did, cause harm to bystanders. Representations of interactions between mad cure-seekers and those around them form a hagiographical pattern of violent mad behaviour. The binding of the mad was a 'savage' act in that it required extreme force to counter that of the mad themselves. Restraint was a necessary reaction to violence and was not itself part of the cure, which was performed solely by the saint. William's intercession restored the mad to a state of calm and quiet: the antithesis of mad behaviour and a clear sign that they had been cured.

In Thomas of Monmouth's account, the malicious savagery of the Jews can be contrasted to the wild actions of the mad. Crucial to the conception of violence were the intention of the perpetrator and the outcome for the victim, both of which were reliant on Thomas of Monmouth's perception and representation of events. In Books One and Two of the *Life and Miracles*, William of Norwich was a victim of the premeditated and intentional violence of the Jews, whose supposed predisposition towards violence was emphasised in the parallels drawn between the boy martyr and Christ. The violently mad, on the other hand, whilst inflicting injuries on others, were also victims, either of illness or, more often in this collection, of demonic torment. They were frequently afforded sympathy from their communities, and assistance was offered (either through prayers or by escorting them to the shrine) to aid their cure. Madness was understood to be curable (through William's intercession), but, nonetheless, those suffering from madness contravened normal social expectations and thus required a cure. The Jews were necessary outsiders (their social role was to act as a reminder to Christians of the consequences of sin), whereas the mad were Christians in need of physical, mental and spiritual guidance. Both displayed violence in their use of extreme force and their violation of perceived boundaries, but the Jews did so with malicious intent, whereas the mad acted beyond their own control.

The violent representations of mad men and women in the *Life and Miracles* are thus products of a different type of saint's cult. Though he shared the advantage of a violent martyrdom, William lacked Saint Edmund of Bury's established reputation as a protector of the faithful. Instead, both in his martyrdom and in his posthumous healing miracles, William was shown to emulate Christ. Unlike Edmund, William did not dispense madness as a divine punishment; it was a sickness for which he provided a cure. Nonetheless, some of the negative physical, mental and spiritual implications of madness that we saw in Edmund's miracle collections endure in the *Life and Miracles*. Madness was not caused by sin, but violent sinful behaviour could be 'savage', as could the ravings of the insane. The violence of mad men and women was often echoed in the violence with which they were restrained, paralleling the biblical Gerasene demoniac who was chained before being cured by Christ. In the chapters that follow, I address whether, as the twelfth century progressed and madness took its place in miracle collections as an illness that could be miraculously cured by the saints, the violence that accompanied it was muted or whether the adverse spiritual connotations of madness and demonic possession persisted even as the language used to describe them evolved.

Notes

1. TM1, V.13, p. 204 ['Cumque illuc uiolentius traheretur, non suo sed maligni spiritus annisu rupit uincula, insurgensque in matrem ipsam humi proiecit, dentibusque per gutter arripuit. Iamque illam morti dedisset, nisi plebs accurrens ereptam liberasset. Tum ille dentibus stridens, toruisque luminibus circumstantes intuens, quos contingere potuit, miserabiliter discerpsit. Qua de re confluentibus plurimis, crudeliter arripitur, alligatur, constrictisque ad pedes manibus, uelit nolit, ab latere sancti sepulcri deponitur']. Miri Rubin's new translation of the text (TM2) has also been consulted, but Jessopp and James has been cited because that is the standard edition of the Latin. I have used Jessopp and James's translation but amended it where appropriate.
2. TM1, VI.4, pp. 223–24; Ibid., IV.3, p. 169.
3. Laharie, pp. 189–90.
4. Koopmans, p. 114.
5. King, pp. 218–20.
6. Ibid., pp. 220–21.
7. Callahan, Jr., p. 221.
8. Jessopp and James, p. lxxxix.
9. Ibid., p. ix.
10. TM1, Prologue, p. 3; Ibid., III.1, pp. 116–17. Thomas received a vision commanding him to revive the fading cult.
11. Ibid., I.16, pp. 46–48.
12. Ibid., III.3, p. 127; Ibid., III.12, pp. 139–41.
13. Rubin, 'Introduction', pp. liii–lv.
14. Ibid., p. lvi.
15. Rubin, 'Making a Martyr', p. 54.
16. Langmuir, p. 210.
17. McCulloh, pp. 706–9.
18. Ibid., p. xii.
19. Ibid., p. 740.
20. TM1, I.5, p. 21.
21. Rose, pp. 104–7.
22. TM1, I.3, p. 16 ['admodum reuera innocentem'].
23. MacLehose, p. 121.
24. Ibid., p. 109.
25. Ibid.
26. TM1, I.5, pp. 20–22 ['in dominice passionis obprobrium'].
27. Ibid., pp. 21–22.
28. Ibid., pp. 20–21.
29. Ibid., pp. 19–20.
30. McCulloh, p. 740.
31. Yuval, p. 170.
32. McCulloh, p. 700; Rose, p. 50.
33. Lewin and the virgin from Dunwich, whose cases are discussed below, are not included in Table 2.1 since Thomas of Monmouth did not directly associate their conditions with madness.
34. TM1, I.15, p. 41.
35. Bartlett, p. 53.
36. MacLehose, p. 109.
37. Ibid., p. 136.
38. Ibid., pp. 135–36.
39. TM1, III.22, pp. 154–55 ['horrendos clamores'].
40. Ibid., VI.8, p. 229 ['oculus uterque uapore quodam igneo corripitur'].

41. Ibid. ['horrendis clamoribus'].
42. Ibid., II.4, p. 68.
43. Ibid., p. 70.
44. Ibid., p. 72.
45. Ibid., II.7, p. 80 ['one of those beings whom they call fairies and incubi, who are prone to lust and are often the seducers of women' / 'eorum quos faunos dicunt et incubos, ad luxum procliues ac sepe mulieribus insolentes']. Later in the miracle account (p. 83), the term *demon* was used.
46. Ibid., p. 81.
47. Coyne Kelly, p. 44.
48. TM1, III.23, p. 156.
49. Ibid., I.4, pp. 18–19 ['His itaque matris acriter pulsabatur animus'].
50. Ibid., p. 17 ['fraudulentis uerborum insidiis', 'fallacibus promissis'].
51. Ibid., I.4–5, pp. 16–19.
52. Ibid., II.7, p. 83 ['Vniueris iam innotuerat demonem esse qui sic eam infestabat'].
53. Ibid., pp. 83–84.
54. Ibid., V.13, pp. 204–5; Ibid., VI.4, p. 224; Ibid., VI.6, p. 227.
55. Ibid., IV.3, p. 169; TM2, IV.3, p. 110. Rubin's translation of 'male se habuit' as 'he behaved so badly' is more literal than Jessopp and James's translation as 'he was in such an evil plight.'
56. TM1, IV.3, p. 169.
57. Ibid.
58. Ibid., V.12, p. 203 ['ligatum manus et pedes'].
59. Ibid. ['non solum morbis hominum sed et uersutiis demonum reuera imperiosus existat'].
60. The comparison between William and Christ is discussed below in reference to the restraint of the Gerasene demoniac (Mark 5:3–4).
61. TM1, V.13, pp. 203–4.
62. Ibid., p. 204 ['non suo sed maligni spiritus annisu rupit uincula'].
63. Ibid., V.13, p. 204; Ibid., I.3, p. 16 ['malignitatis'].
64. Ibid., V.13, p. 204.
65. Ibid.
66. Ibid. ['ille dentibus stridens, toruisque luminibus circumstantes intuens'].
67. Ibid., VI.4, p. 224 ['quos contingere poterat, ungulis ac dentibus crudeliter laniabat'].
68. Ibid., p. 223.
69. Ibid., p. 224.
70. Ibid., VI.5, p. 225 ['Ignei scintillant oculi, horrendi personant soni'].
71. Ibid.
72. Ibid. ['Pudenda parent nec pudet, sui impos potenti uirtute plurima exercet'].
73. Ibid.
74. Bailey, 'Miracles and Madness', p. 241.
75. Herman, 3, p. 12.
76. Ibid., 23, pp. 56–57 ['amens prosilit ad terram, uolutans humo uelut maniam passus debachando'].
77. TM1, IV.13, p. 182.
78. Ibid., VI.7, p. 228.
79. Ibid., IV.13, p. 182 ['Vidimus quoque hisdem diebus'].
80. Ibid., VII.3, p. 265.
81. Ibid., VI.4, p. 224.
82. Ibid., VII.3, p. 265.
83. Ibid., V.13, p. 204.

84. Ibid., VI.4, p. 224.
85. Ibid., VI.6, p. 226.
86. Ibid., pp. 226–27.
87. Ibid., p. 226 ['clamores ineptos repressit'].
88. Ibid., IV.3, p. 169.
89. Ibid.
90. Ibid., V.12, p. 203.
91. Ibid., V.13, pp. 203–4.
92. Ibid., p. 204.
93. Ibid. ['Mox ut sacrum locum attigit, mirum dictu, nec uoce nec uultu uel minimum furoris signum demonstrauit. Pertransito uero hore unius spacio, blande atque humiliter ut solueretur expetens, a quodam ecclesie famulo solutus est, atque postmodum adeo placide ac mansuete se habuit ac si nichil antea furoris habuisset'].
94. Turner, p. 85.
95. Parlopiano, p. 269.
96. Ibid., pp. 270–71.
97. *Leges Henrici Primi*, p. 245.
98. George Rosen, for example, argues that, even in the late Middle Ages, the mad remained 'members of a community' and were entrusted to the care of their families so long as they did not disturb other members (p. 139).
99. TM1, IV.13, p. 182; Ibid., VI.4, pp. 223–24.
100. Ibid., V.13, p. 204; Ibid., VI.5, p. 225.
101. Bailey, 'Wives, mothers and widows', p. 199.
102. TM1, VI.6, p. 226 ['a suis adducitur'].
103. Pickett, p. 31.
104. Parlopiano, pp. 262–63.
105. Herman, 3, pp. 12–15 ['perosus celo ac terre'].
106. Ibid. ['Nor, like all the wicked, shall he survive the Judgement, for the Lord's vengeance will be like an axe at the root of the tree' / 'Quique non resurget in iudicio cum impiis, iam enim erit uindicta Domini ut securis ad radicem arboris'].
107. TM1, II.12, pp. 136–45.
108. Ibid., VII.18, pp. 279–81.
109. Ibid., VI.4, pp. 223–24; Ibid., VI.5, p. 224.
110. Ibid., VII.18, p. 280.
111. Ibid., VI.6, p. 227.
112. Ibid.; Ibid., V.12, p. 203.

Bibliography

Primary

Herman the Archdeacon, 'Miracles of St Edmund', in *Herman the Archdeacon and Goscelin of Saint-Bertin. Miracles of St Edmund*, ed. and trans. by Tom Licence (Oxford: Oxford University Press, 2014), pp. 1–125

Leges Henrici Primi, ed. and trans. by L.J. Downer (Oxford: Clarendon Press, 1972)

Thomas of Monmouth, *The Life and Miracles of St William of Norwich*, ed. and trans. by Augustus Jessopp and M.R. James (Cambridge: Cambridge University Press, 1896)

Thomas of Monmouth, *The Life and Passion of William of Norwich*, trans. by Miri Rubin (London: Penguin, 2014)

Secondary

Bailey, Anne E., 'Miracles and Madness: Dispelling Demons in Twelfth-Century Hagiography', in *Demons and Illness from Antiquity to the Early-Modern Period*, ed. by Siam Bhayro and Catherine Rider, Magical and Religious Literature of Late Antiquity, 5 (Leiden: Brill, 2017), pp. 235–255

———, 'Wives, mothers and widows on pilgrimage: categories of "woman" recorded at English healing shrines in the High Middle Ages', *Journal of Medieval History*, 39 (2013), 197–219

Bartlett, Robert, 'Symbolic Meanings of Hair in the Middle Ages', *Transactions of the Royal Historical Society*, 4 (1994), 43–60

Callahan, Thomas Jr., 'The Impact of Anarchy on English Monasticism, 1135–1154', *Albion: A Quarterly Journal Concerned with British Studies*, 6 (1974), 218–232

Coyne Kelly, Kathleen, *Performing Virginity and Testing Chastity in the Middle Ages*, Routledge Research in Medieval Studies, 2 (London and New York, NY: Routledge, 2000)

Jessopp, Augustus, and M.R. James, 'Introduction', in *The Life and Miracles of St William of Norwich*, ed. and trans. by Augustus Jessop and M.R. James (Cambridge: Cambridge University Press, 1896), pp. ix–xc

King, Edmund, *King Stephen* (New Haven, CT and London: Yale University Press, 2010)

Koopmans, Rachel, *Wonderful to Relate: Miracle Stories and Miracle Collecting in High Medieval England* (Philadelphia: University of Pennsylvania Press, 2011)

Laharie, Muriel, *La folie au Moyan-Âge XIe–XIIIe siècles* (Paris: Le Léopard d'Or, 1991)

Langmuir, Gavin I., *Toward a Definition of Antisemitism* (Berkeley, CA, Los Angeles, CA and London: University of California Press, 1990)

MacLehose, William F., *"A Tender Age": Cultural Anxieties over the Child in the Twelfth and Thirteenth Centuries* (New York, NY: Columbia University Press, 2008)

McCulloh, James M., 'Jewish Ritual Murder: William of Norwich, Thomas of Monmouth, and the Early Dissemination of the Myth', *Speculum*, 72 (1997), 698–740

Parlopiano, Brandon T., 'Madmen and Lawyers: The Development and Practice of the Jurisprudence of Insanity in the Middle Ages' (unpublished doctoral thesis, The Catholic University of America, 2013)

Pickett, R. Colin, *Mental Affliction and Church Law: An Historical Synopsis of Roman and Ecclesiastical Law and a Canonical Commentary* (Ottawa, ON: University of Ottawa Press, 1952)

Rose, E.M., *The Murder of William of Norwich: The Origins of the Blood Libel in Medieval Europe* (Oxford and New York, NY: Oxford University Press, 2015)

Rosen, George, *Madness in Society* (Chicago, IL: University of Chicago Press, 1968)

Rubin, Miri, 'Introduction', in *The Life and Passion of William of Norwich*, trans. by Miri Rubin (London: Penguin, 2014), pp. liii–lv

———, 'Making a Martyr: William of Norwich and the Jews', *History Today*, 60 (2010), 48–54

Turner, Wendy J., 'Silent Testimony: Emotional Displays and Lapses in Memory as Indicators of Mental Instability in Medieval English Investigations', in *Madness in Medieval Law and Custom*, ed. by Wendy J. Turner, Later Medieval Europe, 6 (Leiden: Brill, 2010), pp. 81–95

Yuval, Israel Jacob, *Two Nations in Your Womb: Perceptions of Jews and Christians in Late Antiquity and the Middle Ages*, trans. by Barbara Harshaw and Jonathan Chipman (Berkeley, CA, Los Angeles, CA and London: University of California Press, 2006)

3 Medical madness? Diagnosing the mad in the miracles of Saint Thomas Becket

> We saw a foolish woman, named Matilda, who was filled with a demon [and] who was brought from the region of Cologne, and we were terrified of the strange madness in our presence. For instance, she tore into pieces the linen smock, the only thing that covered her body, and, with unimagined strength, she struck a blow at anybody who wanted to move her away. She would have suffocated a small child, who ran to meet her, had he not been quickly pulled away by those standing nearby. She was bound and thus raved for four or five hours in the presence of the martyr [Saint Thomas Becket], until he provided her the benefit of sanity. The wicked spirit was truly expelled from her but the expulsion left behind vile traces. She then gradually returned to her normal self and the next day was wholly restored. Though her speech was scarcely intelligible to us, she recalled how she had seen the martyr in her sleep, clothed in papal vestments, having a streak of blood across his face, of which we made mention in his Life, and asking about the nature of her illness, and then she had shown the questioner [i.e. Becket] a suffering of body and mind. Then, the saint had promised her sanity and imposed a journey of pilgrimage to the home of the apostles [Rome] or even to the church of the blessed James [Santiago de Compostela], thus he promised she be absolved. And also when we asked her how she had been made insane, she told us that her brother had killed a young man, who had rashly loved her; and so she herself, seized with madness, had struck her baby, who had been baptised the day before, with her fist, and removed it from the midst [i.e. killed it]. She departed, therefore, from the martyr, healed and happy, and anxious only for forgiveness of her crime.[1]

Matilda's miraculous cure was performed in Canterbury Cathedral at some point in the 1170s and was recorded by Benedict of Peterborough, one of two monks of Christ Church Cathedral Priory who compiled collections of miracles that occurred there in the late twelfth century. The martyr who had appeared in Matilda's dream-vision was Thomas Becket, the murdered archbishop of Canterbury, recognisable by his episcopal robes and bloodied face. Benedict seems to have been hesitant to diagnose the precise cause of Matilda's madness, which was attributed to the involvement of a 'wicked spirit' ('spiritus nequam') and also to the death of her lover, though these causes were not necessarily incompatible. In Becket's recommendation of a further pilgrimage to Rome or to Santiago de Compostela after her cure, there is an indication that Matilda needed further spiritual cleansing, perhaps because of a sinful relationship with her now-dead lover or as penance for the murder of her baby. The saint himself, via the dream-vision, diagnosed Matilda as suffering in body and mind ('corporis passionem et mentis'). As Matilda's case demonstrates, medieval diagnoses of madness were not always straightforward and continued to contain references to demons in the twelfth century. Miracle compilers frequently attributed madness to the work of demons despite the rapidly expanding circulation of Latin medical literature in English monasteries, which historians have connected with an increased use of naturalised language in miracle records.[2] This chapter explores hagiographical diagnoses of madness in relation to the ideas circulating in contemporary medical texts and examines how far these texts sharpened the terminological distinctions that Benedict of Peterborough and William of Canterbury (a second Christ Church monk who also compiled a collection of Thomas Becket's miracles in the 1170s) made between conditions. Madness was distinct, in the eyes of the Canterbury miracle compilers, from other conditions that had similar behavioural symptoms, like epilepsy, because of its effects on the minds (*mentes*) of sufferers. Nevertheless, the frequent associations made between madness and demons indicate that representations of madness in Thomas Becket's miracle records, recognised by some historians as a 'touchstone case' of the so-called medicalisation of miracle texts, may actually reveal something of the limitations of the medicalisation model.[3]

Saint Thomas Becket, who performed Matilda's miraculous cure, was arguably the most famous English saint of the Middle Ages, and his cult dwarfed all others, including that of Saint Edmund at Bury. On 29 December 1170, Becket, the archbishop of Canterbury, was murdered in Canterbury Cathedral by four knights who claimed they were acting on the orders of King Henry II.[4] Becket's career as archbishop had been turbulent. He had spent two of the eight years of his archbishopric in exile following disputes with the king concerning jurisdiction.[5] For this reason, Becket's relationship with the monks at Christ Church was far from warm. Not only was the archbishop rarely in Canterbury, but the monks also resented his efforts to boost the position of the secular clergy and did not appreciate his appointment as archbishop by the king, arguing that the right to elect the archbishop should have been theirs.[6] They could not empathise with a man who had been ordained a priest only one day before he became archbishop.[7]

When the archbishop was murdered, there was no immediate consensus that he had died as a martyr.[8] It was only when, on 30 December, the ecclesiastical robes were removed from the body in preparation for burial, and coarse monastic garments, riddled with lice and worms, were discovered underneath, that the monks of Christ Church witnessed a potential sign of Becket's hidden asceticism and began to suspect that the archbishop who had always been aloof may have been one of them all along.[9] Miracles started to occur within days of Becket's death, and the first miracles were performed using the blood he had spilt in the cathedral.[10] The cult grew rapidly and, under considerable public pressure, Pope Alexander III issued a bull of canonisation at Segni in Italy on 21 February 1173.[11] On 12 July 1174, Henry II came to Canterbury to do public penance for the death of his former rival.[12]

Thomas Becket's cult was new and flourishing, and it spread with such momentum that it surprised even the monks of Canterbury Cathedral. It may have been the sudden emergence and popularity of Becket's cult that had inspired Thomas of Monmouth to add a seventh book to his *Life and Miracles of William of Norwich* in c.1173, over fifteen years after completing the sixth book.[13] In no way could Becket's cult be described as in need of revival in the way that Herman had claimed for Edmund of Bury's.[14] The monks of Christ Church amassed the largest body of miracle literature that has survived from twelfth-century England. They drew not only on their own understandings of illness and miraculous cure but also on the letters of other clerics (and sometimes laymen), who wrote to inform them of, and to corroborate, miracles that had occurred far away from Canterbury.

Two miracle collections were compiled in quick succession to each other (and partly simultaneously) at Canterbury, just as they had been at Bury over half a century earlier: the first, containing the record of Matilda's miracle, by Benedict of Peterborough, and the second by another Christ Church monk, William of Canterbury. There is, therefore, in this chapter as in the first, scope for comparison between the priorities of two miracle compilers, writing within almost the same geographical and chronological context, and for analysis of how these priorities influenced the compilers' portrayals of madness. However, in Canterbury, unlike in Bury, the second collection of Becket's miracles was not a revision of the first and was not intended to replace it. Whilst a few miracles appear in both collections (none that detail cases of madness), the majority of the records are separate and thus do not lend themselves to direct comparison. Nonetheless, because of the sheer number of miracles that were recorded, Becket's miracle collections contain a substantial number of madness miracles from which a meaningful comparison of the terminology used to denote madness can be made. This textual and linguistic analysis reveals how far 'new' medical learning (influenced by ancient Greek medical ideas that had recently been translated into Latin) had an impact on the Canterbury miracle compilers. Both compilers had some contact with contemporary medical texts, but, arguably, the second miracle collection shows a more sophisticated knowledge of contemporary learned medicine. The individual context for the compilation of each miracle collection, and the individual style of each miracle compiler, influenced the ways in which madness was represented as an ailment requiring miraculous cure. Therefore, as we did for Edmund of Bury's and William of Norwich's miracles, we begin with the compilers: Benedict of Peterborough and William of Canterbury.

Miracles and medicine in twelfth-century Canterbury

Custodians of Becket's shrine

Thomas Becket's tomb was opened to the public after Easter 1171, and his shrine custodian, Benedict (later of Peterborough), was in charge of the cult's administration, management of pilgrims and care of the sick.[15] Benedict collected records for the first, and shorter, of the two collections of Becket's miracles compiled in the twelfth century. He was made prior of Christ Church in 1175 but left Canterbury to become abbot of Peterborough in 1177.[16] In opposition to previous assertions that Benedict composed the last three books of his six-book collection in Peterborough, Rachel Koopmans has demonstrated that Benedict's collection was most likely written as a cohesive work in the early 1170s and was almost certainly completed by 1174.[17] It is possible, however, that additions were made to the collection throughout the 1170s, notably miracle IV.6, which likely refers to a fire that occurred in Rochester in 1179.[18]

Benedict's was the more widely circulated of the two miracles collections compiled by Christ Church monks, and it proved to be more popular outside of Canterbury.[19] The popularity of Benedict's collection can perhaps be attributed to the simple style that he employed and his frequent biblical references, which provided familiar signposts for his readers.[20] Benedict's scholarly interest lay mainly in theology, and his personal book collection contained books on theology, classics and, most abundantly, on canon law.[21] He also showed some interest in medicine and bequeathed several medical texts from his book collection to Peterborough Abbey in 1194 when he died there as abbot. These included a copy of the *Ars Physicae Pantegni et practica ipsius in uno volumine* (Constantine the African's eleventh-century translation and adaptation of 'Ali ibn al-'Abbas al-Madjusi's *Complete Art of Medicine*, which was circulating in its single-volume format in the twelfth century) and the *Practica Bartholomei cum pluribus aliis rebus in uno volumine* (*Bartholomaeus' Practice of Medicine with several other things in one volume*).[22] The *Practica* was compiled by Bartholomaeus, a teacher at the medical school in Salerno (modern-day Italy) in the mid-twelfth century, and consisted of a treatise of different medical techniques followed by a head-to-toe examination of diseases. It has been suggested that Benedict brought the collection that he eventually bequeathed to Peterborough Abbey with him from Christ Church, and it is possible that he had access to some of these medical texts when compiling Becket's miracles at Canterbury.[23] Considering that Bartholomaeus's *Practica* was likely composed in the second half of the twelfth century, for Benedict to have had it in his possession by 1194 at the latest demonstrates his acquisition of very contemporary medical material.[24] Benedict's miracle collection is therefore written from the perspective of a scholarly monk with an interest in medicine and theology.

Thomas Becket's second miracle collection was written by William of Canterbury. William held a less senior position at Christ Church than Benedict, having only been ordained a deacon by Becket himself in 1170, shortly before the martyrdom.[25] He joined Benedict in the task of recording miracles in June 1172, when the number of miracles had become too great for one monk to manage alone.[26] The first five books of his collection were completed by 1175, and, when a sixth book was added in 1176–77, the total number of miracles came to approximately 438, a far larger collection than Benedict's, which contains around 265 miracles.[27] Nicholas Vincent has convincingly argued that the version of William's collection as it survives today was originally intended for circulation in the 1180s as part of the preparations for Becket's translation (postponed by various circumstances until 1220).[28] As it happened, circumstances provided a new purpose for William's miracle collection, but it is credible that Benedict's collection, as it stands, was widely circulated at this time.[29] Vincent suggests that William's collection was diverted from its original purpose and presented to King Henry II in 1186 in the context of a dispute between the Canterbury monks and Archbishop Baldwin (1185–90) over the appointment of a new prior.[30] Thus, though the intended audience for both collections at the time of their composition was most likely monastic, William's collection in particular may have been revised in order to appeal to the secular interests of the king and garner his support for the monks' cause.[31] Further analysis of the surviving manuscripts of both Benedict and William's collections is certainly needed but is beyond the scope of this chapter, which turns its attention instead to the varied representations of madness in the collections, bearing in mind that they had most likely undergone numerous revisions and shifts in focus between their original composition and their wider dissemination.

As shrine custodians, both Benedict and William had close contact with pilgrims, and part of their role may have been to tend to the sick.[32] In twelfth-century England, the clergy were taking on an increasingly pastoral role, and many shrine custodians were responsive to both the spiritual and physical needs of the lay pilgrims in their care.[33] According to their own accounts, both compilers asked questions and discussed sickness and healing with the recipients of cures. Benedict of Peterborough was careful to record the details of Matilda's vision despite having problems communicating with her, possibly because she spoke German and was not well versed in English or Latin ('her speech was scarcely intelligible to us'). He also noted the reason she had given for her madness when asked about its causes.[34] Similarly, William of Canterbury asked an epileptic pilgrim called Hingram what he thought had caused his condition but was keen to disagree with Hingram's explanation. Instead, he provided his own diagnosis, maintaining that epilepsy was not, as Hingram had thought, influenced by the cycles of the moon.[35] The collections thus provide insights into the compilers' experiences with pilgrims at the shrine as well as their own interpretations of illness and healing.

In William of Canterbury's miracle collection, Rachel Koopmans has identified 'a platform to dispense medical information to his brethren and other readers'.[36] Koopmans speculates that, having heard Benedict's collection read aloud in the chapter house, William was frustrated by Benedict's 'feeble' discussion of illness and attempted, in his collection, to rectify it.[37] She hypothesises that William must have closely observed and questioned those pilgrims who were healed by Becket, as evidenced by the highly-detailed records of their conditions that he was able to make, in which he noted, for instance, the colour and consistency of bodily expulsions, such as vomit and urine.[38] William was at pains to explain the causes of illnesses to his audience (most likely Christ Church brethren) as well as to provide them with advice regarding their own health.[39] Koopmans has analysed William's diagnostic language at length, and she notes his familiarity with Greek terms, his intense interest in the internal aetiology of disease and his use of far more varied terminology than Benedict.[40] For example, Benedict described the divinely-inflicted quinsy of Thomas of Etton as 'squinantia', whereas William used the Greek term 'synanchia'.[41]

There is, therefore, certainly evidence, in William of Canterbury's collection, of the 'new' medical vocabulary and concepts that we saw, in Chapter 1, in Herman's collection of Saint Edmund of Bury's miracles, in which he referenced Hippocrates and Galen and discussed 'cauteries and eye ointments' ('cauteriationibus ac colliriis').[42] It is unsurprising that William's medical vocabulary was, in several places, more sophisticated than Herman's, given that he was writing around one hundred years later. Those hundred years had seen the production of a large number of Latin medical manuscripts, often translated and adapted from Greek texts, via Arabic medical works. These 'new' medical texts were produced, in large part, in the Benedictine monastery at Monte Cassino (modern-day Italy), where monks were engaged in a massive endeavour to preserve and edit old medical manuscripts, and at the medical hub in Salerno (around 150 kilometres south-east of Monte Cassino), but they were transferred and copied throughout Western Europe.[43] Monica Green has shown that English monasteries and cathedrals held one of the largest bodies of Latin medical literature in Western Europe.[44] Twenty-five percent of the surviving codices were produced in England or Northern France.[45] The circulation of theoretical Salernitan texts, like the *Articella* (a collection of medical treatises, bound together, which, from the thirteenth century, was used almost as a standard textbook for medical students), was more common, with practical manuals emerging in greater quantities towards the end of the twelfth century.[46] It is therefore entirely plausible that Latin medical texts of Salernitan origin could have reached Canterbury by the 1170s, though it is difficult to pinpoint precisely which texts Benedict and William may have had access to at Christ Church. It also must be noted that William, in particular, may have gained his medical knowledge before joining the monastic community in Canterbury.[47]

Medical manuscripts at Canterbury

The extent of Benedict's and William's access to 'new' medical texts can be estimated by looking at records of the manuscripts held at Christ Church. In the twelfth century, no separate library space existed in the priory, and books were kept in cupboards in the cloister, a customary practice in twelfth-century English monasteries.[48] Medical texts may also, for practical reasons, have been housed in the infirmary. A fire in 1067 had destroyed much of the original collection of books, and Archbishop Lanfranc (1070–89) made efforts to rebuild it by commissioning copies of patristic texts written in what would become known as the characteristic Lanfrancian script.[49] Unfortunately, no complete twelfth-century book list survives. A catalogue that can be roughly dated to the mid-twelfth century has survived but only in a fragmented form.[50] The catalogue contains sections on grammar, rhetoric, music, arithmetic, poetry, logic, astronomy and geometry, but sections on theology, medicine and law are frustratingly absent.[51]

In the second half of the twelfth century, many English Benedictine libraries were expanding their book collections to include new medical texts, though this development did not necessarily mean that earlier ideas were entirely displaced.[52] Between 1122–23 and 1200, for example, the Benedictine priory at Rochester increased the number of medical treatises in its possession from zero to twenty-seven.[53] These new treatises included some pre-Salernitan material as well as several Salernitan texts, such as Bartholomaeus's *Practica* and Constantine the African's *Viaticum*.[54] Constantine the African, a monk of Monte Cassino, had translated the text of the *Viaticum* from Ibn al-Jazzar's *Zad al-musafir* in the late eleventh century. It was a short medical compendium, originally designed for travellers, and mixed practical and theoretical knowledge in a head-to-toe format, which was typical of Salernitan medical texts.[55] It is highly conceivable that, like Rochester, Christ Church was expanding its book collection in this period and that Benedict and William may have had access to similar 'new' medical knowledge.

To gain an idea of what specific medical texts may have been available to Benedict and William, we must turn to the complete library catalogue of the thirteenth/fourteenth century. The catalogue was made at the instigation of Henry de Eastry when he was prior, sometime between 1285 and 1331 but most likely in the early fourteenth century.[56] M.R. James has argued that the catalogue consists of subject-based sections up until the time of Becket followed by a list of the books acquired after this time, meaning that the beginning of the fourteenth-century catalogue is, in fact, the twelfth-century catalogue.[57] However, this assessment does raise some problems, most notably in that the beginning of de Eastry's catalogue cannot be categorically matched to the fragment of catalogue that we have from the twelfth century, which is too short to be a reflection of the monastery's entire book collection at that time. For the purposes of this chapter, I assume that none of the books in de Eastry's catalogue were, without doubt, held at Christ Church in the 1170s. Yet many of them may have been present, which is why it is worth briefly looking at the catalogue in more detail.

De Eastry's catalogue contains a large section of *libri de phisica* (books of natural philosophy or medicine).[58] Among the works listed are Constantine the African's *Pantegni* as well as his *Viaticum* and Bartholomaeus of Salerno's *Practica physici*.[59] Both the *Pantegni* and the *Practica* were in Benedict's 1194 book collection and could potentially have been held at Christ Church in the twelfth century, either in his private collection or as exemplars from which his copies were made. At least three full copies of the *Viaticum* are listed in de Eastry's catalogue, though it cannot be determined whether any were in Christ Church as early as 1170.[60] Constantine's *Pantegni* was a far larger text than the *Viaticum*. It was divided into theoretical (*Theorica*) and practical (*Practica*) sections, which then dealt with conditions from head to toe. It is worth noting that the *Pantegni* is listed in the catalogue as two separate items: 'Pantegni Constantini, primus' and 'Pantegni secundus'.[61] This differentiation would suggest that the *Pantegni Theorica* and the *Pantegni Practica* were held as separate volumes rather than in their abbreviated form (the *Theorica* accompanied by Books I, II and IX of the *Practica*). Monica Green has convincingly argued against the existence, or at the very least the extensive circulation, of the *Theorica* and the *Practica* as two separate volumes before the end of the twelfth century, and it seems unlikely that these texts were held at Christ Church in the 1170s.[62] Furthermore, Benedict's copy of the *Pantegni* was 'in uno volumine', and it is more plausible that, had Christ Church held a copy at this time, it would also have been in this format. This evidence is contrary to M.R. James's assertion that the *libri de phisica* were part of the original twelfth-century catalogue, and it affirms that we should not assume the presence of any of these texts in the book collections that Benedict and William had access to without further consideration of their contents. Nonetheless, the possible influence of 'new' medical ideas on the miracle compilers must be considered.

Epilepsy and madness

Various terms were used to indicate madness in both miracle collections, and various symptoms were associated with the mad. Table 3.1 is a summary of those miracles recorded by Benedict and William that refer to madness, whether or not it was the condition for which a miraculous cure was sought. Those miracles that can be categorised as 'madness miracles' correspond to the definition of madness given in my Introduction:

- those states defined as *insania* or *amentia*
- those conditions typified by unusual behaviour
- those disorders of the mind in which reason was perceived to be lacking

Table 3.1 Summary of madness miracles in Benedict of Peterborough's and William of Canterbury's collections of the miracles of Saint Thomas Becket.

Ref.	*Summary*	*Madness terminology*
BP I.14	William Patrick had a tumour that caused him excruciating toothache. Because of the pain, he flung his limbs and shouted out. Under suspicion that he was mad, he was put in chains. Becket later cured his tumour.	*amentiae suspicio*
BP, II.9	Edmund, a youth from Canterbury, was suffering from partial blindness. The twisting and screaming that accompanied his miraculous cure made others believe that he was insane.	*insanire putares*
BP II.13	Henry, a youth from Fordwich, was restored to his senses. He had been insane for several days and was brought, bound and raving, to the shrine.	*insanire*
BP II.31	Elward of Selling, an insane man who believed he could see evil spirits, was cured after crawling inside one of the holes in the side of Becket's tomb, designed for pilgrims to put their hands through and much too small even for a child to fit through.	*mentis agebatur insania*
BP II.54	William of Earley (a knight) and his wife came to give thanks for the cure of a child (most likely their child). The child had been shouting out, "See where they come!" but was restored to his senses when a relic of Thomas Becket was suspended around his neck.	*a mente alienatus*; *amentia*
BP IV. 19	Seven-year-old Hermer lost his mind after recovering from a previous illness. The boy was unsteady on his feet and suffered from continual movement of his head, hands and arms. He was also unable to speak. His father, Tetio, tried consulting doctors but was forced by poverty to turn to the saint. A piece of Becket's hair shirt was kept at the Church of St Nicholas (Wissant, France). Upon drinking water infused with this relic, Hermer returned to full health.	*mente captus*; *passio miranda*
BP IV. 37	Matilda of Cologne came to Canterbury Cathedral suffering from insanity. She tore her linen smock and struck out at people, including a small child who approached her. Matilda raved for four or five hours at Becket's tomb until she was visited by the saint in a vision and told to continue her pilgrimage to Rome or to Santiago de Compostela. After her cure, she told the monks that she had gone mad after her brother had killed her lover, and then she had struck and killed her baby.	*plenam daemonio muliercula*; *insanire*; *corporis passionem et mentis*; *amentia*

(*Continued*)

Table 3.1 Summary of madness miracles in Benedict of Peterborough's and William of Canterbury's collections of the miracles of Saint Thomas Becket. (*Continued*)

Ref.	*Summary*	*Madness terminology*
BP IV. 53	Physicians had struggled to heal the inflamed womb of Mabel, daughter of Stephen de Aglandre. The pain caused her to hurl her limbs and become insane. The holy water of Saint Thomas healed her swelling, and she was healthy but weak.	*uterus inflatus*; *insania*
BP IV. 56	A woman led a blind boy and an insane girl from Wales to Canterbury. The girl was brought back to the way of reason, and the boy was partially cured.	*insana*
BP IV. 57	Walter, a clerk of Hatcliffe, near Grimsby, had been insane for five weeks. His friends and parents vowed to convey him to the shrine, at which point his reason was restored, and he was able to make the journey himself.	*insanire*
WC II.9	William, a youth of St Alban's, suffered with alienation of the mind for three months and was then cured by Saint Alban. After this, he suffered from epilepsy and was cured by Saint Thomas Becket.	*alienatio mentis*
WC II.87	A priest called William, who was suffering from giddiness, feared that he could be inflicted with either madness or epilepsy.	*timebat amentiam vel ephilensiam incurrere*
WC II.89	Some relics of the saint were transferred from Arras to a nunnery in Bapaume. A madman was then returned to the control of his mind.	*furiosum*
WC III. 47	Having dissuaded his shipmates from making a pilgrimage to Canterbury, Ralph the Black was told by a priest that he would be held by madness. Ralph was bound and injured himself fighting against his bonds. His roving eyes were filled with fire. Despite his madness, he was able to make a vow to the martyr and was restored to his mind.	*aliena*; *amentia*; *furor*
WC III. 48	Hugh Brustins, a Frenchman born of an illegitimate union, went to St Denis for a cure, having been possessed by an impure spirit. He was told by the saint that a new saint was performing cures now, and he was cured with water infused with Becket's blood.	*spiritum immundum concipere*
WC III. 49	Robert, a servant of the prior of Colchester, was taken by a demon, which took control of his hands. He drunk from a phial containing the martyr's blood twice and was cured both times (after the first time, he was possessed again).	*a daemonio arreptus*
WC III. 50	Hardwin of Châtillon, a possessed worker, was restored to his mind by the relics of Saint Thomas.	*arreptitius*

(*Continued*)

Table 3.1 Summary of madness miracles in Benedict of Peterborough's and William of Canterbury's collections of the miracles of Saint Thomas Becket. (*Continued*)

Ref.	*Summary*	*Madness terminology*
WC III. 51	In Shenfield, Essex, two possessed women were saved by drinking the holy water of Saint Thomas.	*energumena*; *spiritus arreptus*
WC III. 52	In Gloucester, a young servant of the monks and a woman were cured of madness/possession by the blood of Saint Thomas.	*spiritus furoris dementare*
WC V.38	A youth called Geoffrey was struck by lightning and awoke in a fury. He was ignorant of the people he knew and raged with his teeth and nails. He was cured by Saint Thomas Becket.	*furia*
WC VI.3	Reginald of Estampes wrote of Gerard, a clerk of Liège, who was driven mad by poison. Gerard had a constantly laughing mouth and roving eyes. His arms and fingers shook, and he refused to eat. He was cured by drinking Becket's water.	*cerebri turbatione agitaretur*
WC VI. 86	Roger de Berkeley wrote of a possessed man who was brought back to his mind in the chapel of Saint Thomas. The madman had been scorned by his community and had roamed foolishly as one of the beasts in the wild. He was brought to the chapel by a person of good faith.	*a daemonio vexatus*
WC VI. 87	Osbern, a knight, lost his mind after being deprived of an estate by the bishop of Durham. He was put in chains, and, upon promising an annual payment to the martyr, he was restored.	*alienatio mentis*
WC VI. 113	Alice, the concubine of Ralph, dean of Lindsey, went mad with the pain of childbirth. She raged so much that people feared she would die. Drinking the water of Saint Thomas restored health to her mind and her body.	*alienatio mentis*
WC VI. 130	Two possessed women were restored to sound mind. One had not eaten, drunk or slept for fifteen days. The other had spoken the language of demons in Latin, German and other tongues for eight years.	*energumena*

The range of terms used by Benedict and William to describe conditions of the mind, as shown in Table 3.1, are illustrative of the complex and varying constructions of madness that are found in both miracle collections. Madness could arise from physical illness, mental trauma, divine punishment and demonic possession, if a cause was stated at all. It could cause loss of speech, foul language, laughing, crying, loss of physical control and violence, to name but a few symptoms. These symptoms often were explicitly connected with a problem in the mind, which could be lost, seized, alienated or taken. It was this identification of madness as a condition affecting the mind that differentiated it from the other conditions described by both miracle compilers. Neither compiler was solely influenced, in his interpretations of sickness and health, by contemporary learned medical texts. Both writers took inspiration from discussions with pilgrims themselves, from the letters of attestation written to them by clergymen and leading laymen and from theological and biblical representations of madness, which would have been familiar within the monastic community and further afield.

Perhaps the most intriguing records to begin with are those in which madness is discussed but where the diagnosis of the condition requiring miraculous cure is ambiguous. Benedict described the illness of a seven-year-old boy called Hermer, who was 'suddenly struck with an astonishing suffering', having recovered from a previous sickness.[63] His use of the word 'astonishing' ('miranda') demonstrates Benedict's uncertainty about how to diagnose this condition as well, of course, as emphasising Becket's skill in curing it. The strange illness – which presented as a constant rotation of the hands, arms and head – made the boy appear to be insane ('aspectu insano').[64] This insane appearance made it seem as though the boy's mind had been taken ('mente captus videretur').[65] Similarly, in another miracle record, William Patrick, who was suffering from toothache, flung his limbs about and shouted in pain. Because these signs could also be associated with insanity, William was thought to be mad and was placed in chains. It was only with hindsight, presumably when he explained the cause of his strange behaviour, that his true ailment, which had been cured by Thomas Becket, could be diagnosed.[66] Both of these miracles imply that unusual movements and behaviours were symptomatic of madness. These were not symptoms that were new or unique to Becket's miracle collections. In Saint Edmund of Bury's miracles (compiled between c.1070 and c.1100), a man named Wulmer was mistakenly thought to be insane because of his unexpected movement following an incapacitating illness.[67] In William of Norwich's mid-twelfth-century miracles, two women, Ida and Gilliva, were compared to madwomen because of their extreme behaviour whilst in pain.[68] We can thus see a recurring association between madness and abnormal conduct, though madness itself could only be confirmed if there was no other reasonable explanation for strange behavioural symptoms.

Two records in William of Canterbury's collection reveal a degree of correspondence between madness and the symptomatically-similar condition of epilepsy. Unusual movement of the head and limbs could be a sign of both ailments. In one of the earliest studies of medieval Latin, Charles du Cange drew attention to the interchangeability of terminology for madness and epilepsy.[69] Ronald Finucane went even further by suggesting that no distinction was made between epilepsy and insanity in twelfth-century miracle records and other contemporary texts.[70] However, whilst the two conditions could present similar symptoms and were sometimes the subject of comparison, the distinctions noted in these very comparisons show quite clearly that they were not perceived as the same condition. A priest called William, who was suffering from giddiness, feared that he could be inflicted with either madness or epilepsy; either could have produced his giddiness, but they were not the same thing.[71] Another William, from Saint Alban's, suffered for three months with alienation/stupor of the mind ('alienationem mentis') and was cured by Saint Alban after beatings from his friends and words intended to calm him had no effect.[72] Sometime after his cure, he developed a tremor of the hand and falling sickness ('morbus caducus'), with which he was afflicted for nine years, falling every week.[73] Nonetheless, there is no indication of beatings or attempts to calm him during this time, suggesting that his friends' reaction to epilepsy differed from their reaction to madness. William's epilepsy was diagnosed entirely by his physical symptoms without reference to the state of his mind. William of Canterbury's use of the term 'morbus caducus' is also indicative of the close relationship between the diagnosis of epilepsy and its physical symptoms.

When compiling his miracle collection, William of Canterbury had opted for a thematic approach, grouping healing miracles by illness.[74] Notably, he placed epilepsy miracles and madness miracles in separate sections. Whilst the aforementioned William of Saint Albans's miracle was grouped with other epilepsy miracles, the miracle of William, the giddy priest – who was never diagnosed as suffering from epilepsy or madness – was placed alongside miscellaneous records detailing the miraculous cures of clerics. William of Canterbury prefaced his section on epilepsy, the first illness category he addressed, with a detailed explanation of its aetiology, one of the longest such descriptions in his entire collection.[75] He described epilepsy as a lasting suffering that struck with varied frequency anything from once a year to once a day or sometimes more.[76] He then divided *epilensia* (epilepsy) into three conditions: *ephilensia*, which affected the brain; *catalempsia*, which originated in the hands, arms and legs; and *analempsia*, which agitated the stomach.[77] William's use and definition of these three terms suggests a fairly sophisticated medical understanding of epilepsy, and this medical knowledge was something that he was keen to show to his audience. Shortly after recording his own explanation of epilepsy, he criticised Hingram, the Italian epileptic who had believed that his epilepsy was caused by the cycles of the moon. William stated that the movements of the stars had no effect on the health of an individual. The only link that he could make between epilepsy and the moon was that the crescent moon induced a damp atmosphere that would negatively affect the humoral balance of someone who suffered from epilepsy, which was believed to be a cold and moist condition.[78]

The three terms that William used for epilepsy – *ephilensia*, *catalempsia* and *analempsia* – were of Greek provenance, but *catalempsia* and *analempsia* do not appear to have been used by the ancient Greeks in the context of epilepsy.[79] In the Middle Ages, *analempsia*, in the medical sense, denoted the ascension of vapours from the stomach to the brain.[80] As a medical term, *catalempsia* indicated a subdivision of epilepsy, sometimes involving a fever, which *ephilensia* did not.[81] William's use of all three terms has some similarities with Bartholomaeus's *Practica*, which we know to have been at

Christ Church by at least the fourteenth century, though possibly much earlier. The order of the three terms is particularly noteworthy given that both Bartholomaeus's and William's consideration of epilepsy, catalepsy and *then* analepsy is unusual.[82] The first term used by Bartholomaeus (*epilepsia*) defined the condition as a whole and also the first distinct category, epilepsy of the brain, which corresponds closely to William of Canterbury's first definition.[83] The slight discrepancy between this term and William's *ephilensia* should not be given too much significance since Bartholomaeus also used the term *epilemsia* in his description of epilepsy.[84] For Bartholomaeus, catalepsy, the second category of epilepsy, was defined by its origin in the legs, hands or arms, and analepsy, the third state, affected the stomach.[85] Furthermore, William's description of the frequency of epileptic seizures is very similar to Bartholomaeus's. William stated that suffering could 'disturb once a year, or once a month, or once a week, or once a day or even more' ('semel in anno, vel semel in mense, vel semel in hebdomada, vel semel in die vel amplius infestans'), which can be compared to Bartholomaeus: 'once a year, once a month, once a week, once a day, twice, three times, or four, however many times' ('semel in anno, semel in mense, semel in ebdomada, semel in die, bis, ter, vel iiij quampluries').[86] The evidence is not substantial enough to identify the *Practica* as William's source, and he may well have encountered the *Practica*'s theories indirectly via another text, but the similarities between the two texts demonstrate that William was familiar with theories taught at the Salernitan schools and at the cutting edge of medical learning in twelfth-century England.

Following his initial explanation of the frequency of epileptic seizures, William of Canterbury was keen to include details of how frequently cured epileptics had suffered before coming to Becket's shrine. Petronella, an epileptic nun who was brought to Becket's shrine by her sisters, fell nine times a day, Hingram (the Italian epileptic) fell once a week but only at night, and an epileptic canon, also called William, suffered with epilepsy for twenty years with up to a year between seizures.[87] Of course, William's reasons behind including such details may not have been solely related to his interest in diagnostic precision and his familiarity with learned medical texts. The cessation of seizures was often the only way to tell that epilepsy had been cured, so, to corroborate the occurrence of a miracle, it was useful to know how frequent seizures had been prior to cure. Details of the frequency or even the unpredictability of seizures served to emphasise the suffering of the sick individual and thereby enhance acclaim for the miraculous cure.

Despite William's detailed definition of epilepsy, the terms *ephilensia*, *catalempsia* and *analempsia* were not the only terms he used to describe the condition. Of William's six or seven[88] descriptions of pilgrims suffering from epilepsy, the term *epilensia* was used twice and *ephilensia* was used only once.[89] *Analempsia* and *catalempsia* were not used at all outside of their initial definition. On one occasion, William used the term *morbus comitialis* (the epileptic sickness) and, on another, *morbus caducus* (the falling sickness).[90] There was some overlap between these terms, and pilgrims could be described using more than one term. For example, Hingram's condition was labelled both 'ephilensia' and 'comitialis morbus'.[91] Originally a popular term, *morbus comitialis* had become generally accepted in medical works, though not necessarily as the preferred term used by physicians. Gariopontus (fl.1035–50) listed it as another name under which epilepsy might have been known by non-specialists.[92] The term *morbus caducus* was used similarly by medical writers. Bartholomaeus wrote that epilepsy was called 'morb[us] caducus' by the common people.[93] The *Viaticum* stated that ancient writers had named epilepsy after the falls that were experienced by sufferers.[94]

Thus, though William's terms for epilepsy were not always consistent with his own definitions at the beginning of his section on the condition, they were consistent with contemporary medical texts. Furthermore, the use of these terms and the inclusion of epilepsy in its own distinct section demonstrates that William recognised it as a condition with clear signs and symptoms that set it apart from other disorders. William's final two descriptions of epilepsy – *morbus epilenticus* and *morbus caducus* – were terms borrowed from others who had written letters to the monks at Christ Church to attest to the miracles, which were then copied into the collection (one letter came from the monks of Oseney, west of Oxford, and the other was written by the abbot of Pontigny, a Cistercian monastery on the River Serein in France).[95] As we saw in the case of Hingram, William was keen to make it clear when he disagreed with another's terminology or beliefs concerning illness, and, in both of these cases, he did not question the terms used in the letters. Nonetheless, we should remember that both letters were written by clerics, whereas Hingram was a layman, so William might have been more inclined to trust their diagnoses and to copy their letters in full, as uncontested proof of the miracles.

Benedict of Peterborough's concept of epilepsy was arguably less well defined than William's. He used the term *morbus caducus* twice, and he described one woman as having *epilepsia* and another as being *epilentica*.[96] All three terms can be found in Bartholomaeus's *Practica* and are not inconsistent with Benedict having had access to it.[97] The two epileptics who Benedict described were both women. One, a woman in the family of Peter of Alnward, was said to be epileptic ('epilentica') and was cured of her falls by drinking the water of Saint Thomas.[98] Another, the wife of Henry de Longueville, suffered with epilepsy ('epilepsia') and was fatigued by the illness almost every day. Her husband sympathised with her condition and sought a cure for her.[99] The two distinct features of epilepsy thus seem to have been falls (without hysteria) and long-term suffering. However, Benedict did not explain the symptoms of epilepsy, as William of Canterbury had, and several instances of spontaneous falling were recorded in his miracle collection that were not linked to epilepsy. Whilst not attempting any retrospective diagnosis of the pilgrims, it is useful to compare these falls to the cases of epilepsy in order to establish why Benedict chose not to define them as such.

Some collapses and falls were not experienced in the same way as epileptic falls, though they could be similar. The daughter of Aylward of Canterbury filled the cathedral with her cries for two days, falling to the floor ('cadens in terram') and hurting herself unknowingly.[100] Mary of Rouen suffered sudden bouts of crying followed by periods of laughter and hand-clapping. She would then fall to the ground in rapture ('corruens in extasi') and remain lying there for half an hour to an hour.[101] Both of these cases involved falling (though *cadere*, the most common verb used in cases of epilepsy, was not used to describe the falls of Mary of Rouen). However, neither description mentions particularly long-term suffering. Aylward's daughter suffered for two days, and Mary of Rouen's symptoms of crying and laughter were not typical of medieval epilepsy. Nonetheless, the sudden strange behaviour experienced by both sufferers was not connected with madness either. Benedict may have believed that these falling attacks differed from epileptic or mad collapses, or he may have been unsure of these diagnoses and so left the precise nature of the conditions ambiguous. He may even have felt that a more precise diagnosis was not important for his record, which focused on Becket as a healer rather than on the healed themselves.

Regardless, pilgrims who suffered from epilepsy had their own perceptions of the illness – as in the case of Hingram – and the miracle compilers were keen to discuss these with them. Some pilgrims themselves struggled to ascertain the difference between epilepsy and madness, and some symptoms were indicative of both conditions. Most importantly, both miracle compilers focused on the physical signs of epilepsy, which were shown on the body, and paid little attention to the effect of the condition on the mind. Thus, when Petronella of Polesworth left Becket's tomb, she was unsure whether or not she had been cured of her epilepsy.[102] There was no clear change in her mental health, as there was when mad people were healed, and no instantaneous physical relief, as there was, for example, for sufferers of wounds or skin conditions. To be cured of epilepsy, Petronella had to show the absence of both her seizures and her long-term suffering, and, for this, she needed patience and faith.

Body and mind

The effect of madness on the minds of sufferers was far more prominent in the miracle records than it was for epilepsy, as evidenced by the use of terminology related to the mind. Rather than associating madness with the body or with a particular part of the body (e.g. the brain or heart), both miracle compilers tended to focus on the disconnection of the mind from the body and on the disordered state of the mind itself. The most common term Benedict of Peterborough used to denote madness was a variant of the verb *insanire* (to be mad), the noun *insania* or the adjective *insanus*. He also used the terms *amentia* and *alienatio mentis* – both explicitly referencing the mind – but with less frequency. Benedict employed the term *insania* in five records of madness and the term *amentia* in three. Notably, none of these terms were etymologically linked with the physical symptoms of insanity as the term *morbus caducus* (the falling sickness) was for epilepsy.

This concentration on the mind does not mean, however, that physical signs and symptoms of insanity are absent from Benedict's miracle records: far from it, in fact! Matilda of Cologne tore her linen dress and attacked a small child in the cathedral, both visible signs of her madness.[103] Mabel, daughter of Stephen de Aglandre, suffered from a painfully inflated womb/abdomen, and 'at last, such a great intensity of pain tormented her [who had been] put to bed that, with certain astonishing and unusual flingings of limbs, she suggested [in her behaviour] that she was already being transformed into insanity.'[104] Here, insanity was associated with the physical flinging of Mabel's limbs; the same physical symptom was observed in William Patrick when he was writhing from the pain of his toothache, which is why his condition was wrongly attributed to insanity.[105] A Canterbury youth called Edmund was similarly believed to be insane ('insanire putares') because of the twisting and screaming that accompanied his miraculous cure from partial blindness.[106] In William of Canterbury's collection, the dean of Lindsey's concubine, Alice, lost her mind because of the pain of childbirth.[107] Physical pain could, therefore, drive people mad, or the physical behaviour of those in pain could make them appear mad to others.[108]

Nonetheless, despite Benedict's frequent references to the visible signs of madness, in his descriptions of cures, he focused on the effect of the miracle on a sufferer's mental state and ability to reason. Henry of Fordwich, the mad youth who we met at the beginning of this book, was restrained during his madness but, upon cure, was restored to his mind ('menti restituit'), demonstrating that the source of his suffering lay in his mind and that it was this suffering that had caused him to act insanely ('insaniens').[109] Similarly, a young insane girl from Wales was restored to the way of reason as the culmination of her pilgrimage to Canterbury ('Puella in via menti restituta est').[110] Walter, a clerk from Hatcliffe, was unable to make a vow of pilgrimage to the saint because of his lack of reason, so his friends and parents made one on his behalf. His reason was then restored ('rationem recuperavit'), and he was able to make the pilgrimage himself.[111] According to a summary of English law compiled during the reign of Edward I (1272–1307), the insane were among those not capable of giving their consent to enter into a 'contract or obligation'.[112] Therefore, Walter's renewed ability to make his own contract with the martyr, via a vow of pilgrimage, was indicative of his cure from madness.

William of Canterbury also referred to the restoration of mind when describing cures from insanity. Interestingly, he most commonly used language pertaining to restoration in cases where the sufferer had previously experienced an alienation of the mind (*alienatio mentis*). When Alice suffered from an alienation of the mind brought on by the pain of childbirth, the saint's holy water induced a sleep that restored her mind and body to health.[113] A knight called Osbern, who had suffered from an alienation of the mind, was restored to himself ('sibi redditus est') by the saint, to whom he promised an annual payment.[114]

Only one case of madness from both collections was explicitly inflicted as a divine punishment. A seaman called Ralph persuaded his shipmates not to partake in a pilgrimage to Canterbury and, because of this offence, was told by a priest that he would be kept mad ('aliena tentus').[115] Though penal representations of madness are uncommon in Becket's miracles, similarities can certainly be drawn between Ralph's madness and that miraculously dispensed by Saint Edmund, whose miracles were recorded at the turn of the eleventh century and included many cases of divine punishment. Sheriff Leofstan, for example, was inflicted with madness by Saint Edmund and was therefore unable to carry out his duties as sheriff (which had involved an attempt to remove a criminal from Edmund's sanctuary).[116] In a similar way, Ralph's madness impaired his capability to work as a sailor and resulted in further physical suffering, since he was chained and imprisoned in such squalor and abjection that his body began to rot. Despite his madness, and unlike Walter of Hatcliffe, Ralph was able to make a vow of pilgrimage to the martyr. Ralph was not incapacitated in the same way as Walter, and yet he remained socially isolated because he was seen to be mad. Upon making his vow, Ralph was restored to his mind ('menti redditus').

Whereas Petronella, the epileptic nun from Polesworth, had never suffered another fit because of her faith in the martyr, these mad men and women were miraculously healed through the restoration of their minds. Their cures indicate that the cause of their madness lay in their minds or in the disconnection between their minds and their bodies.[117] Upon Matilda of Cologne's restoration to sanity, she was asked by Benedict to explain what had caused her madness. She described how her brother had killed her lover and declared that this act had sent her insane. Whilst seized by madness, she had struck her newly-baptised baby with her fist and killed it.[118] Benedict did not state whether it was the trauma of this experience or the potential sins of fornication and infanticide (sins that could have resulted from demonic possession or, even if they were not demonic in their origins, could have left Matilda more vulnerable to demonic attack) that had sent Matilda mad, but, either way, when Matilda was placed, bound and raving, at Becket's tomb, she was found to be suffering in body and in mind.[119] Madness, then, was specifically understood as a condition affecting both the mind and body.

Medical and theological precedents

Salernitan medical texts of the late eleventh and twelfth centuries did discuss conditions of the mind and the brain but did not typically classify *insania* or *amentia* (the terms used most frequently by Benedict to denote madness) as stand-alone conditions. The *Viaticum* of Constantine the African, several copies of which were held in the fourteenth-century library at Christ Church, defined specific conditions, like frenzy, stupor and lovesickness.

Terminology of the type employed by Benedict was used to describe signs or aspects of these conditions.[120] For example, *frenesis*, caused by a hot brain abscess, could be accompanied by 'alienationes'.[121] Bartholomaeus's *Practica* was similar to the *Viaticum* in that it listed the symptoms and cures of conditions like *frenesis* and *mania* but also used terms like 'insani' (insane) in relation to these conditions.[122] Whilst Benedict of Peterborough was aware of multiple terms for madness, he did not diagnose any of the specific conditions outlined in these medical texts, nor did he describe any of their humoral causes or symptoms. His imprecision is understandable given that the differences between brain conditions in medical texts were often subtle, and, to distinguish them, one needed some knowledge of the brain and perhaps also of urinary examination.[123] Diagnostic precision was not a characteristic of Benedict's miracle collection, regardless of the condition, and it may have been that he lacked the specific medical knowledge to distinguish between frenzy and mania.[124]

Furthermore, precisely diagnosing the conditions suffered by pilgrims may not have been important for Benedict given that the focal point of each miracle record was not the pilgrims themselves but Becket's role in their miraculous cures. Despite the diagnostic uncertainty in Matilda of Cologne's miracle record, her vision of Thomas Becket was strikingly clear, from the ecclesiastical vestments he was wearing to the streak of blood across his face.[125] Similarly, in his record of a miracle experienced by Elward of Selling, a man suffering from insanity, Benedict focused on Elward's miraculous interaction with Becket's tomb rather than on the specific nature of his condition. Elward was described as a man of great height ('staturae grandis'); it was necessary to emphasise his physical size to substantiate the miracle that would occur. His madness was connected with demons ('the enemy of the human face' – 'humani generis hostem'), which he believed he could see in front of his face, snarling at him.[126] To escape this demonic onslaught, Elward was able, despite his size, to crawl inside one of the holes in Becket's tomb, which were designed for pilgrims to put their hands through to be close to the relics.[127] It was this element of the miracle that was tested, to confirm its miraculous nature, when a small boy was asked to repeat Elward's feat and could not. No details were given of Elward's cure from insanity despite the simple fact that he was cured.

In contrast to Benedict, William of Canterbury, as we have seen in his discussion of epilepsy, did dedicate large sections of his miracle collection to the diagnosis of specific conditions, using terminology found in contemporary medical texts. Nonetheless, William provided no detailed explanation of madness as he did for epilepsy. In some instances, his language is similar to Benedict's, and, as we have seen, he used terms that signified an alienation of the mind (*alienatio mentis*).[128] The only occasion that William mentioned the brain (*cerebrum*) in relation to madness was in his record of the cure of Gerard, a clerk of Liège, who was 'shaken by a disturbance of the brain' ('cerebri turbatione agitaretur') as a result of poison. Gerard displayed similar behaviours to the other mad men and women whose miraculous cures were recorded by William of Canterbury. Like Ralph, the sailor who had been punished by madness, Gerard suffered from roving eyes and other behavioural symptoms, such as a continually laughing mouth and agitation of his arms.[129] Nonetheless, the language used in this account cannot be attributed directly to William of Canterbury since he claimed to have quoted it word for word from a letter of Reginald of Estampes, a clergyman who had written to confirm the miracle. William's use of varied terminology to describe madness may, in part, have been due to him drawing on written accounts and attestations of miracles, like Reginald's, rather than relaying information first-hand. In his final book of the *Life and Miracles of William of Norwich*, written in the 1170s, Thomas of Monmouth used the term 'cerebri turbati' to describe the insanity of a man called Robert, so the term was clearly known to and used by clerics at the time William was writing.[130] It is perhaps surprising, then, that he did not use it himself when describing insanity in his own words.

Alongside using more general terms, like *amentia*, William documented several cases of *furor* or *furia*: terms that implied a violent or frenzied form of madness. A madman ('furiosum') in Bapaume, in Flanders, was cured by some relics of Thomas Becket, though we have no other details of this man's condition.[131] A much more detailed account was given of the miraculous cure of a youth called Geoffrey who was struck by lightning and awoke, 'shaken by fury' ('furiis agitans').[132] Geoffrey was ignorant of those he had previously known (friends or acquaintances) and raged with teeth and nails, which showed the violent nature of his madness.[133] Notably, Benedict of Peterborough did not use the terms *furor* or *furia* to describe any of the cases of madness in his collection, including that of Matilda of Cologne, who had torn at her clothing and attempted to attack a child. Instead, Benedict used language that was more closely aligned with biblical representations of violent madness. The biblical Gerasene demoniac, who was possessed by an unclean spirit ('spiritu inmundo'), was so untameable that he could not be held down by chains (Mark 5:2–4). Similarly, Matilda's 'wicked spirit' ('spiritus nequam') left behind vile traces ('inhonesta vestigia') even after its expulsion.[134]

Nonetheless, the closest parallel to the Gerasene demoniac, as regards terminology, is found in William of Canterbury's collection. A Frenchman named Hugh Brustins was taken by an unclean spirit ('spiritum immundum') and sought the divine assistance of Saint Denis. The great French saint told him that a new martyr was performing miracles and that he would be best served by calling on Thomas Becket.[135] There are several reasons why William may have used such a clear biblical analogy here but not elsewhere in his collection. First of all, the miracle has a moralistic undertone in that Hugh was of illegitimate birth, and thus the unclean spirit that possessed him reflected his unclean conception and the tainting of his family line. Furthermore, it is not entirely clear whether Hugh came to Canterbury in person, and William may have been working from another written account of the miracle and borrowing language from there (however, he did not explicitly state that this was the case as he did when he copied other written accounts verbatim). Finally, Saint Denis's self-subordination to the new English saint may have appealed to King Henry II, to whom William's collection was most likely presented, or, alternatively, it may have been intended as further evidence of the legitimacy of the king's former rival. For both rationales, the comparison between Becket and Christ, who cured the Gerasene demonic, further emphasised Becket's sanctity.

Demonic possession

William of Canterbury frequently discussed madness as a form of demonic possession. Terms like *arreptus* (taken/seized) and *captivum* (captured), when used in relation to possession, imply that the person was taken against his or her will. For example, a servant of the prior of Colchester called Robert was 'arreptus est a daemonio' and then was returned to himself ('redditus sibi') upon drinking Becket's holy water.[136] An artisan named Hardwin was simply 'arreptitius' and was then 'restored to his mind' ('menti restitutus est') by Thomas Becket's relics.[137] More explicitly, four women were referred to as 'possessed by the devil' ('energumenae'), and 'demons' (*daemones*) were mentioned multiple times.[138] In total, William recorded nine cases of madness that were linked to demonic possession and eight cases that were not.[139] Benedict of Peterborough, by comparison, recorded two cases of demonic possession and six cases of non-demonic madness.[140] Notably, neither compiler linked epilepsy with demons.

These cases of demonic possession should not be dismissed as a rejection of medical theory or as demonstrative of a lack of knowledge of medical ideas about madness. Anne E. Bailey has noted that, as the influence of Galenic medicine was increasingly felt in miracle records towards the end of the twelfth century, demons did not disappear from such narratives, which suggests that contemporaries saw no contradiction, as modern observers would, in running medical and demonic discourses side by side.[141] A lack of specific medical terminology for madness was not necessarily indicative of a departure from learned medical theories, which would certainly have been surprising for William of Canterbury, since he was very keen to display his medical knowledge elsewhere in the collection. It is, therefore, necessary to view demonic language alongside the medical terminology used in the Canterbury miracle collections as products of the same healing environment rather than as conflicting diagnoses emerging from opposing belief systems.

Matilda of Cologne came to Becket's tomb 'filled with a demon' ('Plenam daemonio'), and, as part of her cure, 'the wicked spirit was truly expelled' ('Expulsus vero spiritus nequam').[142] Nonetheless, aside from its interaction with Matilda, Benedict paid little attention to the physicality of the demon itself; he did not refer to its appearance or to its movements. This approach is true of every case of demonic possession in the two collections; there is not one physical description of a demon in the madness miracles. It was most common, in both miracle collections, for demons to be encountered as disembodied voices, audible only to the mad, or as non-specific figures that lurked outside of the bodies of the mad. Before taking shelter in Becket's tomb, Elward of Selling (the man of great height who was miraculously able to fit through one of the holes in the side of the shrine) was fleeing evil spirits that he could see snarling around him.[143] In another miracle, a child astounded his family by repeatedly crying, '"See where they come, see where they come!"', though no other members of the household could see anything, demonic or otherwise.[144] These sufferers were those in the collections who were closest to encountering physical demons, and yet the demons were never explicitly described as anything more than delusions in the minds of the insane. Benedict did not state that demons physically followed Elward into the cathedral but only that Elward *believed* he saw them there.[145]

There was some learned medical basis for demonic apparitions being connected with the delusions of the mad, especially melancholics.[146] In such cases, delusions involving demons were a symptom of madness but not a cause of it.[147] Benedict was certainly aware that supposed demonic attacks could be diagnosed by physicians as delusions. Stephen of Hoyland, a knight who had suffered from terrifying nocturnal visions for thirty years, believed his condition was caused by demons. Physicians, however, were sure that Stephen's nightmares were *ephialtes*, the Greek term for the condition known in Latin as *incubus*, in which a sufferer felt as though he were being crushed in his sleep.[148] Though *incubus* was connected with demons by medieval writers Benedict seems to have been using the Greek medical term to indicate that the physicians' diagnosis did not involve demons.[149] Of course, the physicians proved to be ineffectual, and Stephen was liberated from his demons by Thomas Becket.

The most common term used in relation to demonic possession was *arripere* (to seize), which indicates that victims of demonic possession were taken forcibly, without their complicity. Such possessions were often accompanied by descriptions of violence, beast-like behaviour or superhuman skills, as though the introduction of the demonic presence into the human body temporarily suspended its humanity. Demons exerted a control over the physical body that was distinctly inhuman. Upon cure, Robert, the servant of the prior of Colchester who had been seized by a demon, reported that someone else had been in control of his hands and tongue.[150] One possessed woman lost the ability to eat and drink for fifteen days (and therefore may have been physically preserved by the unnatural presence of the demon, though this explanation was not explicitly stated), and a second spoke the language of demons for eight years in Latin and German (we do not know whether she knew these languages prior to her possession or whether she had obtained the gift of tongues from the demon).[151]

Another madman, who was troubled by a demon, was scorned by his community and left to roam as one of the beasts in the wild.[152] The allusion, here, to the madness of Nebuchadnezzar, the biblical king who was divinely inflicted with an insanity that caused him to live outside and behave as an animal would (Daniel 4:33), again demonstrates how narratives of demonic possession were influenced by biblical precedent. This miracle was copied into William's collection from a letter by Roger de Berkeley, likely of the Gloucestershire noble family with whom Henry II had been in dispute in the 1150s. De Berkeley's letter is perhaps indicative of the prevalent influence of biblical precedents on lay interpretations of madness. Since saints healed by means outside of those used in contemporary medicine, the inclusion of demonic possession in miracle texts does not mean that hagiographers were not familiar with terms like *frenesis* or *mania* but instead shows that physical, mental and spiritual suffering was believed to take on many forms. William of Canterbury wrote that Thomas Becket was a 'good and faithful doctor' ('bonus et fidelis medicus') who healed pilgrims using 'celestial medicine' ('coelesti medicina').[153] Given the interplay of medical and spiritual language throughout William's collection, it is unsurprising that he could interpret illness as both anatomical (as he had when defining epilepsy) and demonic (as he sometimes did for madness).

As we know, when Matilda of Cologne was visited by Thomas Becket in a vision, he diagnosed her as suffering in body and in mind, which required physical, mental and spiritual healing.[154] The physical body of the possessed man or woman was an expression of the tormented internal state of his or her mind. Consequently, the terminology of possession cannot necessarily be linked to the physical presence of a demon. Instead, terms like 'arreptitius' may have been labels used by Benedict and William – from whose collection the two examples below are taken – to describe a set of symptoms involving violent and inhuman behaviour that was indicative of trauma in the mind, which had been *taken* from the body. Hardwin, the artisan who was restored to his mind by Becket's relics, was described as 'seized' ('arreptitius'), though the involvement of demons was not specifically intimated.[155] In Gloucester, the spirit of madness had driven two people out of their minds ('spiritus furoris duos dementaverat'), though the 'enemy of the human race' (i.e. the devil) was also mentioned.[156] Similarly, in the final book of the *Life and Miracles of William of Norwich*, compiled in around 1173, a man called Robert was cured of 'the madness of the Bacchic spirit'.[157] In the miracles of Saint Frideswide, recorded within twenty years of Becket's miracle collections and heavily influenced by his cult, a young fuller was disturbed by the spirit of madness ('spiritu furoris exagitatus') and was lacking all human reason ('humanae prorsus expers rationis').[158] These cases demonstrate that both demons and madness itself could seize the minds of sufferers and cause them to lose reason.

Conclusion

Compiled over seventy years after Saint Edmund's miracles at Bury, Thomas Becket's miracle collections present a different understanding of madness. Whereas, in Edmund's miracles, madness was represented most frequently as a divine punishment, Becket, like William of Norwich, most often encountered madness as a condition or illness to be cured. Certainly, a comparison of these three cults corroborates Benedicta Ward's thesis that, through the twelfth century, there was an increasing trend towards the recording of healing miracles as opposed to miraculous punishments.[159] Nonetheless, despite both Benedict of Peterborough and William of Canterbury's likely access to 'new' medical texts, in their records of madness, we do not see the 'medicalisation' of terminology that we might have expected.

Specific terms that were associated with conditions of the mind in medical tracts (*frenesis*, *mania*, *melancholia*) were not used by either compiler. Furthermore, though William of Canterbury defined some specific terms relating to epilepsy (*ephilensia*, *catalempsia* and *analempsia*), he did not apply these terms to the conditions he recorded in his collection. Several cases of madness in both collections were attributed to the presence of demons, and both compilers used language pertaining to possession. Such language was used alongside other terms – *amentia*, *alienatio mentis* – that etymologically pointed to a problem in the mind of the sufferer. The demons in Becket's miracles were not physical entities in that they were not described as taking a corporeal form or even, in the majority of cases, as creating an illusion of corporality. Instead, unseen demons agitated the minds of their victims through trickery and delusion. Madness, demonically induced or otherwise, was defined by its effect on the mind of a sufferer, and its effects were most often seen through unusual – or even inhuman – behaviour. Demoniacs could develop superhuman abilities or be prone to outbursts of spontaneous violence. It is possible, in some cases, that language associated with possession was used figuratively to describe such behaviour rather than to indicate the literal presence of a demon.

Whereas Saint Edmund of Bury's miracle compilers had likely drawn on older material, including Abbo of Fleury's tenth-century *Life of Saint Edmund*, Benedict of Peterborough and William of Canterbury were composing hagiographical material for a new and very popular cult. The sheer volume of miracles that they were dealing with might indicate that they could not possibly have spoken with each miracle recipient directly, but there is evidence that both compilers interacted with pilgrims and listened to their stories. Of course, their engagement with contemporary oral testimony does not mean that Benedict and William did not draw on older precedents, including biblical narratives of Christ's miracles. It is likely that such precedents were also influential in the oral dissemination of Becket's cult, which had a far-reaching impact. Several accounts of and testimonies to Becket's miracles came to Benedict and William in written form via letters, some of which they quoted directly and others which they were no doubt influenced by. In this context, the varied terminology used to describe madness in both collections is hardly surprising but is, nonetheless, reflective of multifaceted contemporary understandings of madness and of an enduring connection between madness and demonic possession.

Notes

1. BP, IV.37, pp. 208–9. All translations from Benedict of Peterborough and William of Canterbury are my own. My thanks go to Lena Wahlgren-Smith for her advice regarding this passage.
2. Koopmans, p. 183.
3. Ibid. Koopmans refers to William of Canterbury's collection as a 'touchstone case of what has been termed the "medicalization" of miracle collections in the late twelfth century', though, as will be shown, his explanations for madness were not dissimilar to Benedict's.
4. Staunton, *The Lives of Thomas Becket*, pp. 30–31.
5. Ibid., p. 15.
6. Southern, pp. 10–12.
7. Ibid., p. 11.
8. Ibid., p. 13.
9. Barlow, pp. 313–14.
10. Gibson, p. 62; Urry, pp. 150–51.
11. Anne Harris, p. 243.
12. Hearn, p. 48.
13. Thomas of Monmouth's *Life and Miracles of William of Norwich* is the focus of Chapter 2.
14. The cult of Saint Edmund at Bury is the focus of Chapter 1.
15. Hearn, p. 50; Ward, p. 90.
16. Bull, p. 113.
17. Koopmans, pp. 139–59; For former dating of the collection, see Staunton, *Thomas Becket*, p. 50.
18. Vincent, p. 374.
19. Staunton, *Thomas Becket*, pp. 50–51.
20. Bull, p. 114.
21. King, p. 218.
22. Swapham, pp. 98–99. The combination of the *Theorica* and *Practica* in the same volume suggests that Benedict's copy was made up of the *Pantegni Theorica* and the *Practica* books I, II and part of IX. See Green's thesis regarding the composition of the ten-book *Practica* in 'The Recreation of *Pantegni*'.
23. Knowles, p. 524.
24. Glaze, pp. 248–49.
25. Staunton, *Thomas Becket*, p. 51.
26. Ibid., p. 49.
27. Koopmans, p. 181; Finucane, p. 125.
28. Vincent, pp. 384–85.
29. Ibid.
30. Ibid., p. 385.
31. Ibid.
32. Bull, p. 111; Harvey, p. 112.
33. Wilson, p. 136.
34. BP, IV.37, p. 209.
35. WC, II.8, pp. 165–66.
36. Koopmans, p. 187.
37. Ibid., p. 185.
38. Ibid., p. 188.
39. Ibid., p. 187.
40. Ibid., pp. 184–93.
41. Ibid., p. 186; BP, II.44, p. 92; WC, I.13, p. 153.

42. Banham, pp. 228–29. Banham's use of the phrase 'new medicine' is discussed in Chapter 1.
43. Green, 'Medical Books', p. 279.
44. Green, 'Salerno on Thames', p. 221.
45. Ibid. I would like to offer special thanks to Monica Green, who has provided me with information on the availability of medical texts at Christ Church, Canterbury, and on the circulation of the *Pantegni* and *Viaticum*. At the date of her article, 375 codices were noted, totalling at least 145 distinct texts. In May 2018, her list stood at 570 individual manuscripts.
46. Ibid., p. 222.
47. Koopmans, p. 183.
48. Ramsay, p. 350.
49. Ibid., pp. 146–47; Margaret Harris, pp. 159–60.
50. CUL, MS Ii 3.12, fols 74^{r}–76^{r}, (facsimile printed in James, pp. 3–6).
51. James, p. xxxii.
52. Glaze, pp. 187–261.
53. Ibid., pp. 254–55; *English Benedictine Libraries*, pp. 463–526.
54. Ibid., pp. 497–526.
55. Green, 'The Recreation of *Pantegni*', p. 131.
56. Ramsay, pp. 353–62; MS Cotton Galba E.IV (printed in James, pp. 13–145).
57. James, p. xxxix.
58. Ibid., pp. 55–61.
59. Ibid.
60. Ibid., p. 57.
61. Ibid., p. 55.
62. Green, 'The Recreation of *Pantegni*', p. 144.
63. BP, IV.19, p. 198 ['repente percussus est passione miranda'].
64. Ibid.
65. Ibid.
66. Ibid., I.14, p. 46.
67. Herman, 37, pp. 104–9. Wulmer's case is discussed in more detail in Chapter 1.
68. TM1, III.22, pp. 154–55; Ibid., VI.8, p. 229. Ida and Gilliva's miracles are discussed in Chapter 2.
69. Du Cange, IV (1885), 377 [*insaniose* – connections between the appearance of falling sickness and insanity]; II (1883), 14 [use of the term *cadiva insania* for epilepsy].
70. Finucane, p. 107.
71. WC., II.87, p. 249 ['timebat amentiam vel ephilensiam incurrere'].
72. Ibid., II.9, p. 166.
73. Ibid.
74. Finucane, p. 125; Ward, p. 90.
75. WC, II.6, pp. 162–63.
76. Ibid., p. 162.
77. Ibid.
78. Ibid., II.8, pp. 165–66.
79. Temkin, p. 120.
80. Ibid.
81. Ibid.
82. I am grateful to Thomas Gloning for bringing this distinction to my attention.
83. Bartholomaeus, pp. 355–56 ['Cuius autem tres sunt species, ut totius nominis partis. Est una que habet principium a cerebro, que proprie epilepsia dicitur'].
84. Ibid., p. 355.

85. Ibid., p. 356 ['Secunda species est cathelempsia, cuius origo est a cruribus et manibus et brachiis {…} Tertia species est que dicitur analepsia, cuius principium est a stomaco'].
86. WC, II.6, p. 162; Bartholomaeus, p. 355.
87. WC, II.6, p. 163; Ibid., II.10, p. 165; Ibid., VI.122, p. 508.
88. One record is a further confirmation of the miracle reported in the previous record.
89. WC, II.6, p. 163; Ibid., VI.122, p. 508; Ibid., II.8, p. 165.
90. Ibid., II.10, p. 167; Ibid., II.9, p. 166. Simon of Genoa (late thirteenth century) defined *comitialis* as an ancient term for epilepsy (<http://www.simonofgenoa.org/index.php?title=Comitialis_morbus>, accessed 25 August 2018). The term came from ancient Rome when the *comitia*, or assembly of the people, could be halted by an epileptic seizure, which required cleansing (Temkin, p. 8).
91. WC, II.8, p. 165.
92. Gariopontus, I.7, fol. 4^{r}.
93. Bartholomaeus, p. 355.
94. Constantine, fol. cxlvij^{r}.
95. WC, VI.123, p. 509; Ibid., VI.125, p. 513.
96. BP, IV.43, p. 255; Ibid., III.37, p. 143; Ibid., IV.26, p. 202.
97. Bartholomaeus, pp. 355–56.
98. BP, IV.26, p. 202.
99. Ibid., III.37, p. 143.
100. Ibid., III.1, p. 118.
101. Ibid., IV.21, p. 199.
102. WC, II.6, pp. 163–64.
103. BP, IV.37, p. 208.
104. Ibid., IV.53, p. 221 ['Tanta denique doloris vehementia lecto receptam cruciavit, ut miris quibusdam ac insolitis membrorum jactibus in insaniam se jam jamque converti insinuaret].
105. Ibid., I.14, p. 46.
106. Ibid., II.9, p. 63.
107. WC, VI.113, p. 504.
108. Cohen, pp. 136–39.
109. BP, II.13, p. 66
110. Ibid., IV.56, p. 223.
111. Ibid., IV.57, p. 224.
112. Turner, p. 58.
113. WC, VI.113, p. 504 ['Unde aqua martyris potata est, potata confestim soporem cepit, soporata mente[m] corpusque sanata recepit'].
114. Ibid., VI.87, p. 481.
115. Ibid., III.47, pp. 303–4.
116. Herman, 3, pp. 10–15. Leofstan's case is discussed in more detail in Chapter 1.
117. WC, II.6, p. 163.
118. BP, IV.37, p. 209.
119. Ibid.
120. Constantine, fols cxlvi^{r}–cxlvij^{r}.
121. Ibid., fol. cxlvi^{v}.
122. Bartholomaeus, pp. 374–75.
123. Ibid.
124. Koopmans, p. 186.
125. BP, IV.37, pp. 208–9.
126. Ibid., II.31, pp. 82–83.
127. Ibid.

128. WC, VI.87, p. 481.
129. Ibid., III.47, p. 303 ['oculos ignitos circumferret']; Ibid., VI.3, p. 410 ['Crebri risus oris et oculorum motus, brachiorum et digitorum agitationes videntibus et stupori et moerori erant'].
130. TM1, VII.3, p. 265. This miracle is discussed in more detail in Chapter 2.
131. WC, II.89, p. 250. Bapaume was transferred to the direct control of the King of France in 1191.
132. Ibid., V.38, p. 405.
133. Ibid. ['ipse notos ignoraret, dentibus et unguibus saeviret'].
134. BP, IV.37, p. 209.
135. WC, III.48, p. 304.
136. Ibid., III.49, p. 305.
137. Ibid., III.50, p. 305.
138. Ibid., VI.130, p. 519; Ibid., III.51, p. 306.
139. Seventeen individuals in total, though some of their cures were recorded within the same miracle account. Hardwin of Châtillon's madness has been classified as non-demonic because demons were not specifically mentioned, though he was 'arreptitius' (III.50). The two people from Gloucester, who the spirit of madness had driven out of their minds ('spiritus fuoris dementaverat'), have been classified as demonically possessed since the devil ('hostis humani generis') was implicated in their madness (III.52).
140. The madness of the child who cried out, '"See where they come!"' (II.54) has been classified as non-demonic here because his strange utterances were not specifically attributed to demons.
141. Bailey, p. 252.
142. BP, IV.37, pp. 208–9.
143. Ibid., II.31, p. 82.
144. Ibid., II.54, pp. 102–3 ['"Ecce ubi veniunt, ecce ubi veniunt!"'].
145. Ibid., II.31, p. 82 [humani generis hostem opposita fronte sibi occurrere putabat'].
146. Rider, pp. 56–57.
147. Ibid., p. 56.
148. BP, I.13, pp. 44–45; MacLehose, pp. 67–68; For more on the medieval *incubus*, see van der Lugt.
149. van der Lugt, p. 183.
150. WC, III.49, p. 305.
151. Ibid., VI.130, p. 519.
152. Ibid., VI.86, pp. 480–81.
153. Ibid., II.6, p. 164; Ibid., II.7, p. 164.
154. BP, IV.37, p. 209.
155. WC, III.50, p. 305.
156. Ibid., III.52, p. 307 ['Gloriatur hostis humani generis, ad ignominiam ejus quem arripit, multorum manibus custodum contrectari, mollibus blandisque loris interim coarctari, donec igneis catenis in futuro constringatur'].
157. TM1, VI.5, p. 225 ['debachantis spiritus insania'].
158. *Miracles of St Frideswide*, p. 581.
159. Ward, p. 36; Ibid., p. 67.

Bibliography

Manuscripts

Cambridge University Library (CUL), MS li 3.12, fols 74r–76r
London, British Library, MS Cotton Galba E.IV

Primary

Bartholomaeus, 'Practica Magistri Bartholomaei Salernitani', in *Collectio Salernitana*, 5 vols (Naples: Salvatore de Renzi, 1852–59), IV (1856), 321–406

Benedict of Peterborough, 'Miracula Sancti Thomae Cantuariensis', in *Materials for the History of Thomas Becket, Archbishop of Canterbury*, ed. by James Craigie Robertson, 7 vols (London: Longman, 1875–85), II (1876), 21–281

Constantine the African, 'Viaticum', in *Omnia Opera Ysaac* (Lyon: Trot, 1515), fols cxliiij[r]– clxxj[v] [in the second set of foliation]

Gariopontus, *Passionarius Galeni* (Lyon: n.p., 1526)

Herman the Archdeacon, 'Miracles of St Edmund', in *Herman the Archdeacon and Goscelin of Saint-Bertin. Miracles of St Edmund*, ed. and trans. by Tom Licence (Oxford: Oxford University Press, 2014), pp. 1–125

Miracles of St Frideswide, ed. by Josepho van Hacke, Benjamino Bossue, Victore de Buck and Antonio Tinnebroek (Brussels: Alphonsi Greuse, 1853), Acta Sanctorum, 8 October, pp. 568–589

Simon of Genoa, *Clavis Sanationis* <http://www.simonofgenoa.org/index.php?title=Simon_Online>

Thomas of Monmouth, *The Life and Miracles of St William of Norwich*, ed. and trans. by Augustus Jessopp and M.R. James (Cambridge: Cambridge University Press, 1896)

William of Canterbury, 'Miracula Sancti Thomae Cantuariensis', in *Materials for the History of Thomas Becket, Archbishop of Canterbury*, ed. by James Craigie Robertson, 7 vols (London: Longman, 1875–85), I (1875), 137–546

Secondary

Bailey, Anne E., 'Miracles and Madness: Dispelling Demons in Twelfth-Century Hagiography', in *Demons and Illness from Antiquity to the Early-Modern Period*, ed. by Siam Bhayro and Catherine Rider, Magical and Religious Literature of Late Antiquity, 5 (Leiden: Brill, 2017), pp. 235–255

Banham, Debby, 'Medicine at Bury in the Time of Abbot Baldwin', in *Bury St Edmunds and the Norman Conquest*, ed. by Tom Licence (Woodbridge: Boydell, 2014), pp. 226–246

Barlow, Frank, *Thomas Becket*, rev. edn (London: The Folio Society, 2002)

Bull, Marcus, 'Criticism of Henry II's Expedition to Ireland in William of Canterbury's Miracles of St. Thomas Becket', *Journal of Medieval History*, 33 (2007), 107–129

Cohen, Esther, *The Modulated Scream: Pain in Late Medieval Culture* (Chicago, IL and London: University of Chicago Press, 2010)

Du Cange, Charles, *Glossarium mediae et infimae latinitatis*, 10 vols (Niort: L. Favre, 1883–87)

Finucane, Ronald C., *Miracles and Pilgrims: Popular Beliefs in Medieval England* (New York, NY: St. Martin's Press, 1977; repr. 1995)

Gibson, Margaret, 'Normans and Angevins, 1070–1220', in *A History of Canterbury Cathedral*, ed. by Patrick Collinson, Nigel Ramsay and Margaret Sparks (Oxford: Oxford University Press, 1995), pp. 38–68

Glaze, Florence Eliza, 'The Perforated Wall: The Ownership and Circulation of Medical Books in Medieval Europe, ca. 800–1200' (unpublished doctoral thesis, Duke University, 1999)

Green, Monica, 'Medical Books', in *The European Book in the Twelfth Century*, ed. by Erik Kwakkel and Rodney Thomson (Cambridge: Cambridge University Press, 2018), pp. 277–292

———, 'The Recreation of *Pantegni, Practica*, Book VIII', in *Constantine the African and 'Ali ibn al-'Abbas al-Madjusi: The* Pantegni *and Related Works*, ed. by Charles Burnett and Danielle Jacquart (Leiden, New York, NY and Köln: Brill, 1994), pp. 121–160

——— 'Salerno on Thames: The Genesis of Anglo-Norman Medical Literature', in *Language and Culture in Medieval Britain: The French of England, c.1100–c.1500*, ed. by Jocelyn Wogan-Browne (Woodbridge: York Medieval Press, 2009), pp. 220–231

Harris, Anne F., 'Pilgrimage, Performance, and Stained Glass at Canterbury Cathedral', in *Art and Architecture of Late Medieval Pilgrimage in Northern Europe and the British Isles*, ed. by Sarah Blick and Rita Tekippe, Studies in Medieval and Reformation Traditions, 104, 2 vols (Leiden: Brill, 2005), I, 243–281

Harris, Margaret A., 'Lanfranc and St Anselm', in *Benedict's Disciples*, ed. by David Hugh Farmer (Leominster: Gracewing, 1980), pp. 154–174

Harvey, Barbara, *Living and Dying in England, 1100–1540: The Monastic Experience* (Oxford: Oxford University Press, 1993)

Hearn, M.F., 'Canterbury Cathedral and the Cult of Becket', *Art Bulletin*, 76 (1994), 19–52

James, M.R., *The Ancient Libraries of Canterbury and Dover* (Cambridge: Cambridge University Press, 1903)

King, Edmund, 'Benedict of Peterborough and the Cult of Thomas Becket', *Northamptonshire Past and Present*, 9 (1996), 213–220

Knowles, David, *The Monastic Order: A History of Its Development from the Times of St Dunstan to the Fourth Lateran Council, 943–1216* (Cambridge: Cambridge University Press, 1950)

Koopmans, Rachel, *Wonderful to Relate: Miracle Stories and Miracle Collecting in High Medieval England* (Philadelphia: University of Pennsylvania Press, 2011)

MacLehose, William F., 'Fear, Fantasy and Sleep in Medieval Medicine', in *Emotions and Health 1200–1700*, ed. by Elena Carrera, Studies in Medieval and Reformation Traditions, 168 (Leiden: Brill, 2013), pp. 67–94

Ramsay, Nigel, 'The Cathedral Archives and Library', in *A History of Canterbury Cathedral*, ed. by Patrick Collinson, Nigel Ramsay and Margaret Sparks (Oxford: Oxford University Press, 1995), pp. 341–407

Rider, Catherine, 'Demons and Mental Disorder in Late Medieval Medicine', in *Mental (Dis)Order in Later Medieval Europe*, ed. by Sari Katajala-Peltomaa and Susanna Nirranen, Later Medieval Europe, 12 (Leiden: Brill, 2014), pp. 47–69

Sharpe, R., J.P. Carley, R.M. Thomson and A.G. Watson, eds., *English Benedictine Libraries: The Shorter Catalogues* (London: The British Library, 1996)

Southern, R.W., *The Monks of Canterbury and the Murder of Archbishop Becket* (Canterbury: Friends of Canterbury Cathedral, 1985)

Staunton, Michael, *The Lives of Thomas Becket* (Manchester and New York, NY: Manchester University Press, 2001)

———, *Thomas Becket and his Biographers*, Studies in the History of Medieval Religion, 28 (Woodbridge: Boydell, 2006)

Swapham, Robert, 'Historiae Coenobii Burgensis', in *Historiae Anglicanae: Scriptores Varii, E Codicibus Manuscriptis*, ed. by J. Sparke (London: Gul. Bowyer, 1723), pp. 97–122

Temkin, Owsei, *The Falling Sickness: A History of Epilepsy from the Greeks to the Beginnings of Modern Neurology*, rev. edn (Baltimore, MD: John Hopkins Press, 1971)

Turner, Wendy J., *Care and Custody of the Mentally Ill, Incompetent, and Disabled in Medieval England* (Turnhout: Brepols, 2013)

Urry, William, *Thomas Becket: His Last Days*, ed. by Peter A. Rowe (Stroud: Sutton, 1999)

van der Lugt, Maaike, 'The *Incubus* in Scholastic Debate: Medicine, Theology and Popular Belief', in *Religion and Medicine*, ed. by Peter Biller and Joseph Ziegler, York Studies in Medieval Theology, 3 (Woodbridge: York Medieval Press, 2001), pp. 175–200

Vincent, Nicholas, 'William of Canterbury and Benedict of Peterborough: the manuscripts, date and context of the Becket miracle collections', in *Hagiographie, idéologie et politique au Moyen Âge en Occident*, ed. by Edina Bozoky, Hagiologia, 8 (Turnhout: Brepols, 2012), pp. 347–388

Ward, Benedicta, *Miracles and the Medieval Mind: Theory, Record and Event 1000–1215*, rev. edn (Philadelphia: University of Pennsylvania Press, 1987)

Wilson, Louise E., 'Hagiographical Interpretations of Disability in the Twelfth-Century *Miracula* of St. Frideswide of Oxford', in *The Treatment of Disabled Persons in Medieval Europe: Examining Disability in the Historical, Legal, Literary, Medical and Religious Discourses of the Middle Ages*, ed. by Wendy J. Turner and Tory Vandeventer Pearman (Lewiston, NY: Edwin Mellen, 2010), pp. 135–165

4 Demonic disturbances in the miracles of Saint Bartholomew in London

> Indeed, as he sleeps, the ancient enemy appeared, transformed into the appearance of the most beautiful woman, who whereby seemed to sit, caressing his head. And when she had charmed him for some time with her destructive caresses, she placed a small bird in his mouth, and thus disappeared. Awakened, he is frightened by the unsolicited vision and the same hour, his mind seized, he is deprived of all the vigour of reason, and being ignorant of what should be done or what abandoned, led by madness, running about, wanders now this way, now that way, and not knowing what he does, rushes headlong where the urge of malign fury drives him.[1]

The unfortunate sleeper in this miracle was a youth named Robert, who had broken his journey to London to rest his limbs and to sleep in the woods. The record of Robert's miracle is demonstrative of an association, already identified in the previous chapters, between madness and demons. Nonetheless, Robert's demon is notably different from the avenging demon that possessed Sheriff Leofstan in Bury or the physically-abstract demons in William of Norwich's and Thomas Becket's miracle collections.[2] Robert was attacked in his sleep and not as the direct result of a sinful act. His demon held, at the very least, the illusion of a physical form, and it used its physicality to charm Robert. Thankfully for Robert, he was captured near London and taken to the priory church of Saint Bartholomew, where he was miraculously cured by the intercession of the apostle. Robert's miraculous cure was not compiled in a vast, stand-alone miracle collection, as those miracles attributed to Thomas Becket had been. Instead, it was recorded alongside other miracles in the *Book of the Foundation of the Church of Saint Bartholomew in London* (*Liber fundationis ecclesie sancti Bartholomei Londiniarum*). The *Liber fundationis* is divided into two parts: the first describes the foundation of the church and the miracles that occurred there during the lifetime of its founder, Rahere, and the second details further miracles that were witnessed after his death. The second book contains five records of miraculously-cured madness, four of which were linked to demons, providing a counter-narrative to the so-called naturalisation of twelfth-century miracle texts[3] and understandings of madness.[4] This chapter focuses on how miraculous cures of madness and demonic possession fit into the larger narrative of a spiritual battle between Rahere and his own 'demons'. It also challenges some popular assumptions about medieval demoniacs; in the miracle records examined, women were not considered any more vulnerable to demonic possession than men, and the binding of demoniacs does not seem to have been a punitive measure aimed at the demon inside them, but rather a practical means of controlling them so that they could receive care or healing.

Despite Bartholomew's apostolic status, his twelfth-century cult did not reach the popularity of Saint Edmund's or Saint Thomas Becket's cults in England, and his miracles have received relatively little attention from historians. The miracles performed through Bartholomew's relics in London were recorded in the immediate aftermath of Thomas Becket's death and the subsequent popularity of his cult and in the context of an upsurge in miracle collecting in England, during which miracle collections were also compiled for Saint Godric at Finchale (County Durham), Saint Frideswide at Oxford and the Hand of Saint James at Reading, among others.[5]

The original Latin text of the *Liber fundationis* was most likely composed by an anonymous Augustinian canon belonging to the priory of Saint Bartholomew in London sometime between the death of Prior Thomas in 1174 (recounted in the prologue to part two) and that of King Henry II in 1189 (no later king is mentioned in the text). The only surviving copy of the Latin text comes from the late fourteenth/early fifteenth century in a manuscript that originally belonged to the priory before it was bought by Sir Robert Cotton (1570–1631).[6] The manuscript contains two versions of the text: a transcription of the twelfth-century Latin in the first forty folios, followed by a Middle English translation.[7] Little is known about the author of the *Liber fundationis* apart from his position as a canon of the priory. Like the men who compiled Saint Edmund's, William of Norwich's and Saint Thomas Becket's miracle collections, he had his own agenda when selecting and composing miracle stories. However, since he remains anonymous, we do not know much about his background or personal influences. Like many clerics of this period, he had extensive knowledge of the Bible as well as some understanding of contemporary medical ideas.

The Augustinian priory of Saint Bartholomew was founded in 1123 and was consecrated in 1129 after the building work had finished.[8] It was originally home to thirteen canons (with a further eight lay brothers and four sisters at the hospital), but, by the time of the composition of the twelfth-century *Liber fundationis*, it supported thirty-five Augustinian canons.[9] Saint Bartholomew's hospital was founded alongside the priory in 1123. Both foundations were made by Rahere, whose life is still the subject of historical debate but who, according to the *Liber fundationis*, was a wayward courtier who had seen the error of his ways following a severe illness whilst on a pilgrimage to Rome and who founded the priory and hospital as recompense for his sins.[10] The hospital was staffed separately from the priory by lay brothers and professed sisters, though Rahere was both prior and hospital master until the mastership was granted to Hagno, a clerk, in 1137. Rahere remained as prior until his death in 1143 and was succeeded by

Prior Thomas, whilst Hagno kept control of the hospital.[11] Nonetheless, the master was held answerable to the prior, and hospital and priory were considered united.[12] From the late twelfth to the end of the thirteenth century, the hospital strove for more autonomy from the priory, something that was repeatedly denied until the fifteenth century.[13]

The hospital of Saint Bartholomew has received substantially more attention from historians than the priory, no doubt because it is still recognised as a leading London hospital today. In their attempts to trace the 'medical' history of Saint Bartholomew's, historians have focused on those events in the hospital's history that illustrate its *progress* towards a modern medical establishment, such as the physician John Mirfield's time there and his compilation of the *Breviarium Bartholomei* (1380–95).[14] Carole Rawcliffe has observed, however, that physicians and surgeons paid little, if any, attention to London's hospitals in their early days, preferring, instead, to visit fee-paying patients in their homes.[15] Saint Bartholomew's hospital was originally intended to cater for the poor and for orphaned children, and, like the priory, its primary function was its service to God.[16] Almost a third of London's medieval hospitals, like Saint Bartholomew's, followed the Augustinian Rule.[17] Before 1100, houses of Augustinian canons were most commonly founded as small monastic communities who had reduced spiritual duties (as compared to the Benedictines) so that they were able to serve a specific local need (e.g. the management of a hospital). The twelfth century saw a stricter way of life introduced in many existing foundations as well as in new foundations like Saint Bartholomew's.[18] As a canon of the priory, therefore, it is not clear whether the author of the *Liber fundationis* would have visited the hospital personally, but he does mention some of the patients there who received miraculous cures from Saint Bartholomew.[19]

Basil Clarke briefly examines the miracles of the *Liber fundationis* in his book *Mental Disorder in Earlier Britain* (1975), but he predominantly uses modern diagnostic techniques to discuss the conditions that were recorded.[20] He focuses on nine miracles, which he terms 'psychiatric-social' and include cases of madness that are analysed here as well as other conditions, like an inability to sleep following the incorrect treatment of blood loss.[21] This chapter pays attention, instead, to medieval categorisations of conditions, counting only five cases of miraculously-cured madness and exploring how this complaint was believed to relate to demonic possession, since demons were linked to four of the five cases.

Playing the fool: the life of Rahere

Feigned madness: Rahere as a 'holy fool'

The first reference to madness in the *Liber fundationis* is not, as one might expect, in one of the records of conditions miraculously cured by Saint Bartholomew. Instead, madness was one of the many discomforts suffered by Rahere in his quest to build the priory and hospital. Rahere was not described as mad or insane but was given the label 'idiote', or 'fool'. Wendy Turner, in her discussion of medieval terminology associated with mental incompetence, focusing largely on legal texts, has noted that the term *idiota* most commonly indicated a prolonged (usually lifelong) period of mental incompetence that often lacked the violence of sudden-onset madness.[22] As a literary figure, the *fol* could be a comic character: prized as an entertainer but never considered capable of military gallantry.[23] This role was held by literary characters like Robert le Diable, who assumed the guise of a *fol* as penance for his sins and feigned madness as part of a penitential spiritual journey.[24] It is likely that the author of the *Liber fundationis* purposefully constructed a comparable redeemed 'hero' in Rahere. Notably, none of the mad pilgrims in the *Liber fundationis*, or in any of the miracle records examined here, were described using this terminology, which suggests that Rahere's 'madness' was considered different from that which necessitated a miraculous cure.

The author of the *Liber fundationis* also made it very clear that Rahere's foolishness was feigned, whereas those who later sought cures from Saint Bartholomew had no control over their conditions. Rahere was forced to hide his true wisdom in order to attract children and servants to help him collect stones and other building materials for the construction of the church.[25] He found this task particularly difficult but did it to please the apostle (Bartholomew) even though it made him feel increasingly worthless ('vilior').[26] Rahere's period of self-imposed foolishness is reminiscent of Arthurian literature of the period, in which the protagonist (Tristan, Lancelot, Yvain) sought spiritual/moral renewal by suffering madness, feigned or otherwise.[27] Rahere's feelings of worthlessness, then, can perhaps be seen as part of his penance for the sins of his previous life as a courtier whilst also protecting him from future sin, such as the pride that could result from founding an establishment like Saint Bartholomew's priory and hospital.

In Rahere, there is something of the Byzantine 'holy fool', who feigned madness with pious intent in order to shun worldly reverence.[28] Sergey Ivanov has demonstrated that altered versions of the Eastern holy fool made their way into Western thought from at least the eighth century, though, unlike his Eastern counterpart, the Western holy fool initially avoided reverence through his foolishness but eventually entered the monastic life to pursue more conventional asceticism, as Rahere did.[29] In contrast to Eastern holy fools, Rahere's social purpose (the building of the hospital), rather than his self-imposed separation from society, was of primary importance. Though Rahere's foolishness repulsed him, it attracted others and may well have fascinated the compiler of the *Liber fundationis*, who dedicated some of his lengthiest miracle stories to the subject of madness.

Rahere's dream-vision

Like several of the mad pilgrims who later visited his priory and hospital, Rahere also suffered from demonic attack. Three chapters of the *Liber fundationis* are devoted to relating Rahere's dream-vision and then to interpreting it. When returning from his pilgrimage to Rome, having recovered from the sickness he had suffered there, Rahere was awoken one night having seen a vision ('visionem'). At first, he almost mistook the divine vision for a 'fantastical illusion, which is more often wont to happen to men in sleep', as he did not deem himself worthy of a divine message.[30] The Augustinian canon who compiled the *Liber fundationis*, however, thought that the divine vision was right to be interpreted as such and noted the frequent examples of divine dream-visions in the Bible.[31]

First, Rahere saw a beast (*animal*), which had four feet and two wings.[32] The author of the *Liber fundationis* understood this beast to signify the devil, who was known as the 'Great Eagle' (Ezekiel 17:7) and whose four feet represented the four passions of the soul: fear, sadness, love and gladness.[33] These passions could 'completely dissipate the quietness of the mind'.[34] The ideal state of mind was one of quiet and calm, and excess passion could lead to imbalance and turmoil. A further reference to balance is in the description of temptation coming in four forms: light and hidden, light and open, heavy and hidden, and heavy and open.[35] The construction of a whole made up of four parts is akin to the organisation of the four elements of the universe (air, fire, earth and water) and to the Hippocratic complexions of the body (moist and warm; dry and warm; dry and cold; moist and cold). Each temptation was trodden into the earth by one of the four feet of the beast-devil; thus, sin was connected to mental instability and demonic interference in the world.[36]

Rahere was taken by the beast-devil to a high vantage point from which he was able to look down into the pit below him. This phase of Rahere's spiritual journey has obvious parallels to Christ's encounter with the devil in the desert; the devil brought Christ to the top of a high mountain, from which he could see the entire world, in the hope of corrupting him with the temptation of worldly glory (Matthew 4:8–9).[37] Rahere was rescued – physically and morally – from the precipice by the Apostle Bartholomew, who appeared to him with 'royal majesty', 'imperial authority' and a countenance of 'wonderful beauty', in stark contrast to the bestial qualities of the devil.[38] Bartholomew delivered a message to Rahere, explaining that it was divine will that Rahere found the priory and hospital of Saint Bartholomew in London.[39] Rahere was thus spared from the wiles of the devil and guided towards the right path by the apostle, which was an important precedent for Saint Bartholomew's later encounters with the devil through pilgrims who were tormented and possessed.

Rahere's divine vision also leads us to consider how medieval theologians distinguished between similar divine visions and demonic visions, which often tormented the mad, and what impact their distinctions had on hagiographical representations of visionary experiences. The twelfth century marked the beginning of an outpouring of spirit literature – which discussed human, demonic and divine spirits – in texts such as Alcher of Clairvaux's *On Spirit and Soul*, which was initially highly influential because of its incorrect attribution to Augustine.[40] Such treatises identified the heart as the seat of the human spirit and discussed the possibility of demonic possession of the human soul, with the consensus being that demons could not enter the soul but could possess it through trickery. Demons took up physical residence in the bowels or the reproductive organs.[41] The Holy Spirit, by contrast, avoided such polluted organs; instead, it entered the heart and possessed the soul rather than the body.[42]

With the intensification of interest in visionary experiences in the thirteenth century, particularly those of female visionaries, there was a growing concern with the discernment of spirits (the practice of differentiating between good and bad spirits, or between divine and demonic possession).[43] Since the behaviours of both visionaries and demoniacs could appear extreme at times, theologians increasingly contemplated the difficult task of discerning a true prophet from a false one. Alcher of Clairvaux observed that the important distinction between a demonic vision and a divine vision was that the victim of a demonic vision was deluded into believing that the content of the vision was experienced physically in his or her body, whereas the recipient of a divine vision was able to rationally perceive the spiritual nature of his or her encounter.[44] Despite almost mistaking his vision for an illusion or a dream, Rahere was aware that what he saw was, in fact, a vision and had no physical substance. By contrast, the mad people who came to Saint Bartholomew's church falsely believed that their visions and delusions were material realities, despite the fact that the source of their afflictions lay in their minds.

Terminology: epilepsy, madness and demonic possession

I have identified five cases of miraculously-healed madness in the *Liber fundationis* (outlined in Table 4.1), all of which were described as 'madness' (*insania*, *amentia*), 'raving madness' (*furor*) or a problem with the mind, which was, for example, 'taken' (*mente captus*). Four of these five cases of madness involved demons. A further three cases of demonic disturbance that were not specifically connected with madness concerned a young girl freed from the malign power ('maligna potestate') that had made her deaf, dumb, blind and crippled, a man who was kidnapped at the instigation of the enemy of the entire human race ('totius humani generationis inimicus') and a dumb youth who was tormented by the work of the ancient enemy ('antiqui hostis').[45] These miracles serve to demonstrate the universal interference of the devil in the lives of humans and his almost limitless ability to cause harm, through sickness or otherwise, something for which there were multiple biblical precedents (e.g. Job 2:7 – the devil inflicted Job with a severe ulcer across his entire body). The Bible also provided a precedent for connecting demonic possession with a lack of reason. For example, the Jews in Judea did not believe the teachings of Christ because they felt that he was led by a demon (John 7:20 and 8:48). The four cases of

Table 4.1 Summary of miracles involving madness and demonic possession in the *Liber fundationis ecclesie sancti Bartholomei Londiniarum*.

Ref.	*Summary of miracle*	*Details of demonic involvement*
II.9	A youth called Robert rested in a wood on his way to London. Upon awakening, he had lost his reason and was mad. He wandered around until he was captured and brought to St Bartholomew's church, where he was cured.	As he slept in the wood, the devil appeared to him in the form of a beautiful woman who placed a small bird in his mouth. Robert's cure was illustrative of Bartholomew's ability to cast out demons.
II.10	A knight called Ralph was travelling through Essex on his way to London when he began raving, throwing coins, tearing his clothes and assaulting people with stones. He was captured and brought to the church, where he stayed for two nights before he was cured.	Ralph was seized by a demon, which rendered him senseless and caused the symptoms described.
II.12	The unlawful daughter of a priest was entrusted to the care of a matron who was to school her in doctrine and to keep her from vice. She was pursued by a demon in the form of a handsome suitor, who she refused. Thwarted, the demon struck her, and her mind was taken, causing disordered movement of the limbs, internal pain and foaming at the mouth. She was inflicted thus two or three times a day. She was brought to the church, which the demon tried to prevent her from entering. The canons prayed for her, and she was restored to full health and returned to her parents.	The demon appeared as a young and beautiful nobleman with royal blood so as to tempt the maiden's womanly weakness. He tried to seduce her with his words, and, when that failed, he tried to force himself on her, but she called out to her servants for help.
II.18	A London handmaid was seduced and then became mad and crippled. She rolled her eyes, tore her clothes and spouted blasphemies. She went to St Bartholomew's hospital and was miraculously cured by the apostle.	Her heart was darkened by the oppression of the devil, and she could not comprehend God.
II.24	A little boy was brought to the church by his mother because he had 'lost all sense of reason' and was suffering from 'madness'. The boy was cured, and his mother was brought joy.	None.

demonic possession in the *Liber fundationis*, therefore, adhered to an already-established tradition of correspondence between the language of possession and the language of madness, which we have also seen in other twelfth-century English miracle records.[46]

Epilepsy

Notably, the one case of epilepsy ('epilepsia') in the *Liber fundationis* was not attributed to demons.

> Now, epilepsy is, the physicians say, a disease which compresses the ventricles of the brain and blocks the vital functions, takes away sight, hearing, and the other senses of the body, and wearies the body itself with terrible suffering.[47]

This epileptic boy was believed to have lost his sight, hearing and other senses as well as the health of his limbs because of a problem in his brain and not as a result of demonic interference. This explanation was attributed to physicians, though the epileptic's cure remained the work of Saint Bartholomew and of God. The compiler of the *Liber fundationis* does seem to have distinguished epilepsy from madness, though his explanation for epilepsy was not as detailed as that given by William of Canterbury in his collection of the miracles of Saint Thomas Becket, written around the same time.[48] Epilepsy affected the 'brain' (*cerebrum*) and the 'senses of the body' ('corporis sensus'), unlike madness, which, as seen in the miracle account with which this chapter opened, affected the 'mind' (*mens*) and 'reason' (*ratio*). Furthermore, the boy's epilepsy was not connected with demons. The use of terms such as 'the ventricles of the brain' ('cerebri ventriculos') suggests a sophisticated understanding of the brain's anatomy in line with contemporary medical theories. According to the simplest anatomical models, the brain was divided into three areas or 'ventricles' (these ventricles were subdivided in more complex models). The front ventricle of the brain housed the common sense, which was also possessed by animals, and allowed people to make basic judgements about the world around them (speed, distance, size). The common sense was fed information by the senses, hence its proximity to the sense receptors in the face. Also in the front ventricle was the imaginative faculty, which formed sensory stimuli into images. This information was passed on to the central, reasoning ventricle, which processed it into concepts and judgements (something that non-rational beasts could not do). Processed images were stored as memories in the back ventricle of the brain.[49] Compression of the brain's ventricles (for example, by fluid) could cause a contraction or blockage of the nerves that transferred messages between the brain and the limbs; hence a person suffering from epilepsy could experience loss of movement, feeling or other sensory functions, as described by the compiler of the *Liber fundationis*.[50]

Whilst employing contemporary medical theories in relation to epilepsy, the compiler of the *Liber fundationis* called into question natural explanations for other conditions. For example, he denied that an outbreak of pestilence had been caused by poor air quality and instead argued that the sickness was brought about as a punishment from God.[51] Of course, these two causes were not incongruous; when the Paris Medical Faculty made their official report in October 1348, following the outbreak of plague, they concluded that, despite the immediate cause of the Black Death being bad air, all pestilence was the result of divine will.[52] When unsure of a diagnosis, the compiler of the *Liber fundationis* would include multiple options, as in the case of a maidservant who was said to have been crippled either because she had kept to her bed for too long through illness or because the sinews of her knees had contracted (again, these two explanations were not necessarily incompatible).[53]

A mad boy brought to the church by his mother

Of the four cases of madness, only one was not attributed in any way to demonic activity. This miracle is the briefest account of madness in the *Liber fundationis* and is located towards the end of the collection (the fourth-from-last miracle). A boy who was insane (*insanus*) and had lost all sense of reason was brought to Saint Bartholomew's church in the period following Saint Bartholomew's Day (24 August), when several other pilgrims were said to have been cured there.[54] The boy's mother, who brought him to the church, was the focus of the miracle record, presumably because it was she who had related her son's story. She had carried him around several saints' shrines and was even beginning to find him burdensome. When she arrived at Saint Bartholomew's church, she kept vigil there for her son. The apostle then granted joy to the mother and health to the boy. Not only did the mother witness the miracle, but she also participated in it: both by personally making a petition to the saint and by sharing in his blessing. Though the boy was the direct recipient of the miraculous cure, it was the mother who felt its benefits. It is not even clear whether, during the festivities, any of the canons had seen the boy before his cure, which might explain why there is no description of his symptoms in the miracle record. Possibly, the mother had not connected her son's condition with demonic possession, and the miracle compiler followed her lead. What is noteworthy is that, in this miracle record alone, the compiler diagnosed a loss of reason without explicitly attributing it to demons.

Four demoniacs

Those pilgrims who were made mad through demonic interference suffered from a comparable set of symptoms to one another, though the precise nature of their possession differed in each case. Robert, who we met at the beginning of this chapter, was a youth who had been travelling from Northampton to London and who was possessed after he spent the night sleeping outside.[55] As we know, Robert lost his reason and succumbed to aimless wandering.[56] Ralph, a knight who was also travelling to London, but this time from Essex, experienced similar deranged wandering when he leapt from his horse, tore his clothes and scattered his coins, proceeding to roam the woods and hills.[57] Likewise, a young handmaid who had been oppressed by the devil into committing the sin of fornication rolled her eyes, tore her clothes and spouted blasphemies.[58] The handmaid was unfortunate in that, having been brought to Saint Bartholomew's hospital, she then suffered a contraction of the limbs, meaning that she became both a madwoman and a cripple. Physical contortions of the limbs were common to three of the four demoniacs, with Robert experiencing loss of control and the daughter of a priest, who had been struck by a demonic suitor, suffering 'disordered movement of the limbs' along with internal pain and foaming at the mouth.[59] Notably, this girl's suffering was labelled 'mente capta' (seized in mind); despite her intermittent falling being similar to modern epilepsy, she was not identified as suffering from epilepsy by the twelfth-century compiler.[60]

Diagnosing demonic possession

Sari Katajala-Peltomaa, in her study of miracles recorded in later medieval canonisation processes, has observed that, whilst madness and demonic possession could appear symptomatically similar, there were some symptoms that were more typical of demoniacs: abnormal powers, convulsions, blaspheming, aggression and abhorrence of sacred objects.[61] All of these symptoms hint at the presence of a foreign being inside the body or an external assault on the body. Abnormal powers (such as xenoglossia and prophecy) belonged to the demon itself, whereas blaspheming (such as that discharged by the handmaid) and abhorrence of sacred objects represented the demon's rage towards God. Convulsions could potentially indicate the violent reaction of the body to demonic onslaught, whether external or internal. The careful recording of such symptoms was crucial to a diagnosis of demonic possession. Demonic possession was evident through the symptoms of the sufferer because the demon itself generally, and certainly in all the accounts in the *Liber fundationis*, remained invisible to onlookers if any onlookers were present. The demoniacs in the *Liber fundationis* were fairly typical sufferers of demonic possession since their encounters with demons conformed to recognised models, drawn from the Bible, as well as contemporary theology and philosophy. They suffered symptoms including some of those identified by Katajala-Peltomaa, which made their demonic possession distinct from non-demonic madness. Nonetheless, the representations of demonic possession in the *Liber fundationis* were not, in all respects, congruous with the demonic possessions of earlier miracle collections, like those of Saint Edmund of Bury, or even with contemporary records of demonic possession, like those compiled at Saint Thomas Becket's shrine in Canterbury. By exploring the unique circumstances of the *Liber fundationis*' compilation as well as shifts in contemporary interpretations of demonic possession at the end of the twelfth century, we can consider the connections between demonic possession and madness, and between physical, mental and spiritual health and healing in the miracle narrative.

Male and female bodies

Nancy Caciola has argued that, in the later Middle Ages, women were believed to be more prone to demonic possession than men.[62] She examines various sources, including exorcists' manuals, which first appeared in the fourteenth century and which, by their use of Latin feminine word endings, implied that the expected victim of a demonic attack was female.[63] The female body was thought to be more open to demonic attack, and the female soul was believed to be more impressionable, meaning that women succumbed to sin more easily than men.[64] Twelfth-century miracle texts present a very different picture of internal demonic possession.[65] In his analysis of miracles from medieval France, largely recorded between 1050 and 1150, Pierre-André Sigal categorises 241 miracles (almost nine percent of his total) as cures of 'les affections mentales', seventy percent of which were caused by demons.[66] Notably, sixty-two percent of those who suffered from madness – demonic or otherwise – were men, suggesting that the predominance of female demoniacs that has been found in later texts may not have been echoed in twelfth-century hagiographies.[67]

Table 4.2 shows the genders of the demoniacs in the miracle collections of all five cults studied in this book. Male demoniacs were twice as numerous as female demoniacs. Except for the *Life and Miracles of William of Norwich*, none of the miracle collections, when taken individually, reveals a great deal of discrepancy in the numbers of male and female demoniacs. Notably, whilst Thomas of Monmouth, who compiled the majority of the *Life and Miracles* in the 1150s, recorded more cases of men who were possessed by demons, he showed women to be subject to demonic attacks in other ways. For example, a virgin was protected from a demonic *incubus* by William of Norwich.[68] This virgin was not possessed by a demon and did not go mad, so her case is not included in the statistics in Table 4.2.

In the *Liber fundationis*, of those cure-seekers whose madness was associated with demons, two were female and two were male. In the wider sample of demonic illnesses in the *Liber fundationis*, four of those afflicted were male, and only three were female, one of whom was a child. C.E. and F.E. Forcén have observed too that, in the miracles of Saint Francis of Assisi, compiled in the thirteenth century, there was no predominance of female demoniacs over male demoniacs.[69] Certainly in the *Liber fundationis* and, conceivably, more widely in hagiography of this period, men were portrayed as vulnerable to demons and were just as vulnerable as women, if not

Table 4.2 Gender of demoniacs in English miracle texts from the long twelfth century.

	Gender of demoniacs	
Miracle text	*Male*	*Female*
Miracles of Saint Edmund, Herman (c.1070s–c.1090s)	2	0
Revised *Miracles of Saint Edmund* (c.1100)	2	0
The Life and Miracles of William of Norwich, Thomas of Monmouth (c.1154–55 and c.1173)	4	1
Miracles of Saint Thomas of Canterbury, Benedict of Peterborough (1170–74)	1	1
Miracles of Saint Thomas of Canterbury, William of Canterbury (c.1172–c.1177)	4	5
The Book of the Foundation of the Church of Saint Bartholomew of London (c.1174–c.1189)	2	2
The Great Life of Saint Hugh of Lincoln, Adam of Eynsham (c.1200s)	1	0
The Life of Saint Hugh, Gerald of Wales (c.1213)	0	0
The Metrical Life of Saint Hugh of Lincoln (c.1220)	2	0
Total	**18**	**9**

more so. It is worth noting that three of those driven mad by demons in the *Liber fundationis* were young (two young, unmarried women and one young man)[70]. There is perhaps a connection here between the physical beauty associated with youth and the sexual nature of the demonic attacks on these individuals.[71] Ralph, the only mature adult demoniac, was also the only sufferer whose demonic possession had no sexual connotations.

The priest's daughter, who was struck by a demon, was of illegitimate birth; her conception had resulted from the sins of her father, who had given in to lustful pleasure ('lubrico voluptati'). Yet she was able to escape the vices of people her age through the guidance of a matron in whose care her father placed her and who was able to 'establish a manly mind in the woman's heart'.[72] The girl was then able to resist sexual desire in a way uncommon among women and, for this reason, was masculinised by the compiler. She developed the combined qualities of beauty and chastity, which were begrudged by the devil, who set about to deceive and tempt her in the form of a demonic suitor.[73] The suitor would certainly have been attractive to many young women, being 'a most beautiful youth and conspicuous as a noble of royal blood'.[74] Throughout the maiden's repeated attempts to resist her suitor, numerous allusions were made to the Fall and to women's weakness in resisting sexual desire. The suitor was not all he seemed and was, in fact, a serpent ('coluber') in disguise, who was 'the enemy of female weakness'.[75] During a lengthy dialogue with the demon, the maiden contested, and eventually resisted, this 'evil pleasure' ('malignae voluptati').[76] She was able to maintain her reason throughout this exchange – even questioning the reason of a potential suitor who would approach her before having obtained the permission of her family to marry her – but her mind was afflicted when the demon physically struck her, angered by her skill in resisting him even when he had tried to force himself upon her.[77]

Another woman, from London, was not able to resist the temptations of the flesh so easily. This handmaid 'willingly' ('sponte') consented to the 'pleasure of unclean sin' ('voluptatem sordidi criminis') that lost her her chastity.[78] Far from being the passive victim of sexual advances and unwanted desires, the young woman was active in giving in to the devil. The twelfth century saw the increased circulation of philosophical and medical ideas that associated the female body with sexual pleasure and complicity and thus gave rise to considerations of female sexual desire.[79] Galen (second century AD) had suggested that both male and female sexual pleasure were necessary for conception, and this theory permeated twelfth-century debates.[80] William of Conches, a French philosopher writing in the first half of the twelfth century, explained that, in order to become pregnant, a woman had to release her 'seed', which, like male semen, was ejaculated in response to sexual pleasure.[81] Law codes and legal records reveal a growing concern with the state of the female body as evidence for whether or not a rape had occurred.[82] Using William of Conches's reasoning, it could be argued that a rape victim who had fallen pregnant may well have resisted her attacker mentally but must have given in to irresistible physical pleasure. Female 'consent' to rape was a physical capitulation of the natural will (of the body), whereas the rational will (of the soul) could remain resistant.[83] The handmaid's miracle was, therefore, recorded at a time when philosophers, physicians and jurists were paying greater attention to understanding the physicality of the female body and its relationship to the mind.[84]

The London handmaid's sin was strongly related to her physical body; she 'prostituted her flesh', and her 'limbs were the weapons of sin'.[85] The handmaid's willing consent to physical pleasure is notable. In a punishment reminiscent of Nebuchadnezzar's, the Babylonian king who was sent mad for dwelling on worldly affairs (Daniel 4), the handmaid lost her mind because she had given in to sin and had failed to stand in awe of God, and thus she was denied comprehension of Him.[86] Despite her increased susceptibility, as a woman, to sexual sin, lack of resistance was a sin nonetheless; it simultaneously left her open to demonic attack and disconnected her from God. Moral transgression could manifest itself physically and mentally: hence the handmaid became a physical and mental cripple.[87] Nonetheless, the case of the priest's daughter illustrates that demons could also attack innocent victims, and demonic possession was not always indicative of personal immorality, though we must remember that, in this case, the victim's father had sinned.

Dyan Elliott has suggested that, whilst women could be complicit in sexual fantasy, men were thought more likely, in the twelfth and thirteenth centuries, to be the passive recipients of intrusive or demonically-inspired sexual thoughts.[88] Such passivity was certainly true of Robert, who went out of his mind upon seeing an 'unsolicited vision' of the devil in the form of a beautiful woman.[89] Notably, Robert was asleep when he received his vision, whereas the two women in the *Liber fundationis* who encountered demons were awake. Robert's condition was perhaps associated with the sexual *incubus*: a demon that visited unsuspecting victims in their sleep. Although the term *incubus* was not used in the *Liber fundationis*, the same concept could be referred to by various terms, and it is feasible that the compiler had tales of nocturnal demonic attacks and of human/demonic procreation in mind when recording the miracle, since both were the subject of renewed theological debate in the twelfth century.[90] In a similar way to Rahere himself, Robert's mind was susceptible to unwanted demonic attack whilst asleep. Sleep had altered Robert's sensual perception, which perhaps made him vulnerable to trickery and illusion: 'As he lay, sleep crept over him: it took the sense from the mind'.[91] The miracle account is strikingly reminiscent of Saint Antony's night-time struggle with a devil in 'the attractive form of a beautiful woman'. The Desert Father, who died in the fourth century and is renowned as one of the earliest Christian ascetics, was tormented with visions by this devil, which sought 'to call him back from his proper intention', the pursuit of Christian virtue.[92] Antony's virtue was proven by his refusal to give in to demonic temptation. Weaker men, like Robert, were not capable of such virtuous resistance. Bartholomew's healing of Robert was an obvious attestation of the saint's virtue, though his sanctity was hardly in doubt, given his apostolic status. Instead, the compiler may have been using this miracle story to confirm Bartholomew's patronage of the priory church or to remind the audience of Rahere's own dream-vision, thus attesting to the founder's virtue.

On the boundaries of society

The highly-influential hagiographical account of Saint Antony's battles with demons, written by the fourth-century bishop of Alexandria, Athanasius, was itself based on Christ's temptation in the wilderness (Matthew 4:1–11) and set further precedents for the ways in which demons were believed to interact with mortals. Antony fought his demons in the desert, and it was, in fact, common for demonic attacks to occur on the boundaries of society, perhaps as places where lone individuals were more vulnerable.[93] The youth Robert and the knight Ralph were both possessed in the woods on their way to London. Sleeping alone in these remote locations was (and still is) particularly dangerous, and Robert was not the only traveller to be afflicted in this way. In his *Life and Miracles*, recorded in the mid-1150s, William of Norwich was credited with miraculously healing a youth who had slept outside and had by so doing allowed a snake to take up residence in his intestines.[94] Plus, of course, Rahere himself had been travelling when he experienced his vision.

The priest's daughter was also alone when she was attacked by her demonic suitor, but she had not crossed a physical boundary; she was in her own room. For women, boundaries could be much more restrictive. Women who moved beyond the boundary of the domestic sphere were seemingly understood to be more susceptible to demonic attack.[95] The priest's daughter had relinquished domestic duties in pursuit of spiritual purity, whereas, at the other end of the spectrum, the London handmaid had flouted the social restriction of intercourse to within the domestic sphere of marriage. The priest's daughter herself represented a broken social boundary in that her conception came about from the unlawful intercourse of a priest who should have been bound to chastity.[96] The First Lateran Council of 1123 had decreed that clerical marriages were invalid, and this decree had been reiterated at the Second Lateran Council in 1139.[97]

Boundaries were also an important consideration when negotiating how a demon had been able to enter the body, which, in itself, presented a physical boundary. Both Robert and the London handmaid were internally possessed by demons, as opposed to the priest's daughter, who received an external blow.[98] The devil placed a small bird inside Robert's mouth, by which we are led to believe it entered his body, causing his madness.[99] The mouth was commonly understood to be a point of entry and exit for demons, as evidenced by manuscript illuminations depicting exorcised demons exiting from the mouths of their victims.[100] For example, a miniature from an eleventh-century French manuscript of the life of Saint Radegunda (a sixth-century Frankish queen who founded the Abbey of the Holy Cross in Poitiers) depicts the saint expelling a demon from a possessed woman; the demon's foot is still inside the woman's mouth, from which it is exiting her body.[101] In such cases, the demon was a physical entity; it occupied a physical space and required a physical opening to enter the body.[102]

Where, then, did demons go once they had entered inside the body? According to Augustine, whose writings on the subject were well known in the twelfth century (hence the incorrect attribution of similar works, like Alcher of Clairvaux's *On Spirit and Soul*, to him), demons were able to penetrate the body and mingle with the thoughts via visions of the imagination.[103] As discussed, from the thirteenth century, the physicality of demonic possession was associated primarily with the bowels and the reproductive organs, whereas divine spirits interacted with the heart and the soul.[104] Nonetheless, there is also evidence in the hagiographic tradition of demons occupying the hearts of their victims.[105] In Alcher of Clairvaux's pseudo-Augustinian *On Spirit and Soul*, the spirit ('spiritus'), which coordinated cognition, originated in the heart and could be deceived by a demonic spirit.[106] In the *Liber fundationis*, the handmaid's miracle clearly demonstrates the author's belief in the primacy of the heart, as the seat of the soul, as well as a demon's ability to dwell there: 'The heart, which is the principal of man, was darkened by the oppression of the demon on account of their uniting.'[107] Nevertheless, twelfth-century miracle records did not universally advocate the primacy of the heart. In the *Life and Miracles of William of Norwich*, compiled in the mid-twelfth century, a healed demoniac felt the benefit of his cure in his brain (*cerebrum*).[108] In this case, the location of demonic activity in the brain was perhaps indicative of the association between demonic possession and madness, or a loss of reason, reason being controlled by the brain's rational faculty.

The demoniac and the saint

The body, mind and soul were intrinsically connected, and it was, therefore, 'natural that the body follows the soul when it is disturbed, and also that the soul follows the body in its accidents.'[109] Demonic possession indicated either that the sufferer had given in to sin through temptation, making their soul vulnerable to demons, or that they had been an innocent victim of demonic intrusion in the heart or brain. Demons were often shown to occupy a physical place in the body and to have an effect on the rational capabilities of the mind. Demonic possession was associated with madness more than with any other condition, including epilepsy, which was, instead, explained in non-demonic terms. Like madness, demonic possession had physical symptoms that affected the body. Because of the similarity between non-demonic madness and demonic possession, demonic possession was best diagnosed by observation and by talking with the victim. The cause of demonic possession could be hypothesised based on the perceived morality of the victim. Notably, however, the saint could act as both a moral guide for the misled and as a protector of the innocent.

The primary function of the *Liber fundationis* was not to offer moral guidance to its readers – though the author was clearly willing to endorse carefully-constructed moral messages – nor was it to provide a spiritual compass for the discernment of spirits. Instead, it was written as a record and justification of the founding of the church and hospital and as an attestation to Bartholomew's influence as patron. The apostle's battles with demons confirmed his ability to protect those under his patronage from demonic attack. This patronage extended to the pilgrims who sought his intercession, though significantly, in the case of the priest's daughter, the apostle acted in response to prayers from the Augustinian canons of his church.[110]

The ability to exorcise demons was an attested indicator of holiness. The Bible contains multiple affirmations of Christ's ability to perform exorcisms. When a group of Jews tried to imitate Christ, their mock exorcism did not work, and the Jews were attacked by the possessed man they had been attempting to cleanse (Acts 19:13). Importantly, in the *Liber fundationis*, the power of exorcism did not lie with Bartholomew himself (the possession of such a power could lead to pride) but was exercised through God.[111] Hence demoniacs were delivered 'by the merits of the apostle' or through 'the mercy of the most blessed apostle' but never *by the apostle*.[112] After Robert was cured of madness, he blessed God for bestowing on his apostles 'the power of healing the sick, cleansing lepers, [and] expelling demons'.[113] In this acknowledgement, the compiler of the *Liber fundationis* reinforced the cosmological hierarchy; demons could possess men, saints could exorcise demons, but only God could bestow the power of exorcism.[114]

Thus, Robert's cure, along with those of the other demoniacs, was a mark of divine favour for the community of Saint Bartholomew's church.

Within the cosmological hierarchy, the demon represented an important antithesis to the saint, which was illustrated in the *Liber fundationis* in the contrasting physicality of the terrifying beast-devil of Rahere's dream-vision and the majestic Bartholomew. Barbara Newman has suggested that demoniacs themselves also presented a 'dark mirror' to the saints 'not by aping their spirituality, but by doubling some of their distinctive social roles'.[115] The relationship between demoniac and saint is particularly complex, in this regard, in the *Liber fundationis* because the text follows two saint-like figures. Saint Bartholomew acted as the patron of the church and hospital, and it was through his intercession that miracles were performed. However, a spiritual journey was made by Rahere. Spiritual journeys were undertaken by the protagonists of the majority of saints' lives, and here again Saint Antony provides a recognisable parallel in his physical and spiritual journey into the desert. It was Rahere, then, and not Bartholomew, who metaphorically gazed into the 'dark mirror' in which the demoniacs were reflected.

Like the priest's daughter, Rahere had taken steps to improve himself spiritually, and like her, he had had to battle demons. Like Robert and Ralph, he was alienated from society by madness. However, Rahere's feigned madness was part of his spiritual journey, whereas Robert's and Ralph's demonic madness represented spiritual estrangement. Whereas Rahere was able to attract assistance through his foolishness (despite his personal disgust at it), Robert and Ralph remained distant, in the woods and hills. Rahere acted under Bartholomew's guidance while Robert and Ralph were led astray by demons. These demoniacs served as reminders of Rahere's sacrifice and to reinforce Bartholomew's reputation for divine intercession. Their presence at Saint Bartholomew's church, therefore, should be considered in terms of their relationship with the saint and their participation in the ritual of miraculous healing.

Demoniacs at the shrine

Violence and restraint

Loss of reason, as well as the social stigma of demonic possession, isolated demoniacs from their communities. Nonetheless, all four demoniacs in the *Liber fundationis* participated in the communal rituals that were required for them to receive a miraculous cure from Saint Bartholomew. There was, therefore, a social element to the interpretation of demonic possession, which needs to be examined alongside the physical, mental and spiritual experiences of demoniacs. For Robert, Ralph, the handmaid and the mad boy who was not a demoniac, the necessity for cure was decided for them, and the process was carried out without their input and, in some cases, without their cooperation. The nature of the source material does not allow us to identify whether these demoniacs thought of themselves as demonically possessed, though, presumably, Robert must have related his vision, if it was not entirely fabricated by the compiler. The communities of these individuals had identified their behaviour as deviant and judged that saintly intervention would provide the appropriate cure (because, of course, this behaviour required rectifying). The priest's daughter – the only demoniac to explicitly self-identify as such – requested that she be brought to Saint Bartholomew's church, most likely as a place where a spiritual cure could be provided for what she understood to be a spiritual condition.

Fury and violence were common symptoms of three of the demoniacs (the priest's daughter was not violent towards herself or others). Robert was driven by the impulse of 'malign fury' ('maligni furoris'), and Ralph assaulted with stones those who were unfortunate enough to cross his path.[116] Not surprisingly, people became afraid to approach him. The mad handmaid was bound but, because of her raging ('furentis'), was easily able to break her bonds, and more were added.[117] The fury of these demoniacs was yet another indication of the devil's influence over their bodies and minds. In Romanesque iconography of the twelfth century, the devil was often connected with anger and fury, which was made evident in grotesque images of the devil, demons and demoniacs, with mouths grimacing and eyes wide and staring, decorating the walls and ceilings of churches.[118] The devil's fury was the antithesis of Christ's just patience, which members of religious communities, like that of Saint Bartholomew's priory, were expected to emulate.[119] Anger without a just cause (God's wrath, for example, was just) was linguistically connected with madness or a lack of rationality; the term *furor* could refer to anger or to madness, and it was used in this context by other English miracle compilers.[120] Thomas of Monmouth (writing in Norwich in the 1150s) described the *furia* of a woman called Gilliva, who rolled around on the floor and tore at her cheeks in pain.[121] William of Canterbury (writing in Canterbury in the 1170s) used the term *furia* to describe the violent madness of a youth called Geoffrey, who, after being struck by lightning, raged with teeth and nails.[122] A glossary of the late tenth century equated *furia* with *insania* and *amentia*, and another from the eleventh century glossed *furiis* as *malignis spiritibus*.[123] The violent anger of the mad or the possessed was therefore a recognised part of their madness or possession.

In this light, the binding of the mad did not indicate their social isolation but was instead demonstrative of the community's efforts to reintegrate them. In miracle narratives, violent demoniacs needed to be bound so that they could be brought to churches and shrines to be cured. Robert was 'captured' ('captus') and brought to Saint Bartholomew's church, where he recovered.[124] Ralph was similarly 'led' ('producitur'), despite his resistance, to the church.[125] The handmaid was carried ('deportati'), in her bonds, to the hospital.[126] The priest's daughter, perhaps because of her lack of resistance, was borne more sedately on a litter.[127] Similarly, Thomas of Monmouth, writing in the mid-1150s, used the passive form of *adducere* (to lead) to describe several mad people who were 'led' to the tomb of William of Norwich in the hope of a miraculous cure.[128] The use of passive verbs to describe these demoniacs' journeys to shrines is indicative of the fact that both demonic possession itself, and the process of cure, were beyond a sufferer's direct control.[129]

Katajala-Peltomaa has suggested that blame was sought for the social deviancy of demoniacs outside of the deviant himself or herself because of the social stigma associated with their behaviour.[130] Writing in the thirteenth century, the Italian theologian Thomas Aquinas argued that a person could be plagued by the illusions of demons for multiple reasons; sometimes personal sin was to blame, but, on other occasions, the malice of demons alone was responsible, and the victim could easily be a faultless Christian.[131] Both Robert and Ralph were possessed whilst making hazardous journeys through woods. There was no explicit moral judgement of their behaviour; they were the victims of their own circumstances. The priest's daughter was the victim of demonic malice; her chastity was begrudged by the enemy of mankind.[132] Even so, details of her father's fornication were no doubt included in the account to throw her chastity into relief and, in this way, intimate a connection between demonic attack and sin. The handmaid's miracle is the only case of demonic possession in the *Liber fundationis* in which there is evidence of the victim's own immorality (and hence some degree of individual blame). The handmaid's sexual fornication was contrasted with the honest labour of her domestic service work.[133] Nonetheless, she was treated in a similar way to both Robert and Ralph.

As shown in the handmaid's miracle, the spiritual implications of demonic possession could have negative connotations for the perceived moral state of a victim. The connection between demonic possession and sin had a long-standing precedent. Written in Bury one hundred years before the *Liber fundationis*, the *De Miraculis Sancti Eadmundi* recorded the case of a sheriff called Leofstan, whose ignominious demonic possession, which continued even after death, was a fitting divine punishment for his immoral transgression against Saint Edmund's sanctuary and highlighted his estrangement from God.[134] Nonetheless, prior to the thirteenth century, when false preachers were increasingly identified as taking their lead from demons, demonic possession was more often suffered by innocent victims than by mortal sinners.[135] The biblical example of the Gerasene demoniac shows a man tormented by demons: a victim (Mark 5:1–20). In miracles recorded in the later Middle Ages, victims tended to be deluded or seduced by demons and then go mad (as a sign of their alienation from God) rather than be possessed by demons as a punishment for sins already committed without demonic influence.[136] The handmaid's madness and subsequent contraction of the limbs resulted from the 'oppression of the demon', which had caused her to sin.[137] Arguably, the demons of twelfth-century London had a more sinister influence than those of tenth- and eleventh-century Bury; whilst Saint Edmund had wielded his authority against the very tangible threat of secular power, Saint Bartholomew was faced with victims of subtle demonic trickery, illusion and deception.

Spiritual battles: saint versus demon

In Rahere's dream-vision, the contrast of saint and demon is depicted very clearly, with Bartholomew acting as Rahere's protector and guide. The tradition of demonic challenges to saintly authority stretched all the way to the eastern Byzantine Empire.[138] The resulting battles were developed in the West in thirteenth-century didactic and spiritual texts, which represented verbal duels between a saint or cleric and a demon.[139] Earlier examples of these duels can be seen in the hagiographic literature of the Early and Central Middle Ages, of which the *Liber fundationis* is a notable example that highlights the ongoing battle between saints and demons in a more prominent way than the miracle texts of my other four case studies.

The priest's daughter's miracle contains two spiritual battles, both of which report direct speech. In the first, the young woman was able to rebuff the advances of her demonic suitor by reasoning with him. The ensuing dialogue has an obvious didactic/moral message, with the maiden informing the demon that courtship without the permission of her family and the Church and sexual intercourse for any reason other than to beget children were both unacceptable. The demon then criticised her recourse to reason, arguing that reason was not applicable in an act of pleasure (the verbal duel itself was an act of pleasure for him). He also challenged her piety, condemning it as superstition ('supersticio').[140] The maiden responded with prayers and, unable to overcome her spiritually, the demon sought to overcome her physically, once again failing and then delivering the blow that sent her mad.

Witnessing her madness, the maiden's parents requested that she be brought to Saint Bartholomew's church. Presumably afraid of being overpowered by the saint, the demon engaged in his second spiritual battle with the maiden and tried to convince her not to enter the church. He began by threatening her with increased pain, but, when she ignored him, he moved to promising her health (*sanitas*).[141] His threats and promises were ignored, and the maiden was restored fully to health ('integre sanitati') by the virtue of Saint Bartholomew, in contrast to the false health promised by the demon.[142] It should be noted, however, that Bartholomew did not engage in battle directly with the demon; physical, verbal and spiritual battles were fought by the maiden herself, though they would certainly have been lost without the apostle's assistance.

Exorcism, as shown above, was a power possessed by saints but exercised through God. Physicians were unable to exorcise demons, so recourse to a holy figure, whether it be a priest or a saint, was necessary for any demoniac requiring a cure. Late medieval physicians, taking their lead from Avicenna, whose *Canon of Medicine* had become a standard medical authority by the fourteenth century, advised practitioners not to concern themselves with demons, except to treat their humoral effects.[143] A divine force was needed to expel the demon itself.[144] For Christian thinkers, the New Testament provided an influential archetype of demonic possession and exorcism.[145] The majority of the exorcisms performed by Christ and his disciples were executed fairly easily, with the exorcist simply ordering the demon to leave. One exception was the case of a deaf and dumb boy who could not be exorcised by the commands of the disciples alone but was exorcised by Christ, who then explained that prayer and fasting had been necessary to expel the 'deaf and dumb spirit' (Mark 9:14–29).[146] Saint Bartholomew's exorcisms seem to have been accomplished with similar ease, though, notably, because they were performed posthumously, Bartholomew was not seen to issue the demons with a command or to converse with them in any way. Robert was cured shortly ('brevi') after arriving at the church.[147] The priest's daughter was cured instantly, Ralph's cure took two days (though whether this included the time he waited for the apostle to answer his prayers is not specified) and the handmaid's cure-time was not stated. All of the exorcisms performed by Saint Bartholomew were, in fact, strikingly similar to the cures he performed for physical ailments and followed a pattern for recording healing miracles that was becoming standard in this period: a sick person was recognised as requiring a cure; the sick person came/was brought to a shrine; some form of ritual contact was made with the saint (often, mad people were bound near to the tomb); the miraculous cure was witnessed and then recorded.[148]

In canonisation records of the thirteenth century onwards, two forms of proof were necessary to confirm that an exorcism had taken place: first, the sufferer was restored from an unstable state of mind to a stable one; and second, there was some indication that the demon had been removed (crying, vomiting, etc.).[149] All the demoniacs in the *Liber fundationis* were returned to a state of sanity: Robert was described as recovering his understanding ('recuperato sensi'), and Ralph's sanity was brought about ('mentis compos efficitur').[150] Bartholomew restored the priest's daughter fully to health ('integre sanitati restituit') and delivered ('absolvit') the handmaid from her madness.[151] However, it was only the priest's daughter who the apostle specifically freed from her demon ('a demonio liberavit') – though he was also credited with casting out demons, among other things, after curing Robert – and even she did not display any physical signs of exorcism, perhaps because she had not been internally possessed.[152]

Following their cures, demoniacs could be reintegrated into society. Brown has argued that, in medieval exorcisms, it was the demon itself that remained separate from human society and that the act of possession and then exorcism was used to reinforce the humanity of the sufferer.[153] The compiler of the *Liber fundationis* specifically contrasted the actions of each individual whilst under the influence of demons with their actions post-exorcism. Robert, who had been captured in order to be brought to the church, chose to stay there for some time after his recovery; from being a passive receptacle for the ritual of miraculous cure, he had become an active participant in church life.[154] The priest's daughter was returned to the care of her parents, who had previously seen fit to commit her to Saint Bartholomew's holy care.[155] The handmaid, who had, prior to her cure, been residing in Saint Bartholomew's hospital, was able to return home.[156] Similarly, those who were cured of physical ailments gained renewed social status. For example, a woman who had become paralysed as a result of palsy was able to take a husband and become a mother of sons after her cure.[157] In this respect, the *Liber fundationis* is representative of twelfth-century English miracle texts; the compiler recorded miraculous exorcisms as he would any other miraculous cure, rather than focusing on the expulsion of the demon itself, as was the case in many of the exorcisms of the New Testament.

Conclusion

Demons were the predominant cause of madness, or a loss of reason, in the *Liber fundationis*. The compiler used the spiritual battle between saint or holy man and demon as a means of illustrating Rahere's path to salvation and to the foundation of Saint Bartholomew's priory and hospital. The demoniacs cured by Saint Bartholomew made evident the apostle's role in restoring spiritual balance. Community reactions to demoniacs and the often forcible taking of the possessed to receive divine cures are indicative of communal associations between dysfunctional behaviour and spiritual unrest, whether this unrest was the moral fault of the sufferer or not. Similar associations are evident in the miracle texts across all five case studies, from the miracles of Saint Edmund, compiled in Bury at the turn of the eleventh century, to the thirteenth-century cult of Saint Hugh of Lincoln, which is the subject of Chapter 5.

Demons and demonic possession affected sufferers physically and mentally, and Saint Bartholomew was capable of healing various ailments regardless of their aetiologies. Certainly, as we have already seen, the arrival of new medical ideas in twelfth-century England did not mean that demonic aetiologies were rejected in favour of a naturalistic approach to illness. Indeed, demons were not necessarily seen to operate outside of nature but rather to manipulate elements of the natural world. In the *Liber fundationis*, and likewise across all five twelfth-century cults, miracle compilers used an amalgamation of terminology, including that associated with demonic possession, to denote a loss of reason, which required the restoration of the minds of those affected. It is tempting, and perhaps even accurate, to argue that demonic possession was equivalent to madness in many miracle accounts. Nonetheless, some miracle compilers noted subtle differences between demonic and non-demonic madness. These differences could most often be discerned by speaking with the victim after his or her cure. He or she may have seen a vision of the demon or have had his or her own interpretation of how immorality had left him or her open to demonic attack. Observers and miracle compilers could also make their own diagnoses of demoniacs, who could be identified by signs that hinted at the influence of the demon over their behaviour: blaspheming, new abilities (such as the gift of tongues) and unusual strength. Furthermore, demons were not only implicated in cases of possession; they could also cause physical illnesses or drive a victim mad through external attacks without possessing them. Therefore, whilst it is important to consider demonic possession as a facet of medieval madness, it is also important to look at demoniacs within the context of individual miracle collections and the miracle compilers' portrayals of demonic activity.

The association between demonic possession and the heart in the *Liber fundationis* locates the heart as the seat of the mind and connects the mind with the rational faculties of the incorporeal soul. Nonetheless, as the one case of epilepsy demonstrates, the compiler also made an association between the brain, vital function and sensation. Here, we can see the influence of Galenic texts, which connected the brain with sensation and control of the body. The location of rationality in either the heart or the brain had an impact on the perceived implications of mental impairment. The heart (*cor*) was spiritually vulnerable and could be darkened by demonic temptation and immorality. The brain (*cerebrum*), by contrast, controlled sensation and could be obstructed by physical compression. The mind (*mens*) was not given a specific physical location in the body. Disorders of the mind were connected with loss of reason, which resulted in abnormal behaviour. Healings of the mind brought about the restoration of sanity and health and delivered the healed person from madness.

It is perhaps surprising to see that both mad men and mad women were represented fairly consistently in all of the miracle collections examined. Women seem to have been no more susceptible to demonic possession or madness than men, and mad women often received similar treatment to their male counterparts. Consistency in the treatment of sufferers implies that, whilst a loss of reason could be caused by various factors, different terms for madness (raving madness, demonic possession, insanity) were comparable and even, together, formed a distinct condition. Whereas physical ailments could be recognised because they made sufferers look different, madness was characterised by the way it made sufferers behave. The cessation of this behaviour indicated that a miraculous cure had taken place.

Notes

1. Vespasian B.IX, II.9, fol. 29^{r} ['Dormienti quippe antiquus hostis in speciem mulieris pulcherrimi transformatus apparvit, qui quare blandiens caput eius visus est assidere. Cumque pestiferis cum blanditiis aliquodiu delinisset aviculam in os eium posuit, et sic non comparvit. Excitus, insolitae visioni terretur, et eadem hora mente captus, omni racionis vigore privatur, et quid faciendum quid ne demittendum sit ignorans, insania ducta nunc hac nunc illac discurrendo vagatur, et nescius quid agat praeceps ruit quo eum maligni furoris impetus impellit'].

2. With the exception of the virgin from Dunwich (TM1, II.7, pp. 79–85), which is discussed below.
3. The idea of a 'naturalisation' of the miraculous is discussed in my Introduction. Historians (e.g. Yarrow and Koopmans) have argued that, with the growing influence of rediscovered ancient Greek natural philosophy and medicine in the twelfth century (see Bartlett, p. 31), miracle records increasingly attributed illness to natural causes (e.g. humoral imbalance) as opposed to the work of demons.
4. Boureau, p. 123. Historiographical arguments concerning the 'naturalisation' of madness in this period are discussed in more detail in my Introduction.
5. Koopmans, p. 134.
6. London, British Library, MS Cotton Vespasian B.IX.
7. The Middle English was edited by Norman Moore in 1886 and revised by M.M. Weale in 1923. There is no edition of the Latin for which I refer to the manuscript. An English translation of the Latin text was made for E.A. Webb by Humphrey H. King and William Bernard in 1923, and this has been consulted.
8. Whitteridge and Stokes, p. 10.
9. Moore, p. x.
10. Vespasian B.IX, I.1–7, fols 1^r–6^v.
11. *Cartulary of St Bartholomew's Hospital*, pp. 4–5; Ibid., pp. 175–77.
12. Page, pp. 520–25.
13. Ibid.; Whitteridge and Stokes, p. 12. Richard Clifford, Bishop of London, acknowledged the hospital's independence in 1420.
14. Waddington, p. 14.
15. Rawcliffe, p. 7.
16. Ibid., p. 2; Ibid., p. 11.
17. Ibid., p. 5.
18. Knowles, p. 175.
19. Vespasian B.IX, I.28, fols 17^v–18^r. For example, Adwyn, a crippled man, was supported in the hospital before his health was restored miraculously, not all at once, but bit by bit over time.
20. Clarke, pp. 143–51.
21. Ibid., p. 145.
22. Turner, p. 7, n. 21.
23. Huot, pp. 70–71.
24. Ibid., p. 69.
25. Vespasian B.IX, I.10, fol. 7^v.
26. Ibid.
27. Saunders, pp. 75–76.
28. Ivanov, p. 1.
29. Ibid., p. 380.
30. Vespasian B.IX, I.5, fol. 3^v ['fantastica illusione que hominibus in sompnis frequentius accidere solet'].
31. Ibid., fols 4^r–4^v.
32. Ibid., I.4, fol. 2^v.
33. Ibid., I.6, fols 4^v–5^r ['quatuor animi passiones figurantur: scilicet timor et tristitia, amor et laetitia'].
34. Ibid., fol. 5^r ['que quietem mentis omnino dissipant'].
35. Ibid.
36. Ibid.
37. Ibid., I.4, fols 2^v–3^r.
38. Ibid., fol. 3^r ['regiam maiestatem', 'imperialis auctoritatis', 'miri pulcritudinis'].
39. Ibid., fols 3^r–3^v.
40. Caciola, p. 180.

41. Ibid., pp. 179–94.
42. Ibid., p. 197.
43. Ibid., p. 56.
44. Alcher of Clairvaux, 28, p. 224.
45. Vespasian B.IX, II.1, fols 21^{r}–22^{r}; Ibid., II.2, fol. 22^{r}; Ibid., II.15, fol. 33^{r}.
46. Kelly, p. 70.
47. Vespasian B.IX, II.11, fol. 29^{v} ['Est autem epilepsia ut phisici tradunt morbus qui cerebri ventriculos compremens et animales actiones praecludit, visum, auditum, et ceteros corporis sensus tollit, ipsum que corpus dira passione fatigare consuevit'].
48. WC, II.6, p. 162. Discussed in Chapter 3.
49. Demaitre, p. 129.
50. Ibid., p. 149.
51. Vespasian B.IX, II.5, fol. 25^{v}.
52. 'The Report of the Paris Medical Faculty, October 1348'.
53. Vespasian B.IX, II.20, fol. 37^{v}.
54. Ibid., II.24, fols 38^{r}–38^{v}.
55. Ibid., II.9, fols 28^{v}–29^{r}.
56. Ibid.
57. Ibid., II.10, fols 29^{r}–29^{v}.
58. Ibid., II.18, fol. 37^{r}.
59. Ibid., II.12, fol. 32^{r} ['inordinato gestu membrorum'].
60. Ibid., fols 31^{v}–32^{r}.
61. Katajala-Peltomaa, p. 109.
62. Caciola, p. 40.
63. Ibid., p. 41.
64. Ibid, p. 40; Elliott, p. 53; Katajala-Peltomaa, p. 120.
65. Newman, p. 740.
66. Sigal, p. 236.
67. Ibid., p. 237.
68. TM1, II.7, p. 80. This miracle is discussed in more detail in Chapter 2.
69. Forcén, p. 267.
70. The priest's daughter was a 'girl' (*puella*) and a 'virgin' (*virgo*); the handmaid was a 'youth' (*adulescentia*), as was Robert (*juvenis*).
71. The relationship between youth, physical beauty, fertility and sexuality is explored in Mazo Karras, p. 153.
72. Vespasian B.IX, II.12, fol. 30^{r} ['vitis etatem'; 'in femineo pectore virilem animum constituat'].
73. Ibid., fol. 30^{v}.
74. Ibid. ['juvenis pulcherrimi et tanquam regii sanguinis generositate conspiciens'].
75. Ibid. ['hostis feminae levitatis'].
76. Ibid., fol. 31^{r}.
77. Ibid., fols 31^{r}–32^{r}.
78. Ibid., II.18, fols 36^{v}–37^{r}.
79. Elliott, pp. 37–40.
80. Kümper, pp. 102–4.
81. William of Conches, VI.8, pp. 206–7.
82. Kümper, p. 88.
83. Ibid., p. 103.
84. Ibid., pp. 104–5.
85. Vespasian B.IX, II.18, fol. 37^{r} ['carnes prostituit', 'membra que fuerunt arma iniquitatis'].
86. Ibid.

87. Katajala-Peltomaa, p. 122.
88. Elliott, p. 36.
89. Vespasian B.IX, II.9, fol. 29^{r} ['insolitae visioni'].
90. van der Lugt, pp. 178–79.
91. Vespasian B.IX, II.9, fols 28^{v}–29^{r} ['Sompnus eius iacenti surrepens: menti sensus eripuit'].
92. Evagrius of Antioch, 5, pp. 11–12.
93. Caciola, p. 50; Katajala-Peltomaa, p. 121.
94. TM1, V.3, p. 190.
95. Katajala-Peltomaa, pp. 119–122.
96. Vespasian B.IX, II.12, fol. 30^{r}.
97. *Decrees of the Ecumenical Councils*, I, 194 and 198.
98. Ralph was 'seized by a demon' ('a demonio arripitur'), which implies that his possession was internal, but it was not explicitly so.
99. Vespasian B.IX, II.9, fol. 29^{r}.
100. Caciola, p. 41.
101. Poitiers, BM, MS 250, fol. 34^{v}.
102. Katajala-Peltomaa, p. 115.
103. Augustine, col. 584.
104. Caciola, p. 200.
105. Ibid., p. 31.
106. Alcher of Clairvaux, 27, pp. 222–23; Caciola, pp. 189–94 for detail on these texts and their reception in the twelfth century; for a twelfth-century example, see MS Royal 5 A I, fols 21^{v}–22^{r}.
107. Vespasian B.IX, II.18, fol. 37^{r} ['Cor quod principale est hominis oppressione demonis sibi uniti ob tenebratur'].
108. TM1, VI.4, p. 224.
109. Ziegler, p. 6.
110. Vespasian B.IX, II.12, fol. 32^{v}.
111. Kuznetzova, p. 48.
112. Vespasian B.IX, II.12, fol. 32^{v}; Ibid., II.18, 37^{r}.
113. Ibid., II.9, fol. 29^{r} ['infirmos curandi, leprosos mundandi, demones eiciendi potestatem'].
114. Katajala-Peltomaa, p. 127.
115. Newman, pp. 737–38.
116. Vespasian B.IX, II.9; Ibid., II.10, fols 29^{r}–29^{v}.
117. Ibid., II.28, fol. 37^{r}.
118. Little, pp. 19–24 (for twelfth-century examples).
119. Ibid., p. 32.
120. Freedman, pp. 176–77.
121. TM1, VI.8, p. 229.
122. WC, V.38, p. 405.
123. Uszkalo, p. 9.
124. Vespasian B.IX, II.9, fol. 29^{r}.
125. Ibid., II.10, fol. 29^{v}.
126. Ibid., II.18, fol. 37^{r}.
127. Ibid., II.12, fol. 32^{r}.
128. TM1, IV.13, p. 182; Ibid., VI.4, pp. 223–24; Ibid., V.13, p. 204.
129. Newman p. 747 for the use of the passive tense in exorcism narratives.
130. Katajala-Peltomaa, p. 126.
131. Aquinas, Tertia Pars, Quaestio 80, Articulus 7, XII (1906), 237.
132. Vespasian B.IX, II.12, fol. 30^{v}.
133. Ibid., II.18, fol. 37^{r}.
134. Herman, 3, pp. 10–15.

135. Newman, p. 738. Discussed above in relation to the 'discernment of spirirts'.
136. Katajala-Peltomaa, pp. 122–23.
137. Vespasian B.IX, II.18, fol. 37^{r} ['oppressione demonis].
138. Kuznetzova, p. 46.
139. Newman, p. 734; Blumenfeld-Kosinski, p. 338.
140. Vespasian B.IX, II.12, fol. 31^{r}.
141. Ibid., fols 32^{r}–32^{v}.
142. Ibid., fol. 32^{v}.
143. Avicenna, 3.1.4.19, fol. 150^{r}; Rider, p. 55; Demaitre, p. 136.
144. Newman, p. 738.
145. Kemp and Williams, p. 23.
146. 'Surde et mute spiritus'.
147. Vespasian B.IX, II.9, fol. 29^{r}.
148. Model based on Yarrow, pp. 18–19.
149. Katajala-Peltomaa, p. 124.
150. Vespasian B.IX, II.9, fol. 29^{r}; Ibid., II.10, fol. 29^{v}.
151. Ibid., II.12, fol. 32^{v}; Ibid., II.18, fol. 37^{r}.
152. Ibid., II.12, fol. 32^{v}.
153. Brown, p. 111.
154. Vespasian B.IX, II.9, fol. 29^{v}.
155. Ibid., II.12, fols 32^{r}–32^{v}.
156. Ibid., II.18, fol. 37^{r}.
157. Ibid., II.19, fols 37^{r}–37^{v}.

Bibliography

Manuscripts

London, British Library, MS Cotton Vespasian B.IX
London, British Library, MS Royal 5 A I, fols 21^{v}–22^{r}
Poitiers, Bibliothèque municipale (BM), MS 250

Primary

Alcher of Clairvaux, 'Treatise on the Spirit and the Soul', trans. by Erasmo Leiva and Benedicta Ward, in *Three Treatises on Man: A Cistercian Anthropology*, ed. by Bernard McGinn Cistercian Fathers Series, 24 (Kalamazoo, MI: Cistercian Publications, 1977), pp. 179–288

Augustine, 'De Divinatione daemonum liber unus', in *Sancti Aurelii Augustini, Hipponensis Episcopi. Opera Omnia*, ed. by J.P. Migne, Patrologiae cursus completus, series latina, 32–47, 12 vols (Paris: Imprimerie Catholique, 1841–49), VI (1846), cols 581–92

Avicenna, *Liber canonis totius medicine* (Lyons: Jacques Myt, 1522)

The Book of the Foundation of the Church of St. Bartholomew, London: Rendered into Modern English, ed. by E.A. Webb, trans. by Humphrey H. King and William Barnard (London: Oxford University Press, 1923)

Cartulary of St Bartholomew's Hospital, ed. by Nellie J.M. Kerling (London: Lund Humphries, 1973)

Decrees of the Ecumenical Councils, ed. and trans. by Norman P. Tanner S.J., 2 vols (London: Sheed & Ward; Washington, DC: Georgetown University Press, 1990)

Evagrius of Antioch, 'Life of Antony by Athanasius', in *Early Christian Lives*, ed. and trans. by Carolinne White (London: Penguin, 1998), pp. 1–70

Herman the Archdeacon, 'Miracles of St Edmund', in *Herman the Archdeacon and Goscelin of Saint-Bertin. Miracles of St Edmund*, ed. and trans. by Tom Licence (Oxford: Oxford University Press, 2014), pp. 1–125

'The Report of the Paris Medical Faculty, October 1348', in *Medieval Medicine: A Reader*, ed. by Faith Wallis (Toronto, ON: University of Toronto Press, 2010), pp. 414–419

Thomas Aquinas, *Summa Theologiae*, ed. by Pope Leo XIII, 8 vols (Rome: Polyglotta S. C. de Propaganda Fide, 1888–1906)

Thomas of Monmouth, *The Life and Miracles of St William of Norwich*, ed. and trans. by Augustus Jessopp and M.R. James (Cambridge: Cambridge University Press, 1896)

William of Canterbury, 'Miracula Sancti Thomae Cantuariensis', in *Materials for the History of Thomas Becket, Archbishop of Canterbury*, ed. by James Craigie Robertson, 7 vols (London: Longman, 1875–1885), I (1875), 136–546

William of Conches, 'Dragmaticon Philosophiae', ed. by I. Ronca, in *Guillelmi de Conchis: Opera Omnia*, ed. by E. Jeauneau, 3 vols, Corpus Christianorum: Continuatio Mediaevalis, 152 (Turnholt: Brepols, 1997), I, 1–273

Secondary

Bartlett, Robert, *The Natural and the Supernatural in the Middle Ages* (Cambridge: Cambridge University Press, 2008)

Blumenfeld-Kosinski, Renate, 'The Strange Case of Ermine de Reims (c.1347–1396): A Medieval Woman between Demons and Saints', *Speculum*, 85 (2010), 321–356

Brown, Peter, *The Cult of the Saints: Its Rise and Function in Latin Christianity*, rev. edn (Chicago, IL: University of Chicago Press, 2015)

Caciola, Nancy, *Discerning Spirits: Divine and Demonic Possession in the Middle Ages* (Ithaca, NY and London: Cornell University Press, 2003)

Clarke, Basil, *Mental Disorder in Earlier Britain* (Cardiff: University of Wales Press, 1975)

Demaitre, Luke, *Medieval Medicine: The Art of Healing, from Head to Toe* (Santa Barbara, CA: Praeger, 2013)

Elliott, Dyan, *Fallen Bodies: Pollution, Sexuality, and Demonology in the Middle Ages* (Philadelphia: University of Pennsylvania Press, 1999)

Forcén, C.E. and F.E., 'Demonic Possessions and Mental Illness: Discussion of Selected Cases in Late Medieval Hagiographical Literature', *Early Science and Medicine*, 19 (2014), 258–279

Freedman, Paul, 'Peasant Anger in the Late Middle Ages', in *Anger's Past: The Social Uses of an Emotion in the Middle Ages*, ed. by Barbara H. Rosenwein (Ithaca, NY and London: Cornell University Press, 1998), pp. 171–188

Huot, Sylvia, *Madness in Medieval French Literature: Identities Found and Lost* (Oxford: Oxford University Press, 2003)

Ivanov, Sergey A., *Holy Fools in Byzantium and Beyond*, trans. by Simon Franklin (Oxford: Oxford University Press, 2006)

Katajala-Peltomaa, Sari, 'Demonic Possession as Physical and Mental Disturbance in the Later Medieval Canonization Processes', in *Mental (Dis)Order in Later Medieval Europe*, ed. by Sari Katajala-Peltomaa and Susanna Niiranen, Later Medieval Europe, 12 (Leiden: Brill, 2014), pp. 108–127

Kelly, Henry Ansgar, *The Devil, Demonology and Witchcraft: The Development of Christian Beliefs in Evil Spirits*, rev. edn (New York, NY: Doubleday, 1974)

Kemp, Simon, and Kevin Williams, 'Demonic Possession and Mental Disorder in Medieval and Early Modern Europe', *Psychological Medicine*, 17 (1987), 21–29

Knowles, David, *The Monastic Order: A History of Its Development from the Times of St Dunstan to the Fourth Lateran Council, 943–1216* (Cambridge: Cambridge University Press, 1950)

Koopmans, Rachel, *Wonderful to Relate: Miracle Stories and Miracle Collecting in High Medieval England* (Philadelphia: University of Pennsylvania Press, 2011)

Kümper, Hiram, 'Learned Men and Skilful Matrons: Medical Expertise and the Forensics of Rape', in *Medicine and the Law in the Middle Ages*, ed. by Wendy J. Turner and Sara Butler, Medieval Law and Its Practice, 17 (Leiden: Brill, 2014), pp. 88–108

Kuznetzova, Anna, '"A Wall of Bronze" or Demons versus Saints: Whose Victory?', in *Demons, Spirits, Witches*, ed. by Gábor Klaniczay and Eva Pócs, 3 vols (Budapest: Central European University, 2005–8), II: *Christian Demonology and Popular Mythology* (2006), pp. 45–53

Little, Lester K., 'Anger in Monastic Curses', in *Anger's Past: The Social Uses of an Emotion in the Middle Ages*, ed. by Barbara H. Rosenwein (Ithaca, NY and London: Cornell University Press, 1998), pp. 9–35

Mazo Karras, Ruth, *Sexuality in Medieval Europe: Doing unto Others* (New York, NY: Routledge, 2005)

Moore, Norman, 'The Book of the Foundation of St. Bartholomew's', in *The Book of the Foundation of St. Bartholomew's Church in London. Edited from the original manuscript in the British Museum, Cotton Vespasian B ix*, ed. by Norman Moore, rev. by M.M. Weale, Early English Text Society, 163 (London: Oxford University Press, 1923), pp. ix–xii

Newman, Barbara, 'Possessed by the Spirits: Devout Women, Demoniacs, and the Apostolic Life in the Thirteenth Century', *Speculum*, 73 (1998), 733–770

Page, William, ed., *A History of the County of London: London Within the Bars, Westminster and Southwark* (London: Constable, 1909)

Rawcliffe, Carole, 'The Hospitals of Later Medieval London', *Medical History*, 28 (1984), 1–21

Rider, Catherine, 'Demons and Mental Disorder in Late Medieval Medicine', in *Mental (Dis)Order in Later Medieval Europe*, ed. by Sari Katajala-Peltomaa and Susanna Nirranen, Later Medieval Europe, 12 (Leiden: Brill, 2014), pp. 47–69

Saunders, Corinne '"The thoghtful maladie": Madness and Vision in Medieval Writing', in *Madness and Creativity in Literature and Culture*, ed. by Corinne Saunders and Jane Macnaughton (Houndmills: Palgrave Macmillan, 2005), pp. 67–87

Sigal, Pierre-André, *L'homme et le miracle dans la France médiévale (XIe–XIIe siècle)* (Paris: Cerf, 1985)

Turner, Wendy J., 'Introduction', in *Madness in Medieval Law and Custom*, ed. by Wendy J. Turner, Later Medieval Europe, 6 (Leiden: Brill, 2010), pp. 1–16

Uszkalo, Kirsten C., 'Rage Possession: A Cognitive Science Approach to Early English Demon Possession', *Bodies of Knowledge: Cultural Interpretations of Illness and Medicine in Medieval Europe*, ed. by Sally Crawford and Christina Lee, Studies in Early Medicine, 1 (Oxford: British Archaeological Reports, 2010), pp. 5–17

van der Lugt, Maaike, 'The *Incubus* in Scholastic Debate: Medicine, Theology and Popular Belief', in *Religion and Medicine*, ed. by Peter Biller and Joseph Ziegler, York Studies in Medieval Theology, 3 (Woodbridge: York Medieval Press, 2001), pp. 175–200

Waddington, Keir, *Medical Education at St Bartholomew's Hospital, 1123–1995* (Woodbridge: Boydell, 2003)

Whitteridge, Gweneth, and Verona Stokes, *A Brief History of the Hospital of Saint Bartholomew* (London: Governors of the Hospital of Saint Bartholomew, 1961)

Yarrow, Simon, *Saints and Their Communities: Miracle Stories in Twelfth-Century England* (Oxford: Oxford University Press, 2006)

Ziegler, Joseph, 'Religion and Medicine in the Middle Ages', in *Religion and Medicine*, ed. by Peter Biller and Joseph Ziegler, York Studies in Medieval Theology, 3 (Woodbridge: York Medieval Press, 2001), pp. 3–14

5 Balance and health: restoring sanity in the miracles of Saint Hugh of Lincoln

> There was a raving ('furit')[1] sailor, who even with his hands and feet tied up would scarcely allow himself to be touched. The bishop [Hugh of Lincoln] gave his mind ('Attendat praesul') to stopping his madness ('furorem') and read the gospel of Saint John to him. The sailor made a twisted grimace and stuck his curving tongue out at the saint, seeming as it were to mock him. The holy father exorcised water, gave a blessing and commanded the delusions of the devil to disappear. After being asperged, the madman ('furens') felt no more traces of his madness ('furoris') and recovered the discernment of human reason ('humanae rationis acumen').[2]

This miracle was recorded in the *Metrical Life of Saint Hugh of Lincoln*, a poem composed in the 1220s to celebrate the canonisation of Hugh, bishop of Lincoln, who had died in 1200. The *Metrical Life*'s description of the mad sailor was adapted from Hugh's official canonisation report, which was drawn up in 1219–20, though the report made no mention of the 'delusions of the devil'.[3] The miracle was also recorded in an earlier *vita* of Saint Hugh, written in the first decade of the thirteenth century, shortly after the bishop's death, by Adam of Eynsham, who had served as his chaplain. In Adam's account, the mad sailor was 'possessed by a very savage demon' ('a seuissimo possessum demone').[4] A third *vita* was compiled in c.1213 by Gerald of Wales, an archdeacon of mixed Norman and Welsh descent, who had taken up residence in Lincoln in the 1190s. Gerald's *Vita* was shorter than Adam's *Magna Vita*, and he did not include the miracle of the mad sailor. He did, however, record more of Hugh's posthumous miracles than Adam had, likely because of the time that had elapsed since the bishop's death. Connections can be drawn between the three *vitae*, and it is possible that Adam and Gerald, both writing in the early thirteenth century, knew of each other's works.[5] The author of the *Metrical Life* certainly had access to the papal commissioners' report, which was put together as part of Hugh's canonisation proceedings and which drew on Adam's and Gerald's *vitae*.[6] Historians have identified an increased use of 'naturalized and medicalized' language in the miraculous healings documented in canonisation records from the thirteenth century onwards.[7] This chapter examines how far Hugh's *vitae* followed this pattern in their representations of madness and what role demons and the devil played in miracle records compiled with canonisation proceedings in mind.

The miraculous cure of the mad sailor was performed during Hugh's lifetime, and, as is typical of many of the miracle records in the three *vitae* of Saint Hugh, it includes specific details of the saint's actions during the process of cure as well as representations of the sufferer's physical and mental state before and after his healing. An association was made between abnormal/demonic behaviour and madness; the sailor's grimacing face and curving tongue were indicative of his demonic ensnarement. Similar associations have been noted in the four previous case studies and prevailed in English hagiographical material throughout the twelfth century. In the mad sailor's case, Hugh gained command over the demon using exorcised water and a blessing. Hugh's miracles differ from those examined thus far since the majority were performed by way of the saint's deeds and not his relics. As miracles predominantly performed by a *living saint*, they illustrate the growing popularity, in the thirteenth century, of 'modern' saints (i.e. those who were canonised soon after their deaths), whose virtuous lives reflected the religious convictions of their contemporaries, who were themselves increasingly concerned with their own personal piety.[8] In this period, the conceptualisation of purgatory as a place where ordinary Christians were afforded the possibility of salvation meant that closer attention was paid to the spiritual well-being of the laity and to the correlation between piety on earth and reward in heaven.[9] This correlation was emphasised in all three of Hugh's *vitae* through the saint's own exemplary piety.

By the end of the twelfth century, it had become generally accepted that no one could be venerated as a saint without official canonisation from the papacy.[10] Under Pope Alexander III (1159–81), papal canonisation procedures were regularised and made clearer.[11] Sanctity was recognised by the demonstration of *virtus*, which could be seen in the physical purity and incorruptibility of the saint's body, and by signs of the saint's intercessory power through miracles.[12] Of the other saints whose cults are examined in this book, neither Edmund of Bury nor William of Norwich was officially canonised, and Saint Bartholomew, as an apostle, did not necessarily require papal endorsement. Thomas Becket, however, was officially proclaimed a saint by Pope Alexander III in 1173, and Adam of Eynsham and Gerald of Wales likely had similar aspirations for Hugh when they compiled their *vitae*.

Papal canonisation committees made extensive enquiries to confirm the veracity of the miracles presented to them. Between 1200 and 1334, despite many people becoming the subjects of local cults, only twenty-six were officially canonised by the papacy.[13] Witnesses were called to give evidence to papal commissioners and interrogated using a set of questions that were designed to verify the miracle in relation to contemporary theological, philosophical and legal standards.[14] For healing miracles to be verified, it was essential to confirm that the recipient had been restored fully to health, something that was emphasised in local miracle collections and papal canonisation records alike. Though the means of cure had to be proven to be non-natural (i.e. miraculous), the end product – health – was defined by contemporary understandings of the natural world.[15] In Hippocratic medicine, a healthy individual was one whose four humours (blood, red/yellow bile, phlegm and black bile) were correctly balanced. The *Isagoge of Johannicius*, which was translated from Arabic into Latin by Constantine the African in the eleventh century and later went on to form part of the *Articella*, the principal medical compendium used by medical theorists and practitioners in the later Middle Ages, classified both health and sickness in terms of balance. Disease and illness were brought about 'when the four humours increase beyond the course of nature'.[16] Health ('sanitas') was determined by balance ('temperamentum') and sickness ('infirmitas') by imbalance ('intemperantia'), which led to harm ('laesio').[17]

Following Galen, in the middle of these two extremes (health and sickness) was the state of *neutrum*: neither healthy nor sick.[18] Health could therefore be viewed on a sliding scale where it was possible for one person to be more or less healthy than another. The central *neutrum* state indicated a 'tipping point' between health and sickness.[19] Health was not equivalent to balance, nor sickness to imbalance, since there was no middle ground between balance and imbalance, whereas there was between health and sickness. Humoral imbalance could cause ill health but did not denote sickness in itself.[20] Imbalances placed the body into a *neutrum* state, in which a person was neither healthy nor unhealthy but could be more prone to ill health. In a sense, imbalance was a risk factor for sickness.[21] Health and sickness were determined by observation of the correct or incorrect functioning of the body.[22] According to the *Regalis dispositio* – a theoretical and practical medical treatise, originally written in Arabic by Haly Abbas and transferred to the Christian West in the translations of Stephen of Antioch (fl. twelfth century) – the perfect state of humanity was one in which the mind functioned in harmony with the body, which could only be achieved if both body and mind were independently healthy.[23]

Of course, Hugh's *vitae* were not medical treatises, and one would not necessarily expect to find a discussion of health and sickness of this type in a hagiographical text. Even so, health and sickness were important concepts in the *vitae*, both in relation to Hugh's own life and to the conditions of those he cured. Adam's *Magna Vita* and Gerald's *Vita*, both composed before Hugh's canonisation in 1220, must have been written in anticipation of canonisation and were likely constructed in light of the more stringent evidential requirements of papal committees. The *Metrical Life*, composed after Hugh's canonisation, was certainly influenced by the canonisation proceedings. In all three *vitae*, Hugh's own management of physical and mental health in the pursuit of spiritual perfection exemplified his sanctity. His hagiographers drew on theological and medical models of health to demonstrate how he restored balance to others through miraculous healing. Nonetheless, the tightening of papal control over the recording of the miraculous did not mean that previous hagiographical standards were set aside or transformed. In Hugh's *vitae*, we see that representations of madness were shaped as much by hagiographical patterns that had been developing throughout the twelfth century as they were by new medical and theological standards.

The three *vitae* of Saint Hugh of Lincoln

Before we turn to the miracles, let's find out a little more about the man. In 1186, Hugh of Avalon was made bishop of Lincoln by King Henry II.[24] At Henry's request, Hugh had come to England from the Grande Chartreuse monastery near Grenoble in 1179–80 to become prior of the failing Carthusian priory of Witham.[25] By the time of his death on 16 November 1200, Hugh had achieved a great deal and had successfully navigated his way through the reigns of three English kings with few complications.[26] At the Council of Oxford in 1197, Hugh famously refused Richard I's demand for knights and declared that he had no obligation to provide men for overseas service. He avoided the confiscation of revenues that Richard wished to impose as penalty for his disobedience by visiting the king in person, whilst he was at mass, and winning his respect.[27]

Hugh had a reputation for fairness and wisdom, so much so that he served as a papal judge-delegate on several occasions, notably overseeing a dispute between the archbishop of Canterbury and the monks of Christ Church Cathedral Priory over the establishment of a new house of canons in Canterbury.[28] Hugh's magnificent funeral was held on 23 November and was attended by two kings as well as many archbishops, bishops, magnates, abbots and nobles.[29] Despite multiple miracles occurring on the day of the funeral and in the years that followed, canonisation proceedings did not start until 1219, perhaps because of the disruption caused by the papal interdict between 1208 and 1213 and by Magna Carta in 1215 and its aftermath.[30] Proceedings progressed fairly rapidly once they had begun, and a bull of canonisation was issued at Viterbo in Italy by Pope Honorius III on 16 February 1220.[31]

Adam of Eynsham's Magna Vita Sancti Hugonis

Two substantial *vitae* were available for the papal commissioners to use in Hugh's canonisation proceedings: Adam of Eynsham's *Magna Vita Sancti Hugonis* and Gerald of Wales's *Vita Sancti Hugonis*. Both texts were written with canonisation in mind, and both Adam and Gerald intended to represent the bishop as a man who bore the necessary attributes of sanctity, which extended beyond the performance of miracles.[32] Adam himself had been very close to Hugh, serving as his chaplain for the last three years of his life, and his admiration for the bishop is very apparent in the text.[33] The community at Eynsham was a small Benedictine order of no more than thirty monks. The bishop of Lincoln had the right of patronage over the monastery so could select his chaplain from among their number, choosing Adam in 1197.[34] Adam began compiling his *Magna Vita* in the early thirteenth century, shortly after Hugh's death, and finished it in c.1212 when he presented his work to Robert of Caveford, the prior of Witham, and to the community there.[35] It was written, by his own admission, at the persuasion of Robert FitzHenry, a hermit at Witham, and Ralph, a sacrist, in order to preserve Hugh's exemplary deeds and miracles for future generations.[36]

Adam came from an Oxford burgher family, and his father may have been one Edmundus Medicus, an Oxford landowner and physician who may have served the Augustinian canons of Oseney Abbey, in Oxfordshire, as their medical practitioner and who died in the Holy Land between 1185 and 1190.[37] The evidence for this paternal connection is circumstantial, but H.E. Salter has been able to identify Adam's brothers, William of Oxford and Edmund the Monk, from *The Vision of the Monk of Eynsham*, a miraculous vision recorded by Adam and included in the *Eynsham Cartulary*. Salter argues that the Oxford background of all three brothers provides a link to Edmundus Medicus, and the rarity of the name Edmund – with only one in every thousand bearing that name – suggests a familial tie between him and Edmund the Monk.[38] A familial relationship with an experienced practitioner could explain Adam of Eynsham's own medical knowledge, which is evidenced in his use of fairly sophisticated medical language.[39] For example, when Hugh was on his deathbed, Adam explained how 'every day he had two paroxysms ['paroxismis'], and his whole body was consumed by the fever, and his internal organs were weakened by dysentery ['uitalia et internorum medullas dissenteria exhauriebat'].'[40]

Gerald of Wales's Vita Sancti Hugonis

Gerald of Wales, who composed a second *vita* of Saint Hugh, did not have such an intimate relationship with the bishop as Adam had, though he was a personal acquaintance and had lived in Lincoln.[41] His admiration for the man and the saint is nonetheless very clear. Gerald's *Vita* was completed c.1213 and is far shorter than Adam's, which there is no conclusive evidence he had read. Gerald focused to a greater extent than Adam on Hugh's shrine miracles as opposed to the *virtus* he displayed during his lifetime; Hugh's death takes place at the end of the first part of the *Vita*, and the second and third parts are dedicated to his funeral and posthumous miracles.

In the preface to his *Vita*, Gerald compared Hugh, as the 'lily of Lincoln', with Thomas Becket, as the 'red rose of Kent'.[42] Archbishop of Canterbury Thomas Becket had famously been martyred in Canterbury Cathedral in 1170 as a result of his conflict with King Henry II, and, through this comparison, Gerald purposefully constructed Hugh's life as part of an ongoing struggle between ecclesiastical and royal authority.[43] As the champion of ecclesiastical power, Hugh was the ideal bishop, something that Gerald himself had never been able to amount to, having failed to obtain the bishopric of Saint David's in 1198–1203.[44] Gerald had been forced to acknowledge his own unsuitability for the role of bishop, and he conceded that he perhaps lacked the grace necessary for such a high-ranking Church position.[45] Hugh, by contrast, was happy, loving, generous, learned and at peace with himself and others.[46] In line with the biblical model of the ideal bishop and in contrast to royal authorities, Hugh was 'not violent but restrained' (1 Timothy 3:3).[47] Hugh's miraculous healings of the insane were not only marks of his sanctity but also expressions of his pastoral role, as a bishop, to maintain harmony in his community and to restore wandering souls to his flock.

The Metrical Life of Saint Hugh of Lincoln

In celebration of Hugh's life, as both bishop and saint, the *Metrical Life of Saint Hugh of Lincoln* was composed sometime between Hugh's canonisation in 1220 and the death of Hugh of Wells in 1235 because Hugh of Wells is referred to in the poem as the current bishop of Lincoln.[48] Though the author of the poem is anonymous, speculations have been made as to his identity. In his edition of the text, the most recent editor, Charles Garton, subscribes to the theory put forward by M.R. James and now 'generally accepted as established fact' that the author was Henry of Avranches, a travelling poet who wrote in England, Italy and France.[49] In his edition of the fourteenth-century *Matricularium* of Peterborough Abbey, James notes an entry for a *Life of St Hugh, Bishop of Lincoln, in verse, by 'Mag. H. de Hariench'* and identifies 'Hariench' as a fourteenth-century rendering of 'Avranches'.[50] He also draws parallels between the *Metrical Life* and Henry's *Life of St Francis* (composed in the first half of the thirteenth century), including an interest in contemporary medicine, which may have influenced Henry's interpretation of madness. Henry was known to have been putting various saints' lives into verse – including *vitae* of Saint Guthlac, Saint Birin, Saint Oswald and Saint Thomas Becket – in around 1220, so he is a plausible candidate for the *Metrical Life*'s author.[51]

It is likely that the *Metrical Life* was written to celebrate Hugh's canonisation, and it is certainly a salutation of his life. It was intended to be performed aloud to a clerical and perhaps a lay audience on Hugh's feast day on 17 November.[52] The poet certainly had access to the report made by the papal commission for Hugh's canonisation since the two examples of madness that he included in the *Metrical Life* are in the report, and one of them does not appear in either the *Magna Vita* or Gerald's *Vita*.[53] The miracles chosen for the *Metrical Life* reveal which events were thought to have the highest significance in the celebration of the saint's life in the context of his canonisation.

Madness miracles in the three *vitae*

The three *vitae* of Saint Hugh contain five detailed accounts of madness (summarised below in Table 5.1) as well as several shorter references. The *Metrical Life* mentions that, among the miracles presented to the papal court as part of Hugh's canonisation process, there were nine accounts of mad people ('furiosi').[54] The use of the word 'furiosi' to describe these

Table 5.1 Summary of madness miracles in the thirteenth-century *vitae* of Saint Hugh of Lincoln.

Summary	*Ref.*	*Symptoms and diagnosis*
A sailor from the village of Cheshunt had been possessed when his ship was near London. Having attacked his shipmates, he was brought home and secured with his head tied to a post, his hands to two stakes in the ground and his legs to a wooden beam. Hugh exorcised the man by reciting the gospels and sprinkling him with blessed water.	AE, V.9 Metrical Life, lines 1079–87	Demonic possession: rolling eyes, twisting mouth, sticking tongue out, gnashing teeth. Mad/furious ('furit'): grimacing, sticking tongue out, would not allow himself to be touched.
A madman who had been driven mad by acute fever had to be restrained by eight sane men to stop him from devouring his wife and children. Hugh used holy water to exorcise him and to cure his fever.	Metrical Life, lines 1088–105	Madness/demonic possession: doubled strength and the desire to harm others.
A mad youth from Ancaster was taken to various shrines by his parents in the hope of a cure. He was brought, bound in chains, to Saint Hugh's tomb. He stayed at the tomb for seven days, praying and gradually improving. He went home, cured and carrying the chains that had previously been used to bind him.	GW, II.7	Mad ('amens'), frenzied ('in frenesim').
A frenzied girl from Wigford was bound and brought to Saint Hugh's tomb. She stayed there for several days, crying out and disturbing the services. Having fallen asleep, she awoke cured and began to behave correctly, covering her head and devoutly praying.	GW, II.12	Frenzied: crying loudly.

recipients of miraculous cures implies that their madness was furious and frantic and that they were possibly, though notably not explicitly, influenced by demons. This term was used for every case of madness in Hugh's canonisation report, and it is likely that the author of the *Metrical Life* reproduced it from there.[55] Despite mentioning nine accounts of madness, the *Metrical Life* itself only gives the details of two cases: the miraculous cure of the mad sailor, which was recorded in Adam of Eynsham's *Magna Vita* as well as the papal canonisation report, and another account of a violent madman that was also in Hugh's canonisation report.

The miraculous cure of the mad sailor (quoted above) was first recorded in the *Magna Vita* and is the only case of madness where Adam goes into significant detail. In fact, he claims that, wanting to avoid idle gossip, he had originally decided not to include it at all but had changed his mind at the last minute when he thought that the story would encourage virtue (*virtus*) and not simply satisfy curiosity (*curiosus*).[56] The miracle was the first miracle in Hugh's canonisation report, and Adam's account was cited as its source.[57] In the canonisation records, we learn that the sailor's name was Roger Colhoppe.[58] On his way to see King Richard I, Hugh had passed through the village of Cheshunt, where the villagers, having been abandoned in the matter by their own bishop, beseeched him to cure one of their neighbours.

Adam described Roger (unnamed in his account) as 'possessed by a very savage demon', whereas, in the *Metrical Life*, he was mad/raving ('furit'), in line with the terminology used in the canonisation report.[59] The term 'furit' did not conclusively denote demonic involvement, though it could be used to describe the ravings of demoniacs, and the linguistically-related term *furia* was sometimes connected with evil spirits.[60] The demonic nature of Roger's *furor* was made more explicit, in the *Metrical Life*, when the poet explained that the 'holy father [Hugh] exorcised water, gave a blessing and commanded the delusions of the devil to disappear'.[61] Both the *Magna Vita* and the *Metrical Life* emphasised that it was necessary to restrain the sailor, though Adam had the freedom of space to go into much greater detail, since, in his prose account, he was not restricted by rhythm and metre. In the *Metrical Life*, the sailor's 'hands and feet were bound', whereas, in the *Magna Vita*, Adam explained how the man's head was tied to a post, his hands to two stakes in the ground and his legs to a wooden beam, resembling the form of a crucifix and rendering him unable to move anything except his face.[62]

The second case of madness recorded in the *Metrical Life* is that of a madman whose insanity was the result of an acute fever, which left him in a state of such derangement that he wanted to devour his wife and children.[63] His condition was described as 'rabiem': a term that could refer to madness in general[64] or to the fatal insanity that led to foaming at the mouth following a bite from a rabid dog (there was no mention of a dog bite in this case).[65] Demonic possession was alluded to by the poet when he described how, upon cure, 'the demon departed' ('abit daemon') from the madman.[66] Nonetheless, the main emphasis of his account of the miracle was the restoration of balance through Hugh's application of holy water. The madman's warm blood shrank away from the cold water, which restored his body to an even temperature, cooling his fever and the raging madness.[67] The poet explained that 'each thing rebounds at the sensation of its opposite', which is perhaps indicative of his interest in humoral explanations for ill health; sickness could be caused by imbalances in the bodily fluids as a result of too much heat, too much cold, too much moisture or too much dryness.[68] Though the demon was mentioned in the canonisation report, this medical explanation seems to have been added by the poet.[69] Additionally, the stabilising of opposites could allude to the juxtaposition of the holy water against the unholy demon. In this way, the exorcism performed by Hugh was as much spiritual as it was physical; the fever was broken, and the demon was expelled.

Though one of Gerald of Wales's two madness miracles was recorded in Hugh's canonisation report, neither was included in the *Metrical Life*, perhaps because it focused primarily on the deeds of Hugh's lifetime, and the madness miracles that Gerald recorded were performed posthumously.[70] In both of his madness miracles, Gerald of Wales used the term 'in frenesim' to describe those afflicted. The first, a youth from Ancaster, was 'frenzied' ('in frenesim') and 'mad' ('amens').[71] In contemporary medical texts, frenzy (*frenesis*) was a specific medical condition that could cause someone to go out of his or her mind (*amens*) and act insanely, requiring restraint.[72] In the canonisation report, the youth, whose name, we learn, was John, was described as 'furiosus', and his madness was attributed to the loss of his property.[73] Gerald may have been unaware of this loss, which he did not mention, if he had not spoken with the youth or his family directly, or, alternatively, he may have felt that this detail was unnecessary in his account. According to Gerald, the youth was bound at Hugh's shrine despite having the wits to pray and to hear mass.[74] Once cured, the youth behaved 'reasonably and discretely' ('sane et discrete') in contrast to his previous madness and frenzy.[75] Similar is true in Gerald's second record of madness; a mad girl from Wigford was also 'in frenesim' but, upon cure, acted 'wisely and discreetly' ('sapienter et discrete'), 'correctly and discreetly' ('recte satis et discrete') and 'wisely and devotedly' ('sapienter et devote').[76] In both miracle records, Gerald contrasted mad behaviour, which necessitated a cure, with desirable traits, such as wisdom, reason and discretion, which were possessed by healthy individuals.

The final case of mental affliction from the *vitae* is not a case of madness but a case of sadness, which is described briefly in the *Magna Vita*. Though the cure was not necessarily miraculous – Hugh's kind words cheered up ('exhilarauit') the afflicted maiden – it is still worth mentioning because it is one of the rare cases in which sorrow or grief is discussed as a condition in need of spiritual attention in a miracle text. The word *meror* – meaning sorrow – was used to describe the maiden's sadness, which was caused by grief following a recent loss.[77] What is most striking is that, following Hugh's intervention, the maiden's mind bore the most happiness ('animum gereret letissimum'), which suggests that her previous sorrow was a condition in the mind that required emotional or spiritual care, something that, in humoral medicine, would have involved restoring the *accidents of her soul* to a state of equilibrium.[78] The accidents of the soul, also known as passions, were one of the six non-naturals of humoral medicine, which, like the humours themselves, required regulation in order to maintain health. The non-naturals were functions that were not part of the body's material substance, like eating, drinking and sleeping (as opposed to natural functions, like breathing, which did not require conscious regulation). Regulation of the non-naturals had a direct impact on humoral balance and thus on health and sickness. The accidents of the soul (*accidentibus animae*) were emotional fluctuations – like anger (*ira*), fear (*timor*), pleasure (*delicia*) and sorrow (*tristitia*) – that were accidents not in the sense that they were contrary to the soul's essence but that they were not essential to its existence.[79] Medieval regimens warned against certain unhealthy passions that caused humoral imbalance.[80] Sadness and anxiety made the body, and especially the heart, too cold.[81] Healthy individuals were encouraged to pursue passions like joy, which could be achieved through, amongst other measures, eating well and seeing friends.[82] Balance and concord between the body, mind and soul were attributes of good health. Hugh's kind words to the maiden were, therefore, a form of healing in the sense that they restored happiness and health.

Virtus and madness in Hugh's *vitae*

During his lifetime, Hugh often made physical sacrifices for the sake of his spiritual welfare. Even on the brink of death, he refused to allow the hair shirt he was wearing on his sickbed to be changed more than was absolutely necessary. The hair shirt caused Hugh obvious discomfort; it forced him to lie in congealed perspiration and covered his skin in scratches.[83] Despite it causing physical sores, which Adam had seen on his body, Hugh claimed that his hair shirt was able to heal sores.[84] In this way, bodily suffering was shown to be of spiritual benefit; the sores that Hugh was referring to were in his soul, and the torment of the hair shirt was penance for past sins. Like Saint Paul's metaphorical thorn in the flesh, which, according to 2 Corinthians 12:7, was a form of torment that acted as a constant reminder of the apostle's humanity and prevented him from succumbing to pride, Hugh's hair shirt represented humanity's path to salvation through suffering.

On his deathbed, Hugh's physical suffering and decline did not coincide with a loss of spiritual and mental clarity. In fact, Hugh's physicians remarked with surprise that his spirit ('spiritus') seemed utterly undefeated by his illness.[85] Throughout his sickness, Hugh made sure that his body, despite his fever and weariness, obeyed his spirit and not the other way round.[86] On another occasion, Hugh explained the importance of self-control to his attendants, who wanted to witness personally a miraculously-bleeding host that they had been told about. By informing them that it was enough to have faith in the miracle without having seen it, Hugh 'restrained their idle curiosity, and, by directing their devotion to inner sight and touch, he instructed his listeners about the true and living food of their souls.'[87]

Hugh's spiritual virtue was apparent in his physical appearance after death. Adam compared his skin to that of Saint Martin in its pureness and beauty.[88] This comparison to a saintly body – remember that, at this time, Hugh had not yet been canonised – denoted the highest level of physical and spiritual purity. Interjections, echoing Sulpicius Severus (a hagiographer and chronicler who composed his *Life of Saint Martin* in Gaul in the late fourth/fifth century), that Hugh's skin was whiter than milk and that his blush was redder than the rose enhanced the connection with Saint Martin and suggested that Hugh's spiritual goodness was reflected in a physical appearance akin to, if not finer than, that seen in nature.[89] Furthermore, the red rose, as a symbol of Christ's Passion, provided a parallel between Hugh's death and that of Christ, and thus, though he had not been martyred, his incorrupt corpse reflected his goodness and the faith for which he had dedicated his life.[90]

Additionally, all three hagiographers took note of Hugh's close association with lepers, again drawing a parallel between him and Christ (Matthew 8:1–3, Leviticus 5:3) and contrasting Hugh's own purity with the physical corruption of leprosy. Gerald of Wales marvelled at how Hugh could bear to kiss the lips of lepers without any horror of a 'form more monstrous than human'.[91] He graphically described the 'monstrous' ('monstruose') physical appearance and 'deformity' ('deformitas') of the lepers, whose mouths had been completely eaten away, leaving only teeth in the space where lips should have been.[92]

It is important to note, however, that Gerald did not record any mental and spiritual weakness in these leprous sick. Certainly, there were those among Gerald's contemporaries who associated leprosy with sin; the twelfth-century *Ramsey Abbey Chronicle* reported that the monks of Evesham had attributed their abbot's apparent leprosy to his sacrilegious attempt to move the relics of Saint Osyth, though the chronicler himself acknowledged that there may have been other causes for the abbot's illness.[93] Nonetheless, writers of the twelfth century increasingly employed a different narrative that associated the leper not with sin but with salvation. Carole Rawcliffe has suggested that this alternative interpretation of leprosy may have been influenced by the more frequent occurrence of the illness among prominent and respected members of the nobility, such as Baldwin IV, the leprous king of Jerusalem (d.1185).[94] The biblical narrative that Christ, upon taking on the sins of mankind, was shunned as a leper ('quasi leprosum') established a parallel between the leper and Christ himself. To extend love to one was to extend love to the other (Isaiah 53:4).[95] In the *Magna Vita*, Adam explained that Hugh himself had declared lepers to be blessed ('felices').[96] Their diseased bodies were signs that they had been singled out by God for spiritual salvation.[97] Just as Hugh's physical suffering on his sickbed ended with his death, leaving his body pure and uncorrupted, so too did the scourge of leprosy end with the death of the sufferer.[98]

If bodily cure was spiritually unimportant, one must ask what Hugh believed his kisses would bring to the ill-fated leper. The short answer is nothing. Gerald explained that Hugh's reason for kissing lepers was not an attempt to heal them in body, as Saint Martin had famously done, but to heal himself in his soul.[99] This point held significance, and, whilst he did not go into such detail about the physical condition of leprosy, the author of the *Metrical Life* repeated it in very similar terms, like Gerald, referencing Saint Martin.[100] Hugh's kissing of the lepers was an act of love ('caritatis').[101] The humility and love that Hugh showed to the lepers by kissing them were indications of his sanctity.[102] Again following Sulpicius Severus's *Life of Saint Martin*, kissing a leper was, certainly by the twelfth century, a literary *topos* that was a recognised mark of sanctity.[103]

Hugh's healing of the mad was also represented as a spiritual pursuit, though the cures he performed on madmen were done not solely for his spiritual gain but also for theirs. In his efforts to cure the mad sailor, who we met at the beginning of this chapter, Hugh was described almost as though he were fighting a physical and spiritual battle. According to Adam of Eynsham, he was a 'vigorous conqueror of the powers of darkness'.[104] In the *Metrical Life*'s second madness miracle, Hugh was not a conqueror but a physician who caused the heated spirit to leave the fevered madman using cold water, which repelled it.[105] Hugh fulfilled the role of physician by bringing balance to the body and mind, which the poet highlighted in the juxtaposition of cool, holy water against fevered, demonic madness, since 'each thing rebounds at the sensation of its opposite'.

In contrast to the saint himself, the mad patients to whom Hugh attended were often portrayed as grotesque and unnatural in physical appearance. Such a representation is especially manifest in Adam's description of the deranged sailor who was cured by Hugh at Cheshunt:

> The unhappy wretch was rolling his eyes, and his mouth kept twisting, now in this direction and now in that, with a ghastly leer. At one moment, he stuck his tongue out and, at the next, he gnashed his teeth, and then, opening his mouth wide, he showed the whole back of his throat, which appeared to the spectators like some horrible cavern.[106]

The rolling of his eyes and the gnashing of his teeth give the sailor an unnatural physical appearance. Depictions of the mad as wild or savage had a hagiographical precedent, as shown in Chapter 2 in the descriptions of violent mad men and women who attacked family members and bystanders at William of Norwich's tomb (1150s). Much of the description also has a demonic overtone: from the sailor's twisted mouth to the vast, unnatural hell of his throat. The author of the *Metrical Life* repeated these unnatural and hellish images in his account of the miracle when he described the sailor's twisted face and curved tongue.[107]

In line with their unnatural physical appearances was the frequent acquisition by the possessed of inhuman capabilities, most commonly extreme strength. We saw in Chapter 2 that, in the *Life and Miracles of William of Norwich*, a possessed man resisted restraint with the strength of seven men, and a possessed woman lashed out with the strength of four men.[108] Similarly, in the *Magna Vita*, it was only with the help of a large number of people that the mad sailor from Cheshunt was secured to a large beam on his ship and taken home.[109] For the man who went mad during a severe bout of fever, whose case was recorded in the *Metrical Life*, insanity doubled his strength, and it took eight sane men to restrain him.[110] Had he not been restrained, the man would have had the strength (and perhaps more frighteningly, the desire) to devour his entire family.[111] Hugh's own self-restraint in the face of physical desire and discomforts starkly contrasts the unrestrained physicality of the insane.

Since they lacked any self-restraint, mad people often required some form of man-made restraint, and many were bound when they were brought to saints' shrines. The mad sailor from Cheshunt was possessed by a demon whilst aboard his ship, near London, and there was perhaps a connection between his possession and the instability of his seafaring lifestyle, which may have put him at greater risk of ill health. Notably, before he was cured by Hugh, the sailor was secured and brought home, thus restoring some level of stability, albeit enforced.[112] Bound in the form of a crucifix, he suffered physically because of the evil spirit ('spiritus malignus') inside him, just as Christ had suffered for mankind.[113] What was clearly a striking image was repeated in Hugh's canonisation report and again in the *Metrical Life*, which stated that the sailor's hands and feet were bound.[114] After his cure, the sailor did his best to amend ('emendare') his life and does not seem to have returned to the sea.[115] Away from the unstable lifestyle of a sailor, he died in peace/harmony ('in pace').[116]

Madness was repeatedly connected, in Hugh's *vitae*, with the necessity for restraint. Gerald of Wales did not mention inhuman strength but, nevertheless, both of the insane people in his *Vita* were bound in some way. The mad youth from Ancaster was bound with chains and tied up.[117] Upon his restoration to sanity, the youth returned home, carrying the chains that had once been used to bind him.[118] For the youth, home may have been a place of stability, as it was for the sailor. The chains were symbols of his madness; whilst mad, he was bound, but, when sane, he carried his chains freely. Thus, his mental incapacity was reflected in his physical incarceration and in his inability to control his body. Similarly, Gerald's mad girl from Wigford was fettered for a long time because of her frenzy.[119] At Hugh's tomb, her cries were so loud that she disturbed the celebration of mass, and those who witnessed her madness prayed for a cure.[120] The girl's lack of regard for the mass parallels the behaviour of demoniacs in other miracle records of this period, who displayed abhorrence towards the Church and its liturgical rituals.[121] However, the girl from Wigford was not a demoniac; she suffered from an illness (*morbus*), and demons were not mentioned. Thus, we see the ungodly behaviour of demoniacs associated, linguistically at least, with natural illness.

The author of the *Metrical Life* wrote that human reason (*humana ratio*) was restored to the mad sailor from Cheshunt after his cure. Hugh had exorcised water, given a blessing and ordered the delusions of the devil ('diabolicas fraudes') to disappear.[122] Despite his cure being spiritual, the sailor's condition had affected him physically (in the gross distortion of his body) and mentally (in his loss of human reason). Madness did not only result in imbalance in the body, the mind or the soul individually; it disturbed the balance *between* them. Thus, when the saint provided a miraculous cure, he treated his patients holistically, managing their spiritual health as much as their physical and mental health.

Miracles, madness and holistic healing

Hugh's spiritual journey

The *Metrical Life* was written in dactylic hexameter, the traditional metre in which classical epic poetry, recounting the deeds of exceptional men, was composed. It opens with the first words of the *Aeneid*, Virgil's epic poem, which narrated the legendary journey of Aeneas, a Trojan hero, and would have been well known in monastic circles in this period.[123] The poet used these techniques to frame Hugh's story as a 'spiritual epic' and to compare Hugh's spiritual journey with Aeneas's legendary journey from Troy to Italy, where he became ancestor to the Romans.[124] The story of Hugh's life in the *Magna Vita* was also constructed as a spiritual journey, on which his biggest personal battle was with his own lust. In his struggle with lust, the situation of later miracles was reversed, and Hugh took on the role of the impure sinner. The young Hugh received a vision of Basil, the prior of the Grande Chartreuse monastery, who had died in 1174 and who acted as Hugh's spiritual healer. Adam of Eynsham's familiarity with medical language is apparent here; Basil took on the role of a 'medicus' and cured Hugh in both mind and body ('in corde et in carne') of his earthly lust.[125] The 'heavenly doctor' ('celestis medicus') gave Hugh the 'poison' ('venenum') of lust to quell his pride and then the 'balm of celestial medicine' ('balsamum superni medicaminis') to remove the temptation of the flesh.[126] Thus, the mind required the body to fulfil its spiritual potential, and the body needed the mind to guide it and to quell its earthly temptations. Hugh's battle with lust was particularly relevant in light of the clerical reforms of the thirteenth century, when clerical marriage was gradually dying out after its prohibition in the major orders at the First Lateran Council (1123), and 'manly' strength of mind and body was increasingly connected with religious male chastity.[127] In Chapter 4, we saw how, in the foundation book of Saint Bartholomew's priory in London (written c.1174–c.1189), the 'lustful pleasure' of an unmarried priest potentially contributed to the suffering of his illegitimate daughter, who was plagued by a demon.[128] By contrast, as a bishop and prospective saint, Hugh exemplified ideal male virtue in his battle with lust. His strength emerged not from a lack of lust but from an ability to resist and control it.[129]

Following his own battle with lust, Hugh seems to have possessed a virtuous connection between body, mind and soul that led to his spiritual improvement. Even when eating, he did not merely taste food physically but inwardly with his entire soul.[130] When physically asleep, Hugh's spirit (*spiritus*) continued to be alert and prayed constantly.[131] The idea that the mind could be alert whilst the body rested (Psalms 16:7) was repeated again later in the *Magna Vita* and also in the *Metrical Life*.[132] When receiving a dream-vision of the life he would lead as bishop of Lincoln, Hugh's 'mind was the more free in proportion as his limbs were weighed down by sleep'.[133] When eating and when sleeping – both bodily functions – the mind could engage in spiritual improvement.

Hugh frequently played a role in the spiritual journeys of others, and his hagiographers highlighted his pastoral role in recognising harmony and disharmony in the bodies, minds and souls of those he met. One of the most striking spiritual connections that Hugh experienced in the *Magna Vita* was with infants, and Adam emphasised this connection by dedicating a lengthy discussion to it.[134] Even timid infants were said to be relaxed in Hugh's company, as they were in Christ's (Matthew 19:14), and onlookers were amazed by the happy connection he shared with them.[135] Their amazement indicates that it was unusual for an adult stranger to be able to connect with babies in this way. Those who witnessed the connection attributed it to the fact that the infants' pure souls allowed them to perceive Hugh's sanctity when others could not (Matthew 5:8 – *Blessed are the clean of heart: for they shall see God*).[136] Not only does this biblical reference set up a comparison between Hugh's spirituality and God's perfect state of being, but it also denotes infants as being pure of soul. The implication is that young souls are corrupted from their original state of purity (presumably, after baptism) the longer they are united with their bodies and enticed by sin.

Consideration of the spiritual state of infant souls was particularly relevant in the thirteenth century when dualist heretical movements, like Catharism, were gaining popularity in the regions either side of the Pyrenees. Dualists denied infant baptism since, they argued, infants lacked the ability to reason and, with it, the ability to consent to baptism and to share in the Christian faith.[137] Notably, mad individuals were also considered unable to use reason, and there is a parallel here between the madman and the infant. The insane were permitted to partake in the Christian sacraments provided that they had previously given their consent when sane.[138] Using similar reasoning, Christian theologians could argue that it was right to baptise infants since, as they had inherited Original Sin from adults, they could also be granted salvation through baptism performed with the consent of adults.[139] The infants who engaged with Hugh were portrayed as worthy of salvation and were welcomed by the bishop, just as Christ had welcomed the children in Judea despite the scepticism of his disciples (Matthew 19:13–15). Hugh marked the children who were brought to him with the sign of the cross, as though baptising them, and he was able to perceive their potential 'greatness' ('magnum') where others could not.[140] Fittingly, the infant with whom Hugh had the strongest connection grew up to be unusually good.[141]

Hugh's role as a spiritual mentor was a repeated theme in the *Magna Vita*, and he even provided spiritual guidance to King Henry II and King Richard I. Henry II pledged to seek advice from Hugh on all matters concerning the welfare of his soul.[142] Later, as his ships were threatened by a storm at sea, the king turned his prayers to Hugh, and, by Hugh's intercession, the storm was quelled, and the ships were saved.[143] The quelling of a storm was a common miracle for a saint to perform. Nonetheless, the close proximity, in the text, of the pledge for spiritual guidance to the protection of the king's physical body against the storm emphasises the link between protection of the body and protection of the soul. Furthermore, this miracle represents Hugh as providing stability in a nautical setting and can be contrasted with the miracle of the mad sailor from Cheshunt, who had been possessed by a demon whilst aboard his ship.

For Gerald of Wales, Hugh's relationship with the Angevin kings exemplified the bishop's *virtus*; Hugh's fair and just exercising of episcopal authority was juxtaposed against what Gerald saw as the autocratic wielding of royal power.[144] Such was Hugh's 'wonderful [...] grace' that he was able to tame the 'mind' ('animus') of King Richard, an 'unbridled and fierce' ('effrenis et efferus') ruler, who was 'almost a tyrant' ('fere tirannicus').[145] That Hugh could quieten the most unruly minds during his career as a bishop set a noteworthy precedent for his posthumous encounters with the insane via his healing miracles. In the *Magna Vita*, the king's follies were, rather tactfully by Adam, blamed on his bad advisers. It was a standard literary tool in the Middle Ages, from Æthelred II (r.978–1013 and 1014–16) onwards, to blame bad advisers for royal mistakes. Interestingly, it was the minds of such men that were criticised. Richard's advisers were depraved ('peruersas mentes'), and their evil council was thus equated with a failing in the mind.[146] In a similar way, Richard's vicious army captain, Mercadier, who Adam clearly disapproved of because he was a mercenary and therefore unscrupulous, was like a savage beast ('belluine seuitie'): a description that echoes the violent and sometimes bestial language used to describe the mad.[147] Purity of soul was associated with positive behaviour types, such as the laughter and innocence of infants, and instability and depravity in the mind were associated with negative behaviour types: the givers of bad advice, the savage and, as we shall now see, the heretical.

Sickness and sin

Heresy was a growing concern for the thirteenth-century papacy, and Adam's condemnation of heretics would have appealed to a papal canonisation committee and may even have ameliorated Hugh's chances of canonisation.[148] By associating heresy with the dysfunction of madness, Adam was able to undermine heretical beliefs. One such case in the *Magna Vita* is that of Andrew and Alexander, two ex-Carthusians who had deserted the order and who were described as 'spiritually children' ('ueritate paruuli'), though they were in fact grown men, when they criticised Hugh.[149] Here, the association with childlike qualities was negative because the minds of these men had failed to develop alongside their bodies. For rejecting the Carthusian way, the men were described as 'perverse and insane men' ('hominis peruicacia uesani').[150] That they were stubborn implies that they had the ability for spiritual improvement but lacked the willpower, and that they were mad suggests that their spiritual feebleness lay in the failure of their minds to exercise reason. Once again, a connection was drawn between madmen and children; here, both were deemed spiritually deficient, like the heretics, because of their lack of reason.

In the miracles of Saint Edmund of Bury, compiled at the turn of the eleventh century and discussed in Chapter 1, an association was made between illness and transgression, and madness was linked to transgressions resulting from folly. In the foundation book of Saint Bartholomew's priory in London, compiled a hundred years after Saint Edmund's miracle collections and discussed in Chapter 4, a connection between sickness and sin persisted, though, in Saint Bartholomew's miracles, as in others recorded in the twelfth century, madness was more often miraculously cured than it was delivered as a divine punishment. In Adam's *Magna Vita*, associations between sickness and sin were still prevalent. For example, an adulterous parishioner was described as 'morbida' (diseased/unhealthy), implying that the sin of adultery was an illness.[151] The most common sin to be associated with madness in Hugh's *vitae* was heresy or an error of belief. Adam described how heretics 'madly dream' ('delirando sompniant') that they can be saved from hell by the intercession of any saint.[152] Though the heretics, in this case, were presumably not mad in reality (and it is noteworthy that the word 'delirando', though denoting madness, was not used specifically to describe any of the mad people cured by Saint Hugh), their beliefs lacked reason and were therefore described as being mad. Adam connected sleep and dreaming with a lack of rationality, and the heretics can be contrasted with Hugh himself, who, as we know, was able to keep his mind active when asleep. In contemporary medicine, dreams were considered to be irrational since they were believed to be a result of the continued production of images by the imaginative faculty, whilst the rational faculty was inactive and unable to interpret them.[153] The heretical men were perceived to be irrational because they did not let their rational minds guide them in correct belief in the same way that mad people did not allow their rational minds to guide them in correct behaviour.

An association between lack of reason and sin can be seen elsewhere in the *Magna Vita*. In 1198, a sinner was absolved and healed in body and mind by Hugh at Rochester.[154] Unusually, the record of the man's cure was constructed in the first person as though it were the sinner's own words. The man described himself as suffering 'confusion of the mind' ('mentis confusionem'), though he was not necessarily mad and was able to converse with Hugh via an interpreter (his dialect was unfamiliar to Hugh).[155] The man's mental confusion was brought on by demons, which he mentioned frequently in his account. When he met Hugh at Rochester, the man described how he had been ensnared by the tricks of the devil.[156] Under the influence of the devil, he had committed a terrible crime.[157] We are not told what the crime was, though an accompanying gangrene-like disease that rotted the flesh on his thighs could have been a hint that his sin was of a sexual nature. The physical rotting of the man's body was symbolic of his spiritual corruption, as a result of sin, and of his confused mind; decay of the body was simultaneous with decay of the mind.[158] The sinner feared his fate in hell and was so deeply deceived by the devil that, as a result of a demonic vision, he almost committed suicide before following the advice of a vision of the Virgin Mary to seek cure from a priest.[159]

Demonic enticement towards suicide had a well-known precedent in the tale of the Santiago Suicide, widely circulated from the twelfth century in, among other texts, William of Malmesbury's *Miracles of the Blessed Virgin* (compiled in England, c.1135) and the *Codex Calixtinus* (composed around the same time in Lyons).[160] In the tale, a simple ('simplex') French pilgrim, on his way to Santiago de Compostela to unburden himself of his sins at the shrine of Saint James, was intercepted by the devil, in the guise of the apostle, who persuaded him that suicide was a faster and easier path to salvation.[161] The description of the pilgrim as 'simplex' may allude to his weak mental capabilities, which again connects him to the 'confused' man who sought Hugh's help. Unlike Hugh's 'confused' man, the French pilgrim went through with his suicide but was resurrected by Saint James and the Virgin Mary, and he was able to return to his life as a tailor.[162] The urging of the devil, the temptation of the next life and the involvement of the Virgin in the healing all correspond with the case in the *Magna Vita*. It is possible that Adam of Eynsham wanted to direct his audience's attention to the parallels between Hugh and Saint James (the pilgrimage to James's shrine in Compostela was, after all, a renowned spiritual journey) and to emphasise that the true path to salvation was to absolve oneself spiritually, as the sinful man had done when he went to the priest and as Hugh did throughout his life. Hugh was able to heal the man in body and in mind, signifying his dual role as spiritual guide and bodily physician whilst also highlighting, once again, the connection between sickness in the mind and sickness in the body.[163]

Spiritual guidance and cure

Since there was a continued association between madness, sin and depravity, both Adam and Gerald seem to have been keen to demonstrate that Hugh provided spiritual healing, as well as physical and mental healing, for mad patients. Hugh's role in the spiritual journey of another is perhaps the reason that Adam included the miracle of the mad sailor from Cheshunt in his *Magna Vita* against his initial instincts. After his cure, the sailor went on a 'pious pilgrimage' ('peregrinationi pie') and lived 'faithfully' ('deuote').[164] The sailor's own spiritual journey (by way of pilgrimage) and his lifestyle thereafter present a startling contrast to the ghastly and savage demoniac who had originally been presented to Hugh.

In Gerald of Wales's *Vita Sancti Hugonis*, the mad girl from Wigford, whose frantic mental state was made apparent in the language used to describe her ('furibunda' and 'in frenesim'), had exposed her spiritual failings by screaming in the church.[165] However, upon cure, she was wise, discreet, correct and devoted; all four traits implied that reason and goodness had been restored to the mind.[166] Such words could easily have been used to describe Hugh himself and are, in fact, remarkably similar to Gerald's model of the ideal bishop: a devoted and learned man. One could say then that, upon her restoration to sanity, the girl was brought closer to God and to the ideal state that Hugh himself embodied.

Following her cure, the girl from Wigford strove to provide others with physical and mental well-being by taking up a position in a hospital in Lincoln to tend to the sick.[167] In much the same way as Hugh had interacted with the lepers, the girl carried out work not solely for the benefit of others but also for the improvement of her soul through the practice of charity. We could even speculate that the girl served in the leper hospital of Saint Leonard without the Castle of Lincoln, which was first documented in 1300 but was certainly founded before then.[168] According to Gerald, the girl's charitable work would win her 'the final golden halo or aureole', a reference to angelic perfection far removed from the girl who had previously disturbed mass in the cathedral with her insane cries.[169] It is likely that Gerald would have been aware of the parallels between this spiritual journey and Hugh's own journey. The miracle appears at the end of the second book, where he originally expected to end his *Vita*, and it was perhaps intended to illustrate Hugh's influence over the most desperate of minds and his guidance in the spiritual journeys of others.

Despite the girl's charitable work, neither she nor any of the other mad people cured by Hugh were explicitly required to atone for their previous deranged behaviour once cured. At Canterbury, in the 1170s, a madwoman was purportedly instructed by a vision of Saint Thomas Becket to continue her pilgrimage, after receiving a cure from him, to Rome or to the shrine of Saint James at Santiago de Compostela, with the implication that such a venture would be spiritually cleansing.[170] Nonetheless, such undertakings were rarely documented in miracle records. It was, of course, not often that a hagiographer recommended the services of another saint rather than the subject of his text. In Hugh's *vitae*, the spiritual journeys undertaken by the insane after their cures were more likely aimed towards further improvement of their minds rather than atonement for sins, which does not seem to fit the context of their stories. Alternatively, the girl from Wigford's charitable work, following her cure, can be interpreted as a means of giving thanks. Gerald closed the miracle with the hope that 'all others who have regained health and those who sincerely seek merciful favours in this place prosper and rejoice in gaining their desire'.

The friends, families, neighbours and communities of the mad people in Saint Hugh's *vitae* were shown to share a desire for a cure to be performed and to join in the joy and thanksgiving upon the fulfilment of this desire. The villagers of Cheshunt rushed out to meet Hugh in order to obtain his help for their neighbour. The girl from Wigford was pitied by those in the cathedral even whilst she was disturbing the celebration of mass.[171] The mad youth from Ancaster was taken round several shrines by his parents and friends.[172] When he finally found his cure in Lincoln, his father was unbelievably gladdened, and his parents, friends and neighbours went to give thanks.[173] The youth's father was among those who testified to his madness and miraculous cure in the report of Hugh's canonisation made by the papal commissioners.[174] The *Metrical Life*, uniquely, does not mention the reactions of friends and neighbours, perhaps again because of restrictions of space or metre. Adam's and Gerald's representations of community reactions to insanity conformed to an established pattern seen in records of miraculous healings across the twelfth century. The mad were pitied, assisted, restrained and feared. By not only healing the mad person but also bringing relief and joy to his or her community, the saint continued to function as a protector of his community. Over a century earlier, Saint Edmund had protected his community at Bury by dispensing madness as a divine punishment. Hugh protected his by curing insanity and restoring individual and communal harmony.

The focus of all three *vitae* was Hugh's own spiritual goodness and his power to intercede with God on behalf of others. The case of the sad maiden in the *Magna Vita* has already been mentioned, but we can return to it here as a final example of Hugh's beneficial influence over others. Hugh's kind words transformed the sorrow that the young woman had been suffering into happiness, and 'henceforth her face and mind ('animum') bore the most happiness'.[175] In this way, a harmony was achieved between body and mind, and the maiden's internal happiness was reflected externally in her face. The sad maiden was Blanche of Castile, the new bride of the French dauphin and future king of France, Louis VIII (r.1223–26) and granddaughter to King Henry II of England (r.1154–89), who had himself sought spiritual guidance from Hugh. Blanche's marriage to Louis was celebrated in 1200 when she was just twelve years old. Hugh's meeting with her took place on a physical journey through France, but it also represented Hugh's rising influence in both temporal and heavenly realms. As demonstrated by his interaction with Blanche of Castile, he used this influence to achieve harmony where he could.

Conclusion

In Hugh's *vitae*, the healthiest minds were shown to be those that were happy and that sought spiritual goodness, just like the infants who valued their connection with Hugh and the sad maiden who benefitted from his words. Depraved and uncontrollable minds were those that submitted themselves to the desires of the body or those that fell into spiritual error. Madness was such a predicament but was not always the direct fault of the sufferer, whose mind could be influenced by the trickery of demons or by the impairment of illness. Unlike many other conditions cured by saints, madness bore no physical mark, either externally or internally. The visible effects of madness were behavioural and included violence, screaming and extreme strength, all of which were irrational behaviours when not provoked by any expected stimuli (such as grief). The behavioural signs of madness went beyond what was considered reasonable and sane. The insane could lack 'human reason', and there was an association between madness and the irrational beliefs of heretics.

Upon cure, a different set of behaviours was seen in the once insane patient; the cured madman was pious, faithful, charitable and discrete. These Christian qualities were attributes of the reasoning mind that demonstrated the mind's resolve to exert control over the urges of the body. Several of the mad men and woman who received cures from Hugh gave thanks and sought self-improvement through pilgrimage, prayer or charitable gestures. Each *vita* was written to glorify the sanctity of Saint Hugh, whose own goodness was shown in the fact that the very practices he followed – his dedication to spirituality even on his deathbed and his charitable care for the sick – were the practices that led to spiritual improvement in others.

Hugh, as a living healer, led both by example and by guidance. His *vitae* strove to attest to his virtuous life and to his ability to perform miracles. Even in the throes of an illness that would prove fatal, Hugh demonstrated the ideal relationship between body, mind and soul. His body and its physical torment served only to strengthen his soul through his self-restraint in the face of physical temptation. In his miracles, Hugh restored balance to the sick. He used cold water to cool the madman whose insanity had been brought on by fever and holy water to exorcise the demon that had possessed him. The parallels between saint and physician are hard to ignore here; both performed their cures through the application of opposites, and both aimed thus to restore balance to their patients. A miraculous cure not only restored balance to the sick but also bestowed healing as a mark of God's favour, worthy of thanks. Even as medical language (that pertaining to doctors, balsams and the balancing of hot and cold) crept into miracle records, the spiritual side of the miraculous was made more prominent through the saint's pastoral role in providing physical, mental and spiritual care to his flock.

Notes

1. Garton translates 'furit' as 'lunatic', but 'he was mad' or 'he was raving' is a more appropriate translation. Below, Garton translates 'furens' as 'lunatic' and 'furoris' as 'lunacy', whereas I have used 'madman' and 'madness' as more literal translations.
2. Metrical Life, 1079–87, pp. 66–68. A literal translation is 'the sharpness of human reason'.
3. 'Canonization', p. 97.
4. AE, V.9, II, 125.
5. Loomis, 'Introduction', p. xxxvi.
6. Ibid., 'Appendix', p. 83.
7. Boureau, p. 123.
8. Bartlett, *Why Can the Dead Do Such Great Things?*, pp. 77–78.
9. Le Goff, p. 232. Le Goff's argument is discussed in more detail in my Introduction.
10. Vauchez, p. 27.
11. Ibid., pp. 25–26.
12. Ibid., p. 427.
13. Goodich, 'The Politics of Canonization', p. 295.
14. Ibid., *Miracles and Wonders*, p. 88.
15. Wilson, p. 40.
16. Johannicius, p. 151 ['quando extra cursum naturalem IV humores excrescunt'].
17. Ibid., p. 164.
18. Kaye, p. 144
19. Ibid.
20. van der Lugt, p. 14.
21. Ibid., p. 15.
22. Ibid., p. 21.
23. Harvey, pp. 14–15.
24. Douie and Farmer, p. vii.
25. Farmer, *St Hugh of Lincoln*, p. 1.
26. Ibid., p. 15.
27. Mayr-Harting, para. 8 of 13.
28. Farmer, *Saint Hugh of Lincoln*, p. 79.
29. Ibid., 'The Cult and Canonization', p. 77; AE, V.19, II, 225 [According to Adam, the funeral was attended by 'regem Anglie et regem Scotie, archiepiscopos, episcopos, principes, abbates et proceres'].
30. Farmer, 'The Cult and Canonization', p. 77.
31. Ibid., p. 82.
32. Ibid., p. 79.
33. Douie and Farmer, p. viii.
34. Ibid., p. ix.
35. AE, I.0, I, 1.
36. Ibid., II.14, I, 88 ['hec posteris de Hugone cognoscenda scripto mandata sunt'].
37. Douie and Farmer, p. viii–ix; Talbot and Hammond, p. 37.
38. Salter, pp. 272–73.
39. Ibid., p. 272.
40. AE, II.16, II, 190.

41. Raleigh, p. 166.
42. GW, Preface, p. 7.
43. Raleigh, pp. 165–66.
44. Bartlett, *Gerald of Wales*, p. 46; Ibid., p. 57.
45. Loomis, 'Introduction', p. xxi; Gerald of Wales, 'Letter to the prior of Lanthony', pp. 254–55.
46. Loomis, 'Introduction', p. xxi.
47. Ott and Trumbore Jones, p. 2 ['non percussorem sed modestum'].
48. Garton, p. 4.
49. Ibid., pp. 4–5.
50. Ibid., p. 4.
51. Ibid., pp. 4–5.
52. Ibid.
53. 'Canonization', pp. 97–98.
54. Metrical Life, 1251–52, p. 76.
55. 'Canonization', pp. 97–104.
56. AE, V.9, II, 124.
57. 'Canonization', p. 97.
58. Ibid., p. 107.
59. AE, V.9, II, 125; Metrical Life, 1079, p. 66.
60. Du Cange, III (1884), 634. A glossary of the late tenth century equated *furia* with *insania* and *amentia*, and another from the eleventh century glossed *furiis* as *malignis spiritibus* (Uszkalo, p. 9), as discussed in Chapter 4.
61. Metrical Life, 1084–85, pp. 66–68 ['Exorcizat aquam sanctus pater, et benedicit;/ Ille diabolicas jubet evanescere fraudes'].
62. Ibid., 1079, p. 66 ['manibusque licet pedibusque ligatis']; AE, V.9, II, 125.
63. Metrical Life, 1088–1105, p. 68.
64. Compare to the *rabies* of Sheriff Leofstan (recorded by Herman in Bury and discussed in Chapter 1), which was also not connected to a dog bite.
65. Constantine, fol. xcix^{v}. In his chapter 'De mania et alienatione mentis', Constantine the African stated that 'si ex morsura canis rabidi hec passio alicui contingat, et spumam reiecerit per os sine dubio die vij morietur'.
66. Metrical Life, 1094, p. 68.
67. Ibid., 1092–1105, p. 68.
68. Ibid. ['ad oppositi sensum res quaeque resultat']. This medical explanation supports M.R. James's theory that the poet was Henry of Avranches, who had displayed an interest in contemporary medicine in his other writings.
69. 'Canonization', p. 98.
70. Ibid., pp. 102–4. Five mad women were recorded in the report, and it is possible that Gerald's mad girl from Wigford was among them, though this hypothesis seems unlikely as her story does not match any of theirs.
71. GW, II.7, p. 54.
72. Bartholomaeus, p. 375 ['Magis insani ligentur fortiter']; Latham et al., I, 76 [as well as indicating someone suffering from madness, the term *amens* could be applied to one who was demented or greatly excited].
73. 'Canonization', p. 102.
74. GW, II.7, p. 54.
75. Ibid.
76. Ibid., II.12, pp. 62–65.
77. AE, V.13, II, 156.
78. Ibid.
79. Johannicius, p. 160; Pasnau, p. 15.
80. Gil Sotres, p. 313.
81. Ibid.

82. Ibid.
83. AE, V.16, II, 190.
84. Ibid., pp. 190–91.
85. Ibid., p. 193.
86. Ibid., V.17, II, 199 ['Hugo artus febre iugiter, ut premissum est, fatiscentes spiritui seruire coegnisset'].
87. Ibid., V.4, II, 95 ['a proposito curiose uisionis illos cohercuit, et ad excitandum deuotionis aspectum pariter et amplexum, as hec uera et uiuifica cordium alimenta mentes audientium erudiuit'].
88. Ibid., V.17, II, 206 ['puritatem uero et decorem'].
89. Ibid. ['lacte candidior', 'rosis [...] uernantior'].
90. Paravicini-Bagliani, p. 82.
91. GW, I.8, p. 30 ['nec rei monstrouse magis quam forme humane osculum inprimere'].
92. Ibid. ['oris seu labiorum forma apparuit ulla, sed tantum dentes extabant et prominebant'].
93. Rawcliffe, *Leprosy in Medieval England*, p. 51.
94. Ibid., p. 54.
95. Ibid., p. 61.
96. AE, IV.3, II, 14.
97. Ibid.
98. Rawcliffe, *Leprosy in Medieval England*, p. 55.
99. GW, I.8, p.30 ['"Martinus osculando leprosum curavit eum in corpore. Leprosus autem osculo sanavit me in anima"'].
100. Metrical Life, 1060–61, p. 66 ['Oscula Martini sanarunt carne leprosum, / Oscula leprosi me spiritualiter aegrum'].
101. GW, I.8, p. 30.
102. Rawcliffe, 'Learning to Love the Leper', p. 239.
103. Ibid., p. 238.
104. AE, V.9, II, 126 ['strenuus potestatis aduerse debellator'].
105. Metrical Life, 1099–1101, p. 68 ['Spiritus in tepido discurrens sanguine frigus / Sentit; ad oppositi sensum res quaeque resultat, / Vimque caloris ibi contrarius excitat algor'].
106. AE, V.9, II, 125 ['Ipsius autem oculi miserabiliter rotabantur in girum; os nunc in hanc, nunc illam in partem, miserabili rictu contorquebatur. Nunc linguam in immensum protendebat ab ore, nunc dentibus stridebat; nunc hiatu faucium immanissimo, patulum gutturis meatum ac si quiddam ingens baratrum et intuentibus horridum, demonstrabat'.]
107. Metrical Life, 1082, p. 66 ['genas torque, linguamque recurvam'].
108. TM1, V.13, p. 204; Ibid., VI.6, p. 226.
109. AE, V.9, II, 126.
110. Metrical Life, 1089–90, p. 68 ['geminat dementia vires: / Insanus sanis vix unus ab octo tenetur'].
111. Ibid., 1091, p. 68 ['Quin velit et valeat pueris et conjuge vesci'].
112. AE, V.9, II, 126.
113. Ibid., pp. 125–26.
114. 'Canonization', p. 97 ['ligatum fuit capud ad postem et manus ad paxillos tam a dextris quam a sinistris et pedes similiter ad paxillum]; Metrical Life, 1079, p. 66 ['manibusque licet pedibusque ligatus'].
115. AE, V.9, II, 126.
116. Ibid.
117. GW, II.7, p. 54 ['astrictus vinculis et ligatus'].
118. Ibid. ['cathenas manibus deferens'].
119. Ibid., II.12, p. 62 ['in frenesim rapta fuit, adeo ut vincta diucius et graviter vexata'].
120. Ibid., p. 64.

121. For example, in the *Life and Miracles of William of Norwich* (see Chapter 2), one demoniac struggled at William's tomb and had to be restrained by several people (TM1, VI.4, p. 224), and a female demoniac could hardly be dragged inside the cathedral by four strong men (TM1, VI.6, p. 226).
122. Metrical Life, 1084–87, pp. 66–68.
123. Garton, p. 5; Metrical Life, 1, p. 8. The poem opens with the line 'Arma virumque cano'.
124. Garton, pp. 5–6.
125. AE, II.2, I, 52.
126. Ibid., II.3, I, 53.
127. Thibodeaux, p. 17.
128. Vespasian B.IX, II.12, fol. 30r.
129. Thibodeaux, p. 17.
130. AE, I.12, I, 36 ['immo impressius gustans et interius dentibus terens, totis anime sue uocibus clamabat [...]'].
131. Ibid., II.9, I, 74–75.
132. Ibid., V.7, II, 116 ['ut constraret eum, corpore etiam soporato, Deo uigili mente iugiter inherere'].
133. Metrical Life, 717, p. 46 ['mens liberior, quanto plus membra gravantur'].
134. AE, III.14, I, 129–33.
135. Ibid., p. 130.
136. Ibid. ['"Beati mundo corde, quoniam ipsi Deum uidebunt"'].
137. MacLehose, *"A Tender Age"*, pp. 58–63.
138. Discussed in more detail in Chapter 2.
139. MacLehose, *"A Tender Age"*, p. 81.
140. AE, III.14, I, 129–30.
141. Ibid., p. 131.
142. Ibid., II.6, I, 68 ['"Tecum enim partiar consilia salutaria, tecum et studia anime mee necessaria"'].
143. Ibid., II.8, I, 74.
144. Raleigh, pp. 172–74.
145. GW, I.8 , pp. 28–29.
146. AE, IV.7, II, 34.
147. Ibid., V.7, II, 114.
148. Goodich, 'The Politics of Canonization', p. 294.
149. AE, II.11, I, 80.
150. Ibid., pp. 81–82.
151. Ibid., I.6, I, 19.
152. Ibid., I.10, I, 33.
153. MacLehose, 'Fear, Fantasy and Sleep', p. 83.
154. AE., IV.2, II, 7.
155. Ibid., p. 8.
156. Ibid., p. 7 ['illaqueauerat dolis hostis humani generis'].
157. Ibid. ['contigit me infelicem ex insidiis aduersarii humane salutis detestabile enormis cuiusdam piaculi incurrisse crimen].
158. Ibid., p. 10.
159. Ibid., p. 8.
160. Murray, pp. 277–78.
161. Ibid., pp. 281–82.
162. Ibid., pp. 282–83.
163. AE., IV.2, II, p. 6 ['De alterius conuersione iuuenis, qui mentis simul et corporis per episcopum nostrum consecutus est medelam'].
164. Ibid., V.9, II, 126.
165. GW, II.12, p. 62.

166. Ibid., p. 64.
167. Ibid.
168. Page, II, 233.
169. GW, II.12, p. 64 ['finalem auream sive aureolam'].
170. BP, IV.37, pp. 208–9. Matilda of Cologne's vision is discussed in Chapter 3.
171. GW, II.12, p. 64.
172. Ibid, II.7, p. 54.
173. Ibid. ['ultra quam credi possit exhilaratus'].
174. 'Canonization', p. 102.
175. AE, V.13, II, 156 ['uultum {...} et animum gereret letissimum'].

Bibliography

Manuscripts

London, British Library, MS Cotton Vespasian B.IX

Primary

Adam of Eynsham, *Magna Vita Sancti Hugonis: The Life of Saint Hugh of Lincoln*, ed. and trans. by Decima L. Douie and David Hugh Farmer, 2 vols (Oxford: Clarendon Press, 1985)

Bartholomaeus, 'Practica Magistri Bartholomaei Salernitani', in *Collectio Salernitana*, 5 vols (Naples: Salvatore de Renzi, 1852–59), IV (1856), 321–406

Benedict of Peterborough, 'Miracula Sancti Thomae Cantuariensis', in *Materials for the History of Thomas Becket, Archbishop of Canterbury*, ed. by James Craigie Robertson, 7 vols (London: Longman, 1875–85), II (1876), 21–281

'The Canonization of St Hugh of Lincoln', ed. by D.H. Farmer, *Lincolnshire Architectural and Archaeological Society Reports and Papers*, 6 (1956), 86–117

Constantine the African, 'Liber Pantegni', in *Omnia Opera Ysaac* (Lyons: Trot, 1515), fols j^{r}–cxliij^{v} [in the second set of foliation]

Gerald of Wales, 'Letter to the prior of Lanthony', in *Speculum Duorum or A Mirror of Two Men*, ed. by Yves Lefèvre and R.B.C. Huygens, trans. by Brian Dawson, Board of Celtic Studies, University of Wales, History and Law Series, 27 (Cardiff: University of Wales Press, 1974), pp. 242–261

———, *The Life of St. Hugh of Avalon, Bishop of Lincoln 1186–1200*, ed. and trans. by Richard M. Loomis, Garland Library of Medieval Literature A, 31 (New York, NY and London: Garland, 1985)

Johannicius, 'Isagoge ad Techne Galieni', trans by. Gregor Maurach, *Sudhoffs Archiv*, 62 (1978), 148–174

The Metrical Life of Saint Hugh of Lincoln, ed. and trans. by Charles Garton (Lincoln: Honywood Press, 1986)

Thomas of Monmouth, *The Life and Miracles of St William of Norwich*, ed. and trans. by Augustus Jessopp and M.R. James (Cambridge: Cambridge University Press, 1896)

Secondary

Bartlett, Robert, *Gerald of Wales 1146–1223* (Oxford: Clarendon Press, 1982)

———, *Why Can the Dead Do Such Great Things? Saints and Worshippers from the Martyrs to the Reformation* (Princeton, NJ and Oxford: Princeton University Press, 2013)

Boureau, Alain, *Satan the Heretic: The Birth of Demonology in the Medieval West*, trans. by Teresa Lavender Fagan (Chicago, IL and London: University of Chicago Press, 2006)
Douie, Decima L., and David Hugh Farmer, 'Introduction', in *Magna Vita Sancti Hugonis: The Life of Saint Hugh of Lincoln*, ed. by Decima L. Douie and David Hugh Farmer, 2 vols (Oxford: Clarendon, 1985) I, pp. vii–liv
Du Cange, Charles, *Glossarium mediae et infimae latinitatis*, 10 vols (Niort: L. Favre, 1883–87)
Farmer, David Hugh, *Saint Hugh of Lincoln* (London: Darton, Longman and Todd, 1985)
———, *St Hugh of Lincoln: An Exhibition to Commemorate the Eighth Centenary of His Consecration as Bishop of Lincoln in 1186* (Oxford: Bodleian Library, 1986)
———, 'The Cult and Canonization of St Hugh', in *St Hugh of Lincoln: Lectures delivered at Oxford and Lincoln to celebrate the eighth centenary of St Hugh's consecration as bishop of Lincoln*, ed. by Henry Mayr-Harting (Oxford: Clarendon Press, 1987), pp. 75–87
Garton, Charles, 'Introduction', in *The Metrical Life of Saint Hugh of Lincoln*, ed. and trans. by Charles Garton (Lincoln: Honywood Press, 1986), pp. 1–7
Gil Sotres, Pedro, 'The Regimens of Health' in *Western Medical Thought from Antiquity to the Middle Ages*, ed. by Mirko D. Grmek, trans. by Antony Shugaar (London and Cambridge, MA: Harvard University Press, 1998), pp. 291–318
Goodich, Michael E., *Miracles and Wonders: The Development of the Concept of Miracle, 1150–1350* (Aldershot: Ashgate, 2007)
———, 'The Politics of Canonization in the Thirteenth Century: Lay and Mendicant Saints', *Church History*, 44 (1975), 294–307
Harvey, E. Ruth, *The Inward Wits: Psychological Theory in the Middle Ages and the Renaissance*, Warburg Institute Surveys, 6 (London: Warburg Institute, 1975)
Kaye, Joel, *A History of Balance 1250–1375: The Emergence of a New Model of Equilibrium and its Impact on Thought* (Cambridge and New York, NY: Cambridge University Press, 2014)
Latham, R.E., et al., eds, *Dictionary of Medieval Latin from British Sources*, 17 fascicules (London: Oxford University Press, 1975–2013)
Le Goff, Jacques, *The Birth of Purgatory*, trans. by Arthur Goldhammer (Chicago, IL: University of Chicago Press, 1984)
Loomis, Richard M., 'Appendix: The Rebuilding of Lincoln Cathedral from *The Metrical Life of St. Hugh*', in *The Life of St. Hugh of Avalon, Bishop of Lincoln 1186–1200*, ed. by Richard M. Loomis, Garland Library of Medieval Literature A, 31 (New York, NY and London: Garland, 1985), pp. 83–95
———, 'Introduction', in *The Life of St. Hugh of Avalon, Bishop of Lincoln 1186–1200*, ed. by Richard M. Loomis, Garland Library of Medieval Literature A, 31 (New York, NY and London: Garland, 1985), pp. xiii–lv
MacLehose, William F., 'Fear, Fantasy and Sleep in Medieval Medicine', in *Emotions and Health 1200–1700*, ed. by Elena Carrera, Studies in Medieval and Reformation Traditions, 168 (Leiden: Brill, 2013), pp. 67–94
———, *"A Tender Age": Cultural Anxieties over the Child in the Twelfth and Thirteenth Centuries* (New York, NY: Columbia University Press, 2008)
Mayr-Harting, Henry, 'Hugh of Lincoln (1140?–1200)', in *Oxford Dictionary of National Biography* <https://doi.org/10.1093/ref:odnb/14060>
Murray, Alexander, *Suicide in the Middle Ages*, 2 vols (Oxford and New York, NY: Oxford University Press, 1998–2000), I: *The Violent Against Themselves* (1988)

Ott, John S., and Anna Trumbore Jones, 'Introduction: The Bishop Reformed', in *The Bishop Reformed: Studies of Episcopal Power and Culture in the Central Middle Ages*, ed. by John S. Ott and Anna Trumbore Jones (Aldershot: Ashgate, 2007), pp. 1–20

Page, William, ed., *A History of the County of Lincoln*, 2 vols (London: Constable, 1906)

Paravicini-Bagliani, Agostino, *The Pope's Body*, trans. by David S. Peterson (Chicago, IL and London: University of Chicago Press, 2000)

Pasnau, Robert, 'The Mind-Soul Problem', in *Mind, Cognition and Representation: The Tradition of Commentaries of Aristotle's* De Anima, ed. by P.J.J.M. Bakker and J.M.M.H. Thijssen (Burlington, VT: Ashgate, 2007), pp. 3–20

Raleigh, Peter, '*Fere tirannicus*: Royal Tyranny and the Construction of Episcopal Sanctity in Gerald of Wales's *Vita Sancti Hugonis*', in *Gerald of Wales: New Perspectives on a Medieval Writer and Critic*, ed. by Georgia Henley and A. Joseph McMullen (Cardiff: University of Wales, 2018), pp. 165–182.

Rawcliffe, Carole, 'Learning to Love the Leper: Aspects of Institutional Charity in Anglo-Norman England', in *Anglo-Norman Studies XXIII*, ed. by John Gillingham (Woodbridge: Boydell, 2001), pp. 231–250

———, *Leprosy in Medieval England* (Woodbridge: Boydell, 2006)

Salter, H.E., 'Vision of the Monk of Eynsham: Introduction', in *Eynsham Cartulary*, ed. by H.E. Salter, Oxford Historical Society, 51, 2 vols (Oxford: Clarendon Press, 1907–8), II (1908), 257–283

Talbot, C.H. and E.A. Hammond, eds., *The Medical Practitioners in Medieval England: A Biographical Register* (London: Wellcome Historical Medical Library, 1965)

Thibodeaux, Jennifer D., *The Manly Priest: Celibacy, Masculinity, and Reform in England and Normandy, 1066–1300* (Philadelphia: University of Pennsylvannia Press, 2015)

Uszkalo, Kirsten C., 'Rage Possession: A Cognitive Science Approach to Early English Demon Possession', *Bodies of Knowledge: Cultural Interpretations of Illness and Medicine in Medieval Europe*, ed. by Sally Crawford and Christina Lee, Studies in Early Medicine, 1 (Oxford: British Archaeological Reports, 2010), pp. 5–17

van der Lugt, Maaike, '"Neither ill nor healthy": The intermediate state between health and disease in medieval medicine', *Quaderni storici*, 136 (2011), 13–46

Vauchez, André, *Sainthood in the Later Middle Ages*, trans. by Jean Birrell (Cambridge: Cambridge University Press, 1997)

Wilson, Louise E., 'Miracle and Medicine in Medieval Miracula ca. 1180 – ca. 1320' (unpublished doctoral thesis, University of Cambridge, 2011)

Conclusion

Madness

> But what is easier, to give health of the mind or of the body?[1]

This rhetorical question was posed by a monk called Benedict, who, in the 1170s, was recording the miracles performed by England's great saint, Thomas Becket. In his collection of over two hundred of Becket's miracles, Benedict committed to writing the miraculous cure of a blind man called Robert, who had come, as a pilgrim, to Becket's tomb in Canterbury Cathedral, hoping that the saint's intercession would heal him. The next miracle that Benedict recorded was the healing of a mad youth called Henry. Benedict prefaced his record of Henry's cure with this question, which emphasised Becket's universal healing power but also made a comparison between mental and physical illness. Madness, as a condition of the mind, required a different cure to blindness, as a condition of the body.

As Benedict's question indicates, miracle compilers in twelfth-century England recognised a difference between corporeal and mental illness. Mental illness (madness) was referred to by many terms, as shown in Table 0.1. Some of these terms (*frenesis*, *furia*, *furor*) implied a more violent or frenzied form of madness, though the vast majority of mad people brought to shrines for cures displayed some form of violent behaviour (biting, screaming, attacking others). Other terms (*amentia*, *insania*) appear to have been interchangeable, and, often, more than one term was used to describe an individual sufferer.

Similarly, there were some overlaps between the terms *anima* (soul), *mens* (mind) and *animus* (mind). Both *mens* and *animus* could refer to the mind, but *animus* was never used in relation to the loss of the mind that resulted in madness. Miracle compilers used *anima* (and occasionally *animus*, though with far less frequency) to denote that part of a human that could be protected and punished by God and influenced by emotions (accidents of the soul) and sin. The term *mens* seems, therefore, to have specifically referred to the cognitive and reasoning ability of a person. The mind (*mens*) was connected to both the body (from which it interpreted sensory stimuli) and the soul (from which it expressed feeling and desire). Nonetheless, we need to recognise that these terms were interrelated and, therefore, present a linguistic challenge to historians, who must remain sensitive to the diversity of their medieval meaning.

Despite being referred to by many terms, madness does seem to have been recognised as a distinct condition that was different from other conditions, like epilepsy. William of Canterbury, who organised his collection of the miracles of Saint Thomas Becket thematically, according to the illness cured by the saint, grouped cures of epilepsy and cures of madness separately. William recorded the miraculous cure of a priest, also called William, who suffered from giddiness and was worried that his symptoms were indicative of either madness or epilepsy.[2] Comparisons between madness and epilepsy, such as this, reveal that, whilst both conditions could present similar symptoms, they were not the same. In general, epilepsy was attributed by miracle compilers and contemporary physicians to a corporeal problem in the brain, limbs or stomach. Common symptoms of epilepsy were foaming at the mouth and abnormal movement of the limbs. It was made clear that epileptics were not perpetually incapacitated, as mad people were. For example, Petronella, a nun who suffered from epilepsy and sought a cure from Saint Thomas Becket, left Canterbury not knowing whether she had been cured.[3] There was no instantaneous and noticeable change in her health; instead, she needed to show, over a period of time, that she had not suffered another fit.

When mad people were miraculously cured, the change in their behaviour was immediately apparent. Madness was recognised by behavioural signs, including crying, hair-pulling, tearing clothes and biting. Mad people could be violent towards themselves and others, and many were bound by friends, neighbours or relatives in order to get them to a shrine. Some symptoms, such as blaspheming and refusal to enter the church, were more typical of demonically-induced madness and were indicative of the demon's control over the sufferer's behaviour. Most mad people were cured instantaneously by the saints, as was typical of miraculous healings. In order to demonstrate that a mad person had been cured, miracle compilers described their behaviour as calm, quiet, wise and discreet. These behaviours were all signs of a healthy mind.

There was a strong association between certain behaviours (weeping, wailing, rolling around) and madness, so much so that people who displayed such behaviours could be compared to mad people without being diagnosed as mad themselves. William of Norwich's mother, Elviva, was compared to a madwoman when wailing with grief at the death of her son.[4] Two women who were screaming and crying with pain were also described as acting madly, as was a priest who was suffering from an agonising toothache.[5] However, despite their seemingly unusual behaviour, none of these people were mad or were cured of madness. It was only when such behaviours lacked a rational explanation (such as grief or pain) that the sufferer was truly thought to be mad.

Despite evidence that, in the later Middle Ages, women were believed to be more susceptible to madness and demonic possession than men, in miracle records from the twelfth century, men were portrayed as just as vulnerable as women, if not more so.[6] Mad women, like mad men, could be violent, though their violence was proportionately less extreme in line with their assumed physical weakness. Sieldeware, a mad woman brought to the tomb of William of Norwich, needed four men to restrain her, whereas her male equivalent required seven men.[7] Furthermore, both men and women could fall victim to demonic deception or to sexual temptation from demons.[8]

By the mid-twelfth century, madness and demonic possession did not necessarily result in the sufferer's alienation from the Christian community. Naturally, because they lacked the ability to reason and consent, mad people could not participate in Christian rituals. One mad girl, for example, screamed so loudly at the shrine of Saint Hugh of Lincoln that she disturbed the celebration of mass.[9] A madman who was troubled by a demon was scorned by his community and left to roam wild before he received a cure from Saint Thomas Becket.[10] Nonetheless, most mad people, of either gender, were accompanied or led to shrines by family members, friends or neighbours, almost always against their own will or without any awareness of their surroundings. Mad cure-seekers were not excluded from shrines (as, for example, a sorceress was in Norwich), nor is there much evidence for them having to atone, after being healed, for any sins committed whilst mad.[11] One exception was Matilda of Cologne, a madwoman who came to Thomas Becket's shrine but who, whilst mad, had committed the mortal sin of murdering her own child.[12] Such a serious sin, whilst treated with more leniency than it would have been had it been committed by a sane person, was likely the reason that Matilda was required to continue her pilgrimage to Rome or to Santiago de Compostela, even though Thomas Becket had already cured her madness.

Medicine

Previous studies of medieval hagiography have concluded that there was a rationalisation and naturalisation of the language used to describe sickness and disease in the twelfth century, which has been attributed to the increased circulation of Galenic medical texts and the tightening of papal control over canonisation processes.[13] The growing influence of the papacy over the canonisation of saints, culminating in 1234 when Pope Gregory IX made canonisation the exclusive prerogative of the pope, led to increasingly stringent processes for the verification of miracles. To be perceived as credible, miracle records had to observe theological, philosophical and legal standards.[14] Verification of healing miracles required details of the sick person's condition before and after cure. According to medieval understandings of Hippocratic medicine, health was regulated by balancing the four humours (blood, red/yellow bile, phlegm and black bile) and the six non-naturals (air, food and drink, motion and rest, sleeping and waking, excretion, and passions or accidents of the soul).

Certainly, miracle compilers saw that restoring balance was an important part of the miraculous healing process and also that imbalance and immoderation could lead to illness. In two collections of the miracles of Saint Edmund of Bury (the earliest collections examined here and the only records to focus on madness as a divine punishment), excessive or sinful behaviour, such as undermining the saint, could be punished with madness. The links between such transgressions and their resulting punishments were made evident. For example, when Sheriff Leofstan was 'mad' enough to break Saint Edmund's sanctuary, he was punished with demonic possession and death.[15] Similarly, when a nobleman rashly tried to seize a manor belonging to the Bury monks, his imbalanced mind was reflected in the chaos of a thunderstorm and in his subsequent punishment with madness.[16]

It is clear that some miracle compilers in this period had come into contact with texts from the 'new' medical corpus, translated in Italy and disseminated from there. For example, William of Canterbury's detailed commentary on epilepsy has close parallels with the work of Salernitan physician Bartholomaeus.[17] Nonetheless, monastic libraries acquired manuscripts at different paces, and awareness of specific medical texts cannot be assumed across English monasteries. Even within one monastery, individual monks may have possessed (or may have felt it appropriate to include in their miracle collections) varying degrees of medical knowledge, as was demonstrated in the miracles of Thomas Becket, compiled in two collections by Canterbury monks Benedict of Peterborough and William of Canterbury. For example, the compilers described the quinsy of Thomas of Etton respectively as 'squinantia' (a fairly common Latin term) and 'synanchia' (a more specific medical term, drawn from the Greek συνάγχη).[18] William of Canterbury, though clearly very familiar with natural aetiologies for epilepsy and other conditions, recorded several cases of demonic possession. Since, for these cases, he did not provide any descriptions of demons or of the process of possession, it is possible that he was using language associated with possession metaphorically to describe demon-like behaviour rather than to indicate the literal presence of a demon. Nonetheless, the continued use of language pertaining to demonic possession illustrates that madness was far from being naturalised in the second half of the twelfth century.

The terms that were associated with madness in medical texts (*frenesis* and *mania*) were not commonly used in miracle records throughout the twelfth century. The earliest miracle collection studied, Herman's *De Miraculis Sancti Eadmundi*, was the only text to use both terms, *frenesis* and *mania*, to denote forms of madness.[19] Only Gerald of Wales, who compiled his *Life of Saint Hugh* in around 1213, used the phrase 'in frenesim' consistently to describe madness, and even he only recorded two cases.[20] Saint Hugh's official canonisation report frequently used the term 'furiosi' to describe mad men and women, which, though it did not specifically indicate demonic involvement, was associated throughout the twelfth century with demonic and non-demonic madness.[21] The *Metrical Life of Saint Hugh of Lincoln*, which used the canonisation report as its source, reintegrated demons more explicitly into the narrative.[22] In the *Metrical Life*, demons caused imbalance in a similar way to excess humours. Hugh cured one demoniac using holy water, which cooled the madman's fevered blood and drove out the unholy demon. The poet explained that 'each thing rebounds at the sensation of its opposite'.[23]

In the miracles compiled in the foundation book of Saint Bartholomew's priory and hospital (recorded in the late twelfth century, after Thomas Becket's miracles), demons were the predominant cause of madness, and their encounters with mortals were described in striking detail. The founder of the priory, a wayward courtier called Rahere, faced his own battles with demons but was guided to salvation by the apostle Bartholomew. He even feigned foolishness as part of his efforts to attract support to the foundation project and to achieve spiritual redemption. The demoniacs cured by Saint Bartholomew made evident the apostle's role in restoring spiritual balance. Demons took on the forms of handsome young men and women so as to tempt their victims into sin.[24] Bartholomew's spiritual battles with these demons served as reminders of Rahere's own spiritual journey and reinforced Bartholomew's reputation for divine intercession. The unusually vivid descriptions of demons in this text, as compared with the others examined, illustrate how individual representations of madness were influenced by the construction of the complete hagiographical narrative.

There was no rejection by any of the hagiographers of demonic aetiologies for madness and, to a lesser extent, for other conditions. Some medical writers acknowledged the role of demons in causing illness, and hagiographers do not appear to have perceived demonic and non-demonic diagnoses as incompatible, as illustrated by the *Metrical Life*'s attribution of one case of madness to both fever and demonic possession.[25] Indeed, seemingly incongruous (to the modern eye, at least) explanations for illness are indicative not of confused hagiographers but of a multifaceted approach to healing in medieval England and to the continued place of the demonic in medieval medicine.

Miracle

Alongside the diffusion of Galenic medical ideas, the twelfth century saw the increased dissemination of Patristic texts in England, which stimulated contemporary theological debates concerning individual human spirituality. Influenced by Augustine, Platonic-Christian concepts of the incorporeal soul prompted writers like Alcher of Clairvaux and William of Conches to consider further the human body and mind in relation to reason, will and morality. The implications for hagiographical representations of madness were twofold. First, reason was a necessary contributor to physical and spiritual health. Reason was lost in cases of madness, and sufferers were affected physically and spiritually. Second, a change in the relationship between saint and miracle recipient was illustrated in the hagiographer's representation of loss of reason. Whereas the madmen who encountered Saint Edmund of Bury at the turn of the eleventh century were deprived of their reason in order to incapacitate them physically and spiritually, the mad men and women who were healed by the saints who followed were restored to full health and to piety and discretion. Saint Hugh himself presented a compelling example of the ideal balance between body, mind and soul. Twelfth-century records of miraculous healings follow the precedents of biblical miracles (most notably, that of the Gerasene demoniac, who was ostracised and chained by his community and then cured by Christ [Mark 5:1–21]) and of earlier saints' lives (such as Athanasius' *Life of Antony*). Miracle compilers embellished, extended and adapted these models to accommodate their immediate settings. There was a gradual, and by no means chronologically uniform, shift in the role of the saint from the protector of the few to the protector of the many. The reason for this shift was that the laity were increasingly seen as capable of attaining salvation.

By taking five cults from across the twelfth century as case studies, we can see that representations of madness were influenced by hagiographical tropes, the local context of saints' cults and the approach of individual hagiographers. Benedicta Ward argues that the twelfth century saw a transition from 'traditional' miracle narratives, in which the saint protected monastic interests by miraculously avenging wrongs, to 'modern' miracle narratives, in which the saint miraculously healed sick pilgrims who came to his or her shrine.[26] Rachel Koopmans presents a slightly different pattern; from c.1140, the focus of miracle recording moved from medium-sized collections of monastic miracles to long miracle collections, with more stories from the laity.[27] Both Ward's and Koopmans's models provide a fair overview of twelfth-century developments. Certainly, the role of the saint was evolving through the twelfth century. There was an increasing trend towards the recording of healing miracles (as opposed to miraculous punishments), and records of lay interactions with saints were more abundant. However, individual adherence to this trend was dependent on the response of each cult and each hagiographer to wider theological and intellectual developments.

For three of the cults examined (those of Saint Edmund of Bury, Saint Thomas Becket and Saint Hugh of Lincoln), multiple miracle collections were compiled by different writers in quick succession. Comparisons between these collections illustrate that, even within a fairly small geographical and chronological context, each miracle compiler had his own priorities when shaping his miracle collection. The most direct comparison can be drawn between the two collections of Saint Edmund's miracles, since the second collection, compiled around twenty-five years after the first, was a complete revision of the same miracle records. The first collection, written by a monk of Bury, showed Saint Edmund protecting monastic interests by avenging transgressions against the monks' sanctuary and possession rights. The second collection, commissioned by the bishop of Norwich, was less concerned with the immediate needs of the Bury monks than it was with demonstrating how punishments on earth protected sinners from eternal suffering. Notably, a nobleman called Robert de Curcun was not punished with madness in the revised account, though he was in the first collection, perhaps because, in the intervening years, he had been restored to the king's favour.[28] Immediate circumstances, therefore, had a direct impact on how the miracle record was constructed.

The three *vitae* of Saint Hugh of Lincoln demonstrate how miracle records could be adapted depending on their intended audience. Adam of Eynsham, writing for a monastic audience, with canonisation in mind, only included one account of madness because, he claimed, he did not want to simply satisfy curiosity.[29] The *Metrical Life of Saint Hugh of Lincoln*, written for a wider audience in celebration of Hugh's canonisation, included two accounts of miraculously-healed madness, though the poet knew of at least nine.[30] Both of the accounts that were included were of particularly violent cases of madness (one madman wanted to devour his entire family), which may have been attractive to a general audience, and both illustrated Hugh's direct role in the healing process since the exorcisms were performed during his lifetime.[31]

We can also see how each of the five cults impacted each other, and there are parallels between the miracle records. Thomas Becket's cult was especially influential and may have inspired the compilation of Saint Bartholomew's miracles as well as Book Seven of Thomas of Monmouth's *Life and Miracles of William of Norwich* (compiled around twenty years after the first six books).[32] Gerald of Wales made a direct comparison between Saint Hugh (the 'lily of Lincoln') and Saint Thomas Becket (the 'red rose of Kent').[33] Notably, Gerald recorded far more of Hugh's posthumous miracles than his other two hagiographers did, perhaps to accentuate the comparison with Becket, who had performed all of his miracles posthumously. Becket's reputation was thus used to enhance Hugh's and to emphasise the Church's continued struggle with royal authority (both Becket and Hugh were known to have stood up for ecclesiastical rights against powerful Angevin monarchs).[34]

If this study were to be extended to include additional cults, it is likely that similar diversity would be found in the language used to describe madness. For example, Saint Frideswide's miracles, compiled in the late twelfth century by Prior Philip of the Augustinian priory in Oxford, provide an interesting illustration of the influence of Thomas Becket's cult, which both Prior Philip and Prior Robert before him looked to as a model.[35] Saint Frideswide's translation in 1180 was presided over by Archbishop Richard of Canterbury, and two miracles occurred on that day in his presence.[36] Saint Thomas Becket himself was seen to endorse the cult through his appearance in visions recorded in the miracle collection.[37] Representations of madness in the miracles of Saint Frideswide show similar variances in language and aetiology to those seen in the miracles associated with the five cults examined here. A mad girl called Emelina was described as being 'alienated in mind' ('mentis alienatione') and suffering from 'madness' ('amentia').[38] Whilst insane, she tried to drown herself, an act influenced by 'diabolic suggestion' ('suggestione diabolicae'), which implied that there was a demonic element to her madness.

A comparison between the findings of this study and representations of other conditions in miracle texts would be a valuable addition to the historiography and would elucidate whether madness was unique in its variability. Miracle texts demonstrate convergence between religious and medical theories, which complemented rather than displaced each other. The variable representations of madness in miracle texts also highlight the importance of paying close attention to medieval terminology and its contemporary context when using hagiography to explore social and cultural history. Though composed with the glory and veneration of a particular saint in mind, miracle records are especially attractive to historians, and presumably also were to medieval contemporaries, because of their engagement with the lives of individuals. From a distance of over eight hundred years, we cannot directly penetrate the realities of those individuals whose miraculous experiences were recorded, but we can consider how individual experience was represented. In miracle records, we can discern the signs and symptoms by which madness was recognised. Sometimes, we are given details concerning the individuals believed to be mad (young, old, male, female, rich, poor) and the circumstances of their madness. We see how individuals – the mad and their associates – were expected to participate in the cult of saints, and we observe the ways in which the saint was shown to interact with his earthly community. We are told how individuals were recognised as being cured and what form the healing process took. In the face of such tempting glimpses of individual lives and social realities, however, we must not lose sight of the often-neglected individuals whose roles were fundamental to the construction of these realities: the miracle record compilers who shaped their observations of the miraculous into enduring records of individual and communal devotion.

Notes

1. BP, II.13, p. 66
2. WC., II.87, p. 249 ['timebat amentiam vel ephilensiam incurrere'].
3. Ibid., II.6, pp. 163–64.
4. TM1, I.15, p. 41.
5. Ibid., III.22, pp. 154–55; Ibid., VI.8, p. 229; BP, I.14, p. 46.
6. Caciola, p. 40.
7. TM1, VI.6, p. 226; Ibid., V.13, pp. 203–4.
8. Vespasian B.IX, II.9, fol. 29^{r}; Ibid., II.12, fol. 30^{v}.
9. GW, I.12, p. 62

10. WC, VI.86, pp. 480–81.
11. TM1, VII.18, pp. 279–81.
12. BP, IV.37, pp. 208–9.
13. See, for example, Yarrow, Koopmans, Bailey.
14. Goodich, p. 88.
15. Herman, 3, pp. 12–13.
16. Ibid., 36, pp. 102–3.
17. WC, II.6, p. 162.
18. Koopmans, p. 186; BP, II.44, p. 92; WC, I.13, p. 153.
19. Herman, 37, p. 108; Ibid., 23, p. 56.
20. GW, II.7, p. 54; Ibid., II.12, pp. 62–65.
21. Uszkalo, p. 9. For example, WC, II.89, p. 250; Ibid., V.38, p. 405; Vespasian B.IX, II.9, fol. 29r.
22. For example, Metrical Life, 1079–87, pp. 66–68 (discussed at the beginning of Chapter 5).
23. Ibid., 1088–1105, pp. 68–69.
24. Vespasian B.IX, II.9, fol. 29r; Ibid., II.12, fol. 30v.
25. Rider, pp. 48–49.
26. Ward, p. 36; Ibid., p. 67.
27. Koopmans, pp. 3–4.
28. Edmund Revised, I.15, pp. 226–29.
29. AE, V.9, II, 124.
30. Metrical Life, 1251–52, p. 76.
31. Ibid., 1088–1105, pp. 68–69.
32. Koopmans, p. 134; McCulloh, p. xii.
33. GW, Preface, p. 7.
34. Raleigh, pp. 165–66.
35. Yarrow, p. 177.
36. Ibid., pp. 177–78.
37. Ibid, p. 177.
38. *Miracles of St Frideswide*, p. 574.

Bibliography

Manuscripts

London, British Library, MS Cotton Vespasian B.IX

Primary

Adam of Eynsham, *Magna Vita Sancti Hugonis: The Life of Saint Hugh of Lincoln*, ed. and trans. by Decima L. Douie and David Hugh Farmer, 2 vols (Oxford: Clarendon Press, 1985)

Benedict of Peterborough, 'Miracula Sancti Thomae Cantuariensis', in *Materials for the History of Thomas Becket, Archbishop of Canterbury*, ed. by James Craigie Robertson, 7 vols (London: Longman, 1875–85), II (1876), 21–281

Gerald of Wales, *The Life of St. Hugh of Avalon, Bishop of Lincoln 1186–1200*, ed. and trans. by Richard M. Loomis, Garland Library of Medieval Literature A, 31 (New York, NY and London: Garland, 1985)

Goscelin of Saint-Bertin[?], 'Miracles of St Edmund', in *Herman the Archdeacon and Goscelin of Saint-Bertin. Miracles of St Edmund*, ed. and trans. by Tom Licence (Oxford: Oxford University Press, 2014), pp. 127–303

Herman the Archdeacon, 'Miracles of St Edmund', in *Herman the Archdeacon and Goscelin of Saint-Bertin. Miracles of St Edmund*, ed. and trans. by Tom Licence (Oxford: Oxford University Press, 2014), pp. 1–125

The Metrical Life of Saint Hugh of Lincoln, ed. and trans. by Charles Garton (Lincoln: Honywood Press, 1986)

Miracles of St Frideswide, ed. by Josepho van Hacke, Benjamino Bossue, Victore de Buck and Antonio Tinnebroek (Brussels: Alphonsi Greuse, 1853), Acta Sanctorum, 8 October, pp. 568–589

Thomas of Monmouth, *The Life and Miracles of St William of Norwich*, ed. and trans. by Augustus Jessopp and M.R. James (Cambridge: Cambridge University Press, 1896)

William of Canterbury, 'Miracula Sancti Thomae Cantuariensis', in *Materials for the History of Thomas Becket, Archbishop of Canterbury*, ed. by James Craigie Robertson, 7 vols (London: Longman, 1875–85), I (1875), 137–546

Secondary

Bailey, Anne E., 'Miracles and Madness: Dispelling Demons in Twelfth-Century Hagiography', in *Demons and Illness from Antiquity to the Early-Modern Period*, ed. by Siam Bhayro and Catherine Rider, Magical and Religious Literature of Late Antiquity, 5 (Leiden: Brill, 2017), pp. 235–255

Caciola, Nancy, *Discerning Spirits: Divine and Demonic Possession in the Middle Ages* (Ithaca, NY and London: Cornell University Press, 2003)

Goodich, Michael E., *Miracles and Wonders: The Development of the Concept of Miracle, 1150–1350* (Aldershot: Ashgate, 2007)

Koopmans, Rachel, *Wonderful to Relate: Miracle Stories and Miracle Collecting in High Medieval England* (Philadelphia: University of Pennsylvania Press, 2011)

McCulloh, James M., 'Jewish Ritual Murder: William of Norwich, Thomas of Monmouth, and the Early Dissemination of the Myth', *Speculum*, 72 (1997), 698–740

Raleigh, Peter, '*Fere tirannicus*: Royal Tyranny and the Construction of Episcopal Sanctity in Gerald of Wales's *Vita Sancti Hugonis*', in *Gerald of Wales: New Perspectives on a Medieval Writer and Critic*, ed. by Georgia Henley and A. Joseph McMullen (Cardiff: University of Wales, 2018), pp. 165–182.

Rider, Catherine, 'Demons and Mental Disorder in Late Medieval Medicine', in *Mental (Dis)Order in Later Medieval Europe*, ed. by Sari Katajala-Peltomaa and Susanna Nirranen, Later Medieval Europe, 12 (Leiden: Brill, 2014), pp. 47–69

Uszkalo, Kirsten C., 'Rage Possession: A Cognitive Science Approach to Early English Demon Possession', *Bodies of Knowledge: Cultural Interpretations of Illness and Medicine in Medieval Europe*, ed. by Sally Crawford and Christina Lee, Studies in Early Medicine, 1 (Oxford: British Archaeological Reports, 2010), pp. 5–17

Ward, Benedicta, *Miracles and the Medieval Mind: Theory, Record and Event 1000–1215*, rev. edn (Philadelphia: University of Pennsylvania Press, 1987)

Yarrow, Simon, *Saints and their Communities: Miracle Stories in Twelfth-Century England* (Oxford: Oxford University Press, 2006)

Index

Note: **Bold** page numbers refer to tables